Inside My Head

© 2013 by Genevieve St. Clair, St. Clair Publications

All rights reserved. No part of this publication may be reproduced or transmitted in any form by any means electronic or mechanical, including telecopy, recording, or any information storage and retrieval system now known or invented, without permission in writing from the publisher, except by a reviewer who wishes to quote brief passages in connection with a review written for inclusion in a magazine, newspaper or broadcast.

ISBN 978-0-9826302-4-2

Published in the United States of America

**St. Clair Publications**
P. O. Box 726
Mc Minnville, TN 37111-0726

http://stclairpublications.com


Cover Design by Kent Hesselbein

© 2011 KGH Design Studio
http://www.kghdesignstudio.com/services.html

# inside my head

What happens when one woman finds out there is freedom beyond living by the rules

## Genevieve St. Clair

Inside My Head

Thank You God for speaking directly to me and relating this story to the world.

Thank you Jimmy Dean, Micheal, Eric and Felicia for all of your love and every day wonders, for your encouragement and faith in me.

I am honored to be your mother.

Thank you Mom for raising me in my amazing Godly heritage, for your constant love and faithfulness.

Thank you Daddy for all your input and encouragement, love and acceptance.

Thank you Matt for being a beautiful part of my life,

my best friend.

I love you all

# PROLOGUE

A lifetime dream of mine was fulfilled when my best friend bought a house for my children and me. It matched the tumultuous state our lives were in. The foundation seemed solid and the exterior was good. We discussed which walls we would tear out and how we would extend the living room, add closets to bedrooms, and include a second bath. My excitement grew with each plan to improve this dilapidated abused home. Old plaster was all torn out to make one large open canvas. Drywall would begin the updates. Hardwood floors needed to be refinished and I could envision grandeur.

Days before the two by fours were going up to frame the rooms, my friend discovered a place where someone had, at one time, cut a square section out of the floor, and put it back. Construction and home repair being his profession, he realized that needed investigating. Once removed that small square revealed rotted, termite damaged floor joists. The hardwood floors I had been so excited about in that room had to be torn out to check the extent of damage.

Right away, it became evident that all floor joists had to be replaced, as well as the four by four base of the home. Each room had to be done methodically as to not allow the exterior walls and second floor to cave in as we worked.

Upon inspection of the eight by twenty foot hole remotely considered the basement, we discovered that the brick foundation was now convex. We chose to remove the hot water tank, fill the plumbing pipe at the bottom, and use only the top one. We discarded the old shelving and useless items we had found down there and filled that space with gravel in order to save the foundation in the back corner of our now much larger project.

Much of the work took place during the second snowiest winter on record in our area. The people making sure our city stays beautiful came around in late winter and sent a letter of concern regarding the exterior. Therefore, early spring work was switched to the outside in order to please these people. Doing all the work ourselves had become tedious and drawn out. We had no idea the cost or time it would demand in the beginning.

A man we know drove up today and remarked at how much we had accomplished. He also commented on it's past beauty. "No," my friend replied, "it was a mess inside. All the floor joists were rotten. The inside was a mess."

"Yeah, well it was beautiful ten years ago," our friend insisted.

In a way, that is what this book is all about. How someone can look solid, sturdy, and beautiful on the outside yet is rotting away inside. We all think things at times that that we don't want anyone to know. Like the floor joists in our house, if our deepest thoughts were exposed, they would be rotten and shaky; many times from our pasts that have all but destroyed us. We tend to build up the outside and appear to the world as strong, capable, intelligent, trustworthy, kind, fun, etc.

In this book, I will lift up a small square of the beautiful but filthy hardwood floor of Constance's life and expose the deterioration of her mind. I will also depict the horrors and bitterness of others in her life which neither she nor anyone else would have ever known. I take you behind the masks of women who, on Sundays, appear to be upper-middle-class two story, three bedroom, two bath homes. In reality, they are run-down shanties in desperate need of repair. Some have been through the demolition and remodeling process, which Constance is beginning.

The master carpenter is gentle and yet he doesn't leave any nook or cranny untouched. He can take a broken down little shack and create an extravagant mansion. The process can be long and tedious. There is the pain of demolishing old walls that have been built. There is also the pain of tearing out the hardwood flooring we so carefully lay to cover-up the infestations of hurt, bitterness, anger, unforgiveness and self-hate that we can't bear to have anyone see. The rewards far-surpass the pain in the end.

My prayer is that this book will help you to get through that process. That you will allow God to point out those secret convex foundation walls you insist are stable and fill you up with His Spirit. I pray that you will not get caught up in the world's idea of beauty; that you won't allow the inner work to slow or even halt so that you can revamp the outer parts. Once God does what needs to be done inside, the outside will follow. The inner peace, joy and stability will exude from every part of your life and others will have to know what's different. Those that insist you were beautiful before will now realize what true beauty really is.

Don't get lost in the first chapter. Constance is like so many people, her mind races constantly from one subject to the next because her body has to remain fixed in one place. There is no rest for her mile-a-minute mind. Follow as our Great Shepherd leads Constance beside the cool clear water into the lush green pastures of rest in her mind.

# Inside My Head

## CHAPTER ONE

*Two hours till I get outta here. Well, two hours and ten minutes to be exact. Let's see, it's Tuesday, dance and foottball. O.K., off to Jades school to pick her up then to Porter, he doesn't get out till 3:30. Did I get gas this morning? Uhh, hmm it's cold and...nope! I figured I'd make it on what I had till this, afternoon. Let's see, where's the closest station to the school? O.K. hmm, oh yeah, there down the road from the school. O.K. first the bank, then to Jade then to get gas and pop, it's so much cheaper there.*

*She works hard for the money, so hard for it honey, she works hard for the money so you better treat her right, alright. Yeah right! O.K., I bet if I timed it tomorrow that same song would be playing at* (my eyes glance toward the clock, whose hands have barely moved since last glance) *11:55 tomorrow and Thursday and Friday and every day. I will hear that same song. I wish I could pick the music. Lift it up, TFK. One Way, Jesus, who's that by???? I think Hillsong. Darlene Zschech, now she's amazing! No, I know who's amazing, Paula White. More than anyone living, I want to meet her. She's THIS American's idol! Well, Lord, not really, I don't worship her or anything I mean you know my heart anyway and know that but I'd sure love to know her. Man, can you imagine being her friend? I know God is her friend. Huh, God? Yep! I knew it! You don't even have to answer. I want to be like her. I'd like to look like her too. Man, I'd have no problem finding a husband if I looked like her. She's beautiful! I bet guys would say she's an 8 or better. Those fingers! They're so long! Mine are short and fat like all of me. I'm not sure whose hands I got, maybe Grandma Kol's. Good thing I didn't get a lot from Grandma Kol. Oh my gosh! Yeah, I'd rather be like Aunt Constance, my name sake, well, except for being dead and all. She was probably 5'7", a good height for a woman, I think, and much thinner. Well, probably* my same weight but 5" helps ya look thinner. She wore it well and always looked proud. Well, pride is wrong anyways. Maybe, I could just look confident. Oooh! Especially if I see HIM outside of here. That's the one thing I look forward to. Kevin. When machines go down, there he is, like Superman! Any time someone's in trouble...Oh, crap, break time. I need a drink anyways. I'll hurry.

"Hey," Tina says in her 'I'm-exhausted-and-glad-it's-almost-over' voice, and she raises her hand slightly as if mocking a wave.

"Hi." I barely mutter back in the same tone. My body hurts everywhere and I'd rather be anywhere than here. My mind races just to be anywhere but on the line. Oh! A line at the pop machine, no one ever knows what they want and then the machine takes forever. I get the same thing every day. I could be different today. Hmm, lemonade, fruit punch, oh, I need the caffeine anyway.

Is he gone or is Superman still fighting the steel monster? Hmm, he's still there, good! I like to watch him squint his eyes and look at the monster before him as if to determine how to defeat it anew each time. Maybe he's looking deep into it with his x-ray vision to find the problem. Could Superman see through steel? I don't know. I don't think so. I think steel was his greatest adversary, that and kryptonite. Maybe he's using his mechanic's telepathic ability to speak to the enormous steel monster, to ask where the problem is. Maybe the monster tells him and he fixes it and they're friends like that old lion and mouse story. I think it was a mouse. Hmm... yep, yep, it was a mouse.

Aww, shoot! There he goes. Oh, well, he'd never look at me looking like this anyway. I mean, I'm no more than a...5 tops, but at work we're all more like 2's and 3's. Well, except him. He's still magnificent, still steel, hmm. The man of steel is still magnificent. I wish I was Lois Lane. I'd like to see him away

## Inside My Head

*from work. Like at the grocery store, when I'm dressed better and wearing make-up and my hair is down. Yeah, like a super-model. Well, plus a few...dozen pounds. My hair blowing in the wind and make-up perfect and me in my little, well, not so little, black dress. I'd say, "Kevin? Is that you?" NO! NO! Maybe... Hey! Don't I know you from work, in the maintenance department at the plant down the road?" NO! That's silly if I said that he'd probably picture me like this and see right through the make-up, dress, and hair. Oh, well, how often do I even put on that dress, let alone wear it to the grocery store. Maybe I'd see him picking out some fruit and say "Hi, I'm Constance" and leave it at that. I'd never say to Superman, "Hi, I'm Connie," how plain. Although, I am plain and no more than a five at any given time, but, maybe, if I said, "Hi, I'm Constance," he'd see me as the super-model-hair-flowing-little-black-dress-wearing woman, rather than the dirty-jeans-torn-tshirt-work-boots-ponytail-safety-glasses-wearing woman. Who knows? Two o'clock, whew, it seemed like today would never end. If it weren't for the benefits I'd quit this job. But, since that ridiculous man I had children with dropped off the planet, I need them. Raising kids now days, they're a must. This is certainly not my career choice though, I mean, I know I've been here five years, but I'd do something else, I don't really know what, but not this. Like today, ten hours on my feet, then to the bank, then to the school for Jade then to get gas, Porter has football so he stays at school, , then to ballet, drop off Jade, then home to shower and change and...Oh yeah! Oh my gosh! I forgot I have that Bible study tonight. Man, why me? How stupid can I be? I don't know how to be a Proverbs 31 woman! Her husband and children will rise and call her blessed. I don't even have a husband and that's not being blessed. I know, God I have other blessings and I should be thankful, and I am, but, a man would be nice, if there were any good ones. Well,...*

"Goodbye, Connie!"

"Goodbye, Joe. Goodbye, Sheila." *I know, God, there are good ones, but good and gorgeous? It's like the two are oil and water. Good seems to equal short hair, even butch cut, and*

## Inside My Head

*dress clothes, office job, soft and friendly...Nothing's wrong with that I guess, but I like long pony-tailed hair, strong men who work and play hard like Steven Segal. Who get dirty and sweaty and, oh my gosh, I'd better stop now! I still have too far to go before I can take care of those thoughts. God, is there anyone out there like that? (sigh) I guess I'll take anybody God, but I'd really like for him to be exciting and sexy. You know, God, 40 is supposed to be like a second 'magic' age for sex for women. You know. I realize my youth was spent on many men and the one I super-glued myself to left after only three years of "marital bliss". Now it's been way too long. I'm fantasizing about a mechanic at work and I don't even know his last name!*

"Hi, mom!"

"Hi, Jade. How was your day, Honey?" I ask habitually, not expecting or listening to her response.

"Good, Keith asked me out."

"What? Did you say Kevin asked you out?" *How weird is that? I like a Kevin and she likes a Kevin. Although, who doesn't like Jade, she's gorgeous, everything I ever dreamed of being, including pure; at 14 I no longer held that title. She loves Jesus and is very vocal about it. I'm so proud of her.* "What do you want to eat?"

"Mom, I just got done telling you that Keith asked if we could meet at Taco Bell. Weren't you listening at all?" Her beautiful green eyes frown in disappointment.

"I'm sorry, Honey, I was thinking of how proud I am of you and I can't imagine why everyone hasn't asked you out. Taco Bell, yeah, we could do that real quick I guess."

"Mom, after dance, I told Keith about six."

"Honey, I've got that Bible study tonight at our house, remember?"

"Oh, no, I'd forgotten. Well, I got his number, I'll just text him. We'll go another night."

"Do you still want Taco Bell?" I glance over to see her long, beautiful fingers texting quicker than I can type. I don't know how she does that.

"Uhh, sure, whatever. He's cool with that, Mom. Thursday right after school then you can meet his mom too, O.K.?"

I barely get out an 'O.K. Honey' before she has her MP3 player attached to her head by way of earplugs. I smile as I begin to drift back into my past.

*"You wanna play truth or dare?" I look around at Shonda, Paul, Tommy, John, and Simone. Everyone agrees and I start. "Tommy, truth or dare?"*

*"Truth!"*

*"Aww! You always say truth." I say disappointed that I still won't be able to dare him to do something. "O.K., have you ever French kissed?"*

*"Yes!" He grins from ear to ear. His turn and he picks me. "Connie, truth or dare?"*

*"Dare!"*

*"Good! I dare you to French kiss me." I was so scared. I'd never done that before. I was only 12 and he was 16. He was so worldly and so wild, and sooo cute. What if I wasn't good at all? I sighed and we kissed. That was the first of many, many to come. Tommy was a good kisser, and...*

*Gas! I can't forget gas. Where was I? Oh, yeah! That kiss, that first wonderful French kiss. That took me by surprise. How much I loved to kiss and be kissed like that.*

*"Truth or dare?" we played again a few months later, and Tommy chose me again.*

*"Dare!" A sly Grinch grin, spanned his face. That meant trouble. I knew it right away. I kind of wanted the trouble, yet was second-guessing that choice. "Truth!" I shouted hoping to change my bid.*

*"No, you can't do that!" The entire group agreed with him and I got stuck with a dare. "I dare you to let me touch your boobs." My jaw dropped and I wasn't sure what to do.*

*"That's not fair." I pleaded with him to no avail. "Well, at least not so everyone sees," I bargained.*

*"O.K. let's go in there." He pointed to the bathroom.*

*"O.K." I said reluctantly and followed him. His touch was caressing more than grabbing like I expected, then he looked me in the eye and told me he'd wanted this since that first kiss so many months ago, and we kissed. French kissed. Stopping was still fairly easy although I liked the way he made me feel.*

"Mom! Where are you going? Did you forget about dance already?" Jade's urgent voice snapped me back to today.

"Oh, yes. Yes, I did, Honey. I was thinking about all I have to do this evening and those ladies coming over. I'm sorry. Umm, could you get in my purse and get out the list of names for me, please, Sweetheart?"

"Yeah, I'm sorry I yelled."

"I understand, don't worry. Do you think Joyce's mom could bring you home since I have that study?"

"Yes." She said pulling the yellow pad, which contains list after list, most of which are never finished, from my purse. Some urgent matter comes up and I discard my list for that day and never get back to it. I've read everything in all the magazines about organizing my house and time with no relief from the constant reminder that I am just never going to be good enough at anything.

"Bye, Honey. I'll see you about six. I love you."

"O.K. Mom. And by the way, I'll have an apple when I get home. Don't buy me anything." She smiles her amazing smile and turns to go. "I love you!" She calls back. How different she is than I was at her age. I was so concerned about what others thought about me; especially Tommy.

*Tommy and I hung out a lot after that day. I was 13 then and he had turned 17. I saw him talking to other girls, but we weren't actually an item so I talked to other guys as well. On an especially cold fall afternoon, I asked mom if I could go for a ride with my friend and she agreed. "Don't be too long. And check in!" She yelled after me before the door shut.*

*We drove all over. There really wasn't much to do, so we ended up at his house to watch some TV His parents were gone with his two sisters and we flipped through nearly every channel then decided on some movie.*

*"Let's play truth or dare." He said with that Grinch grin he'd shown six months earlier. I knew it meant trouble, but I couldn't resist him. Somehow he always knew that.*

*"O.K. but I start this time."*

*"O.K." He flashed that all too familiar grin, and I melted.*

## Inside My Head

"Truth or dare?" I expected a 'truth,' like always. I wanted to know how he felt about me. Really felt. Were we just friends, or could it be more?

"Dare," he said for the first time. He seemed so confident. I was hooked. He laughed at my surprise.

"Dare? You never say dare. In almost two years you have never said dare." I couldn't think. What could I dare him to do? (sigh) (sigh, again) "Then... take your pants off."

"Really?" Now he was the surprised one, but he did it. I'd never actually seen a boy without pants before. It wasn't really what I expected. Of course, I don't know what I expected. "O.K.?"

"O.K." I shrugged. I didn't know what to do or think. I just looked at it. I wanted to touch it, but that wasn't part of the dare and I wasn't sure he would want me to.

"Truth or dare?"

"Aren't you going to put your pants back on?" I questioned, looking down and back up repeatedly..

"No. Now, truth or dare?"

"Truth." That was the first time in two years I had said truth, but I knew a dare at this point would be a bad idea. He still smiled grinchly.

"Do you want to touch it?"

"What?"

"Do you want to touch it?"

"Let's just play." I tried to get out of answering. How could he always know what to ask? It didn't seem fair.

## Inside My Head

"We are playing. Tell me the truth. Do you want to touch it?" He insisted on an answer. Truth wasn't any better. "Thinking?" He wouldn't give up.

"Yes." I looked at it again and it just sort of hung there.

"Yes, you want to touch it, or yes you're thinking?"

"Both, I guess."

"Gas, I can't forget gas. And I should probably pray for this Bible study tonight. I have no idea why I'm doing this, I keep going back to that, but I have no idea what it means to be the perfect wife. I don't even know how to be an O.K. wife. I do think that some of it has to do with having a good husband and obviously I have no idea how to pick one of those either.

O.K. the list, God, help me tonight. I don't know why I am even doing this. Nearly everyone on this list could teach this better than me. God, I want to do what you want me to, but, I don't see me as the one to teach this particular class. Even with a leader's guide, which hmm, I don't have. (sigh) I know you say you won't put on us more than we can take, but I don't see it. What can I teach them? I am not good enough at anything. Proverbs 31 is all about the perfect woman. I am not. I am way not! Help me. Teach me as I study to teach them. I am prepared. All weekend I studied and got verses and extra verses and sayings. I don't want to lack for something to say. Me? Lack for words? Not likely.

God, I know my shortcomings, my failures, my many sins; and I know You do because, well, of course YOU do, being God and all.

Deep breath, O.K. my list, there's Maraschino, the most beautiful woman I've ever seen. God you know she intimidates me completely. I could never be so perfect. Why is she coming? Why isn't she teaching the class? She has a stunning husband. I have none. Man, could she have a better life? Two 'nines' married; both Christians. God, what about me? I'm lucky if someone sees me as a 'five'. At work I may be a 'three'. God, I'm nothing at all. I have no singing voice, and too much body. My hair is short and thin. I have no money either. Couldn't I have something going for me? She's got it all! Why does she have to come? I don't even like her. I don't want her there. I can't teach her anything, I have nothing.

Sarah plain and tall, she doesn't and never has had a husband. What does she need this class for? What do I need it for? Will I get a husband? (sigh)

JoAnne, she's a mountain of a woman. I feel sorry for her, God. How could anyone let themselves go so bad? She is humongous! At least she has a husband, I don't, so how can I say anything? She always seems happy enough. Maybe I would be to if I had a husband; a good one for a change. That jerk I hooked up with was a bad mistake. Porter John. What a rip-off when it comes to a man. He was a let down from the word go, If I'd have only seen it from the beginning. But, no! Not me! I wait till he's gone and my heart is ripped to shreds, then I have two babies and a body that looks like a used balloon that nobody will ever look at the same way again. Then I see what a loser I chose. I was so blind and stupid! Maybe if I'd have been a Christian when I met him... well, I wouldn't have met him if I was a Christian.

Oh, man, the list. I get sidetracked so easily, God, sorry. Martina, (sigh), Martina makes me want a martini. Everyone knows she checks medicine cabinets, under the kitchen sink, the linen closets, and the coat closet everywhere she goes. Nobody wants the perfect priss at their house. I bet she's only coming to check out my house. Hmmph! And after tonight she won't be back I'm sure. My house is lived-in. If she had anything else to do besides order her maid around, her house might appear to have a warm body in it. Of course, there would have to be some warmth in one of those bodies.

## Inside My Head

*And Fancy Pants! Poor stupid blonde. Do you think she'll even 'get it'? She is the typical dumb blonde. I know that's mean, God but I suppose you created her that way. Well, if nothing else I'm smart. Thank you, God.*

*Oh, God, I'll pray for the rest later, but just bless it tonight and help us all get something out of it. I'll do my best. I need to get a shower, and straighten the house, and I only have an hour. I'll pop these dishes right in the oven until they leave. A quick wipe of the counter and voila! A clean kitchen!*

"Hey, Duke! Good boy, you stay outside for tonight. Here's food and water. Good boy. I love you too, Duke. Nice kisses. O.K. O.K. enough! Alright, alright! I'll see you in a little while, boy."

*What do I wear? Hmm, I wear jeans all the time, but I don't want to be too dressed up. These brown pants and this top will do I guess. I just won't look in a mirror. Casual/dressy, jewelry would be nice.*

"La, la, la, halleluiah, halleluiah, I sing to you, Lord while I wash my hair and face. While I clean I sing words I make up to praise your greatness. I praise you above all creation, as the Great Creator. La, la, la, How great Thou art. How great Thou art.

"Oh! I forgot ice. Oh, man! They won't have anything cold to drink. What time is it? Oh, my gosh! I got to get out of here. I'll shave next time, why bother, No one will know anyway. Good thing women wear pants, now. Ahh! I'll run down to the little market, shoot! No time! Hey, I'll call Sarah, she'll pick some up and pop too. She is such a sweetheart. Everyone always counts on her. She'd do anything for anyone. In fact it seems like she's always doing something for someone." I called and she agreed as always.

## Inside My Head

*That's one less thing I have to do. Toilet paper, hmm, not much here. Don't say we're out. Please, please, please, whew! Good, two rolls. I need to put that on my list. Door bell already? Six-thirty five? It's early. It's got to be Martina, trying to see all the cabinets before everyone else arrives. (Heavy sigh and I shake my head.)* "Coming!" Rushing to the door I trip over the area rug and of course, look stupid. *You idiot! Can't even walk in your own house? You're more of a dumb blonde than Fancy!* "Oh, Fancy, come in!" *Good thing I didn't say that out loud.*

"Thanks, Connie. Wow! Ain't never been here before. Ya gotta great place here, hon. Decorate y'urself?"

"Yes, but I never have time to update you know"

"Sure. I'd be happy to come over and help sometime. I kinda gotta knack for that kinda thang, ya know?"

*Oh you've got to be kidding. Fancy decorating my house!? Probably a Duke's of Hazard bar scene. Me in my Daisy Dukes and all. Yeah there's an idea.* I roll my eyes as I turn from her.

"Well when I get time and money maybe I'll give you a call." *When I lose a ton of weight and look good in those Daisy Dukes again. Maybe I'll even bleach my hair and go all the way to country bumpkin.*

"Great. I know how hard it can be to come up with extry cash. I usta be pretty poor m'self"

*My eyebrows scrunch in disbelief. Used to be? Is she rich now? How?*

"What... oh the door. Martina and JoAnne, hello. Come in."

# Inside My Head

"Hi" both ladies say with smiles as they enter. "Hi Fancy!" both greet her together.

"Hey! girls! y'all look fantastic. I didn't know what ta wear. Casual-dressy, or jeans and T-shirt, Ya know? I kinda went a mish mash, see?" She opens her jacket to reveal a fairly nice sweater with plain jeans and slide on sneakers. *Now, I wish... naw, I'm glad I wore this. I'm the leader. Everybody wore jeans. (I shake my head.) That's ok, I'm the leader, I need to look nice.*

"I'll be right back, ladies. If someone would answer the door that would be great." I rush off to the kitchen and rummage through the cupboards trying to track down plastic cups with no luck. *Great, more dirty dishes. I hope this is worth all the trouble I'm going through. I've already got dishes to do. Well, at least there's no food. How many cups again? Fancy, Martina, Joanne, Maraschino, Sarah, and me. 6 O.K. Shoot! I have to wash two. If I weren't so lazy this would all be done. I'm so stupid.* "Here we are ladies, cups for the drinks." I set down the glasses, 4 of one style and 2 of another. *I don't even have matching cups. How lame. I never have enough of anything. These people must think I'm a loser, I don't even know why they're even here. O.K., mirror, hair still wet, finish make up, better. Bible, notes, pens and paper. Got it all. Whew, I'm ready.*

"I'm back! Oh great, looks like most everyone's here already. Ladies if you'd all like to get drinks, Sarah brought them tonight. Then we'll get started with prayer."

"Who would like to open us up this evening?" I look around, hoping I'm not forced to pray in front of these women. "Maraschino, thank you, you can open up for us tonight."

"Father God in Heaven, You alone are able to teach us tonight all that You would have us understand. We welcome Holy Spirit and Wisdom into our presence that we may absorb all that is spoken tonight. We come before You like the dry deserts we are and ask you to pour down Your Living Water into the very depths of our souls and draw us close to you tonight. In the name of Jesus Christ, the most merciful lover of our souls, Amen."

*Oh my gosh! How incredible! I'm so glad I didn't pray. I'd have embarrassed myself with the simplicity of my words.* "Amen, thank you Maraschino. Tonight I thought we could get to know each other just a touch and write out our goals for this group. Here is some paper and some pens if you would each take one and pass them then as I start with the 'rules' and my own introduction you may go ahead and write out what you hope to learn or do as part of this group, O.K.?"

"O.K." everyone says as their heads nod and they pass along paper and pens.

"Oh yeah, please take enough paper for notes as well. O.K. now for my story, Umm." I stammered… "Well…." I wring my hands looking around at the floor, the ceiling anywhere but their faces. *This is stupid we all know each other! How dumb and embarrassing. I'm usually good about talking to people but I am not good enough to do this class. What in the heck was I thinking?"*

"I like my name Constance better than Connie because it sounds so much more eloquent. I have been a Christian for ten years. I was married to a bad excuse for a man for only three years. I didn't marry till I was twenty-four and of course we had two children, Jade and Porter, right away. Mother and I were never very close but she told me stories about my father's abuse. He died when I was only four. She remarried a wonderful man who I always considered to be my daddy. He was a good man. I somehow believed and I guess in a way I still do, the first is the worst, so I planned not to marry too young. Of course, I was not a Christian so I married Porter only because I was pregnant. God changed my life after Porter left. I was in the hospital and my roommate led me to the Lord. So during the next six weeks of this Bible study I would like for you when you are ready, to give your testimonies.

"Now, the rules. Number one: What is said here stays here. Gossip is strongly spoken against in the Bible and I don't want anyone to be apprehensive about sharing anything here. We are all friends and I hope that our friendships can grow and strengthen as our spirits do. Number two: well, not that it's a rule but please make this a discussion. If anyone has something to add to what I say please jump in. How does that sound" (I look around at blank faces.)

"O.K. then, my goal for this group is that we can develop relationships with each other that will surpass all our imaginations. My personal goal is to learn from this and to become a better woman; a stronger and yet more sensitive, godly woman. I do hope to marry again and I want to know what a godly wife should be like. So I hope each of you will bring to the table your individual wisdom and teach me as well. O.K.?" *Whew that went O.K., I think. I hope it sounded good. Man, being a leader is tough. As Constance, I think I can do it but as Connie I am weak and worn. I don't know. Their eyes are all on me. What if I really mess up; what if they already see me as bland or stupid. Oh crap! Why did I say I'd do this? I am no good at teaching, God. What was I thinking? Why didn't You stop me?* "Geez," Sarah spoke up softly with her eyes bouncing from mine to the floor and back while she fiddled with her hands which had been neatly folded on her lap. "I am thankful that you chose to lead this group because I know that you are so good at this kind of thing. I am hoping to learn from you so that when I do marry and have children I will be as good a mother as you are." She smiled, looking almost apologetic. I return the smile.

"I appreciate your kindness," *but I know how wrong you are. I have no idea why my kids are so good. I pretty much suck at life and at being a mom. I certainly can't pick a good man but, whatever, I guess she hasn't had much luck either since she's still single. She's not ugly just plain.*

"O.K.," (deep breath) "let's begin with Proverbs 31:10. Do you all have Bibles with you? I look around and everyone does. JoAnne gets up to pour herself some more pop. *Of course if she didn't drink pop so much she probably wouldn't be as big as a house. Doesn't she get that?* "Good, I figured you all would since it is a Bible study but, I have a couple of extras just in case. Anyway...who can find a virtuous wife? In the NIV Bible it says a wife of noble character. I may go back and forth between the King James and the NIV so I just wanted to let you know.

"'For her worth is far above rubies.' Let's pause here for a moment. This was written to a king. His mother was trying to tell him what to look for in a perfect woman/wife. Proverbs 12:4 says 'A virtuous woman is a crown to her husband: she that maketh ashamed is as rottenness in his bones.' A virtuous, moral, chaste woman is his crown. His crown! This is also translated as a wife of noble character. This nobility in a woman is a fine character, a high quality moral woman. The crown of a prince tells his ranking in society. His crown is majestic and beautiful it tells the world he is heir to a throne. He is yet to be king at which point he will don the heavy multi-jeweled crown of a king. When he walks in a room even before seeing his face his crown is seen. It is a point of pride for him. The more jewels and the heavier it is the more attention that is drawn to him. We are those crowns for our husbands."

"That's so excitin'!" Fancy blurted out. *Whew, they are listening. Or at least she is.*

"Wow! That's incredible. I never understood it that way before; me a crown. How cool! I wouldn't have ever expected to be a crown for my husband." Sarah spoke with more passion than I've ever heard from her before. *That's encouraging. Maybe I can do this. As I look around everyone is nodding and some are still writing frantically.*

"Well, Jack sure got the biggest crown; he must be a king, Ha, ha, ha," JoAnne remarks with her usual self-deprecating humor. *I don't know how she can joke around. If I were that heavy, I'd be depressed.*

Everyone does that half laugh; that 'that's-not-funny-but-for-your-sake-I'll-laugh' laugh. I notice eyes rolling and foreheads wrinkling. *They all agree with me. It's not funny that she takes up the whole love seat by herself, it's just gross.*

"Verse 11 says, 'the heart of her husband safely trusts her; so he will have no lack of gain.' Any ideas from you ladies about this verse?" I look around hoping. *Martina? Maraschino? Come on. You guys are more capable than me to figure this out. Of course I did study all weekend. Maybe God just dropped it in me. I don't know.* "Well, trust is the number one issue here. How well do you understand the trust thing? Is it still important? And if so, how important is it? And Why? And while you're all writing, who is this issue more important to, husbands or wives? And how does it differ? Do you want any questions repeated?"

"Yes, all of them. I'm sorry, I wasn't writing at first and have forgotten them." A smile crosses Maraschino's perfect face. I re-state all the questions at a slower pace. "Anyone have any answers to start the discussion?" I look around. *Everyone seems to be afraid to answer. Like a junior high classroom! What if I'm wrong? How embarrassing.*

"Well, I ain't never been married..." starts Fancy, "but, I hear that trust is the most important issue in every marriage. Now, in my parents' marriage, there was great trust between 'em. They're still married after thirty-five years. I believe trust has kept 'em together. Daddy worked with a lotta women at a department store for years. He's a very handsome man and had many a' chance to cheat but he didn't. It took a lot of trust from Mama. If she'da accused him or been jealous, they'da never made it."

"Good. So you believe it's more important to men?" *I have to get a discussion going on or I'll have to do it all myself.*

"Yeah, I guess, but if Mama hadda worked outside the home, daddy woulda had ta trust her too."

"Makes sense," I started.

"Well, I know in my marriage trust is important to both my husband and me. But I do know that he has accused me on many occasions of cheating and I can't make him understand I would never do that. He stays with me but our lives are not happy." Maraschino openly states. *What? Model marriage in jeopardy because of his jealousy? I don't get it. They're both Christians and both beautiful. Why would she cheat on him? He's gorgeous! If he were my husband I'd make sure he knew how happy I was. Man, I don't expect I'll ever get a '9' for a husband. Nines don't even look my direction. I'd... I'd, mmm, mmm, mmm, oh my gosh, what I wouldn't do is a shorter list. If I could just touch him, I'd be on fire for days.*

"Why does he think you'd cheat on him" Martina asks dumbfounded at his accusation. "You love Jesus, don't you?" *Martina, martini, you got balls girl.*

"Yes, I love Jesus now, but, my past is a very dark and hurtful one and he doesn't trust me. I'd have to say that, with trust in place our marriage would be much more pleasant for us both."

"Thank you for your openness. Anyone else?" No one follows that and I don't blame them.

"O.K., both of you are correct in that trust is of the utmost importance in both husband and wife and in today's western world…. Well, in today's world period. That is the first trust issue we'd think of, however, we will have to look at part "B" of the verse to get even more meaning from it. 'So he will have no lack of gain.' Further into the passage we will see how his wife took care of the house and finances. He trusted her to gain wealth for the family. Not to go out and spend all they had. As this study continues, we'll see that everything he has is entrusted to his wife! She is smart and wise and hardworking and faithful. He trusts her implicitly with every part of his life. And she is capable of handling it all. Help me explain this in today's terms." No one offers anything. I look and look. *Martina you're wealthy, you understand this don't you?*

"Martina, how about you? Do you have any examples of trust your husband places in you?"

"Well," she pauses…" I do make sure the maid gets her job done." *We must all look dumbfounded at the ridiculousness of that statement.* "And!" she nods and smiles to herself, "I keep our calendar! It's up to me if we can make an engagement. If I forget to put something down, we could miss something important. Is that what you mean?" *You've got to be kidding! That's it! All that money, that big house, only one child and that's what you do?!"*

"Yes, that's a good start. Anyone else who's married?"

"I keep the books for our home" JoAnne says, "it's been that way since we got married. He doesn't even know where the money goes. He gives me his check minus an agreed upon amount for his personal spending needs like gas and lunches and I pay the bills, do the shopping, make sure we have what we need for the house."

"Now that's an honor. Your husband trusts you with his ... well... your money. Do you invest any of it?" *Oh boy, that could be personal. I shouldn't have asked that.*

"Yes, I do. I pay tithe to the church and invest the second ten percent in the market. I don't use a broker though." *And it's doing well?*

"No broker?" Martina perks up. "How do you invest with no broker?"

"Well, I took a course at a community college years ago in business and investing. I have researched different places and have been investing for years. It's quite simple really."

"Could ya teach us?" Fancy asks.

"Sure!" Joy beams from JoAnne's face like I'd never seen. Not the fraudulent laughter following a self-deprecating quip, but real joy.

"Looks like we've already got ideas for the next group, huh?" I say, hoping to fan the flame of thought for

JoAnne. To see her that happy even brings me joy and I could use the help anyway. "Tonight is just the beginning of a very interesting study. Are there any questions or more comments about either of these two verses?" I pause for a bit but no one else speaks. "Well, who thinks they would be willing to give their testimony next week? Hmm, no one? Well, remember, we're here to learn from each other. So, please, someone help me out." Sarah Plain and Tall raises her hand sheepishly.

"I will, Connie, but I don't have a real lot to talk about, O.K.?"

*Whew! Anybody helping is good and I can always count on Sarah plain and tall.*

"Excellent! Would anybody volunteer to bring snacks next week?"

"You all know me. I'll bring some kind of sweet treat and a drink, how's that?" JoAnne volunteers in her usual tone.

"Great, JoAnne! We all know you make the best goodies around. Also, next week, if you'd like to bring friends, you can. Eight signed up and there are only six of us. I can fit 10-12 with dining room chairs. O.K?" I look around and every head nods in a way that says there will be six next week too.

"Can we pray ta close?" Fancy suggests.

"Of course, Fancy, would you like to lead us?"

"Sure. Daddy, we love You and are so grateful that You brought each one a y'ur daughters together tonight. Please let all we learnt bounce 'round in our heads this week and change each of our lives to make us more like You. Thank Ya, Daddy. Jesus, lover of ma soul, reach deep

## Inside My Head

in our hurtin' hearts and prepare us to be Y'ur bride. Teach us ta be like th' five wise virgins and gather extry oil fur this here long night, we love You, our betrothed. Holy Spirit, fill us up with You, the only everlastin' oil, and fan th' flame of revival in us that we would be jump-started fur what Y'u're brangin' to our homes and our church and our community. We love You. Amen."

"Wonderful, thank you. I look forward to seeing each of you and your guests next week. And Sarah, I look forward to hearing all about you. Goodnight, everyone."

.........

*Oh, my gosh! I thought they'd never leave! I thought after my -I look forward speech-, they'd go but they all wanted to chat at my house. I gotta be up by three a.m. so I can drop my kids off before going to work. Man like I got nothing better to do than chat. Whew, I mean I want it to be enjoyable but, you know, lets end at a reasonable time, too. Kids are home and in bed. Lunches all made, already had a shower. It's 11:00 p.m. already. Oh, my gosh, I'm tired.*

*God, what did you think? Went well tonight, Huh? Hey, oh, my gosh! Fancy's prayer. Wow! I didn't know she had it in her. What a creative prayer. Same with Maraschino. I can't pray like that. I just sort of talk to You. I don't know. Where did they learn to pray like that? I wonder if they do that when they're not in front of people. I bet not. I know how it is. They just don't want to be embarrassed so they make up fancy prayers to say while we're all discussing other things. They both did well. Hey, God could You please put it on everyone's heart to get out earlier next week. Man, I need sleep. Goodnight, God.*

# CHAPTER TWO

Beep, beep, beep smack!

Beep, beep, beep smack!

"Ten minutes already? I hate that clock! Three thirty. There's just something wrong with the idea of getting up this early to go to a place you hate just to pay bills. I hate my job." *Man, I can't even walk right. Years ago if I were walking like this at 3:00 a.m., it was because I was getting home, not getting up to leave,* sigh, "those were the days."

"Jade, wake up, honey."

"O.K. ,Mom, thanks." *I can hear the smile without even looking. Of course, looking is impossible with my eyes closed.*

"Porter honey, wake up." *I'll stand right here. I'm kinda like his snooze button, I guess. I wish I wasn't.* "Porter, you have to get up, hon." Yawn.

"O.K. mom," *his eyes aren't open yet. I can tell because he sounds like I do, and my eyes aren't open yet.*

"Porter, I'm going to the bathroom and when I get back you better be up." *It would be nice if this wasn't the norm, but every day this is it. I smack the alarm, wait ten minutes and smack it again. I remind myself of just how much I hate my job, then wake up Jade, then Porter. She gets right up and I practically have to pull him out of bed. I wonder what it would be like to have a job I loved.*

"Porter, I'm out. Are you up?" I peek now that my eyes are open.

# Inside My Head

"Yeah, I'm up."

"Good." I shuffle back to my room with slippers sliding across the floor. Picking my feet up is way too much work at this time of the day. Porter and Jade both sound like me on the way to the bathroom. The argument begins. Who takes longer? Why they take longer? They always try to involve me, but I quit being the referee on this one a long time ago.

*What to wear, what to wear. The choices are limitless, this pair of jeans or this pair. Odd, when holding them between me and the mirror, they all look the same; t-shirt, hmm... which one; blue, black, gray or .... green. Or should I say boring, boring, boring or ugly? I guess it's those and boring number 2 for today. This reminds me of 'do you want what's behind door number one, number two, number three, or do you want to take a chance on the box' some stupid whore model, wearing as little as possible on daytime television, just brought up behind you.*

*Man, I'd love to just sit and watch TV for a week straight, but if I take a day off I usually run like crazy the whole day. Pick up one of the kids, take them to the doctor or dentist, then home or back to school, then to the store; and from there, who knows? It just gets crazy!*

"Here are your lunches that I made last night. Eat the 'good for you' stuff first and save the best for last. Oh, my gosh! Look at the time. We have to leave now. We'll be late and I can't be late today."

"It was Jades fault. She wouldn't get out of the bathroom and I had to go," Porter starts in.

"Porter, you should have gone back in your room till I finished. It's not my fault you're so late." *Jades defense is solid. Maybe she'll be a lawyer and I won't have to work anymore. Of course, that'll be at least eight to ten years* *before she even starts her practice. Of course, as a lawyer she could be rich immediately if someone falls at a store or has a baby with a birth defect. Lawyers are all about the blame game. 'Oh, you were just sliding your feet across the floor after the person in front of you dropped a bottle of fruit punch and you fell and broke your pinky and cut your knee? Well, we'll sue for $1.3 million and we will probably settle for $750,000 of which I'll take the first $250,000.'*

"You guys tell Aunt Bonnie hello."

"K, mom, love you."

"See you this afternoon, I love you too." Kisses all around and out they go. "Whew, how do I get up at 3:30 and run late? I guess I'm just too slow." *It seems they're right. Since 35, it's all been downhill. Especially when you're alone. I don't have a good reason to get up. Well, besides Jade and Porter. I do love them with all that is in me. If it weren't for them, I don't know what I'd do. Life wouldn't be worth living. As it is, this is what I got* (I raise my hand pointing toward the parking lot). "Work. A factory. My home away from home. Five years. It wasn't supposed to be this way. Porter was supposed to stay. I got pregnant! I figured that was my destiny. All those other guys and I'd never gotten pregnant, then..." I sigh deeply.

"Hi, Connie." Sheila says in passing.

"Hi."

"Good morning, Connie."

"Good morning, Ron." He's always so friendly. *How is anyone that cheerful at 5:00 a.m.? I barely force a smile. There it is...music. Delta Dawn, what's that flower you got on? ... She's 41 and her daddy still calls her baby... I wonder if my dad would still call me sugarplum. I miss him so much. He was somebody I could talk to. He was too young to die. They do say*

## Inside My Head

*only the good die young. Of course, that's not true. That kid just got shot downtown the other day during a drug deal gone bad, according to the news. Obviously he was no good.*

*God, I don't get it. My dad was great. He treated mom like a queen and me like a princess. I loved him. I was sure he'd be so angry when I got pregnant with Jade, but he wasn't. He walked me down the aisle looking so proud. Like I was a virgin. I suppose he'd have died sooner if he'd have known about all those other guys. He probably would've killed Tommy if he knew about us...(sigh). Those were the days. Sneaking around and doing it every chance we got, wherever we could. It was so exciting to think we could get caught. So sexy to pretend we were just friends then get down the road and have to pull over 'cause we both wanted it so badly he couldn't concentrate on driving. Every time we kissed it was hotter than any time before. I still get hot just thinking back.*

*Oh, my gosh! He was an incredible kisser. He taught me so much. Of course, I'd be horrified if Jade ever found out. Oh, my gosh. If I even thought she was making out with some guy in the backseat, or anywhere for that matter, I'd have a fit.*

*She's awesome. I know all the signs and she's not hiding anything. God has made such a good thing come from me. I don't even know why or how. I'm no good, how can my kids be so great? I think it was a little over a year ago Jade started really changing. That camp she went to with church. She came back different. I mean she was good, but could be sassy and ornery with Porter. Now she's softer, gentler, something, I don't know. Like this morning "O.K. mom, thanks." Waking up with a smile. I shake my head and smile. She's great.*

*I should send Porter to that camp this year. Well, next year, I think it's every other summer. It'd be worth any amount of money if he'd be nicer and not so much like his dad. Well, if he turned out like his dad I don't know what I'd do. I don't know what I'm going to do now. I don't know how to raise a boy. I slept with every boy I ever knew after fourteen. That's not what I want Porter to be like.*

*I don't want some woman standing around thirty years from now getting hot over thoughts of her and Porter when they were kids. Tommy's mom, hmm, she thought he was a good boy, and we really were just friends until she walked in on us making out on his bed.*

*Oh, my gosh, I'll never forget that day. We were out swimming in Tommy's pool. He looked so fine in his Speedo and I looked so fine in my bikini. We splashed each other. Nothing can get me hotter than a pool. I don't guess that'll ever change.*

*Of course, I've changed. I wouldn't be caught dead in a bikini. But I sure would like to play again. What could be better than a warm pool and a hot body?*

Buzz, buzz, buzz, hmm. Break.

"Hi," Ronnie says.

"Hi" I wave as I make my way over to the pop machine. Diet pop with my 100 calorie snack.

"Hey Connie, what are you eating?"

"Hey Sheila, a pack of Oreo-like cookies. One of those 100 calorie packs. Have you seen those commercials where the guy dresses like a snack fairy?"

"Yeah, they are kinda funny, huh?" she snorts.

"Well, hmm. What are you doing tonight?"

"I got church tonight."

"Oh,.." Sheila looks at her hands on the table as she

picks at some stuck on morsel left from days gone by.

"Why, what's up?" I ask as I take another big gulp of my pop and then offer the bag of cookies to her.

She shakes her head without looking up. "Just wondered... I haven't got anything to do. I thought maybe we could hang out or something."

"Oh, sorry, yeah I go every week to that big church across town. You know that Calvary Hill Church?"

"Oh, yeah. I've never gone there."

*Is she wanting to go? Nah.., not her. She wouldn't be caught dead in church. I'm sure she'd much sooner be found at a bar than a church. I'd ask but I know how she is. So does every man here.*

"These breaks are never long enough are they?" I say quickly as I glance up. "By the time you get your drink and eat a snack, you don't really have time to go to the bathroom. I'm sorry, Sheila, but I'll see you back on the line, O.K.?"

"Yeah."

*She doesn't act like herself. I wonder what's up. Sheila never lacks for company. Well, at least male company. Oh, I hate this bra. Bzz, bzz, bzz. I knew I wouldn't get back on time. Even our breaks are rushed. What I wouldn't give to be able to stay home. I thought when Jade was a baby, I'd get to, but, No!! Porter had other thoughts and most of them didn't include me. I can't believe him and Darlene have been together for so long now. What was it with her? Why didn't he stay with me? I mean I know he said I was a whore but that's why we got together in the first place. Besides I was thinner than Darlene. Of course, I haven't been for the last eight years. What a cow! I'm busy doing*

## Inside My Head

*all kinds of things I don't want to do. I look like a pig. My house is never clean anymore because I'm never home. I don't know if I remember how to cook using a stove or oven. I nuke everything.*

*I don't wear make-up 'cause why bother. My hair... I lost track of the natural color years ago. Although people tell me red is good. I've tried them all. I guess red is as good as any other. You don't have to be a star baby, to be in my show... what a stupid song. That's all guys want for real, a star, a drop dead gorgeous movie star; a porn star preferably. Someone that'll knock their socks off every time. But they don't care if they knock your socks off.*

*I want sex. Good sex. I know the old saying how pizza and sex are alike. They're both good, hot, cold and with anything on them. Something like that anyway.*

*I guess sex could be like pizza. Oooh, there's Tony. Now he'd be a meat lovers pizza. Something you could really sink your teeth into. I like my men with some meat. I guess just cheese is O.K. with a lot of cheese. Well, a guy that's a cheese pizza would be maybe just a bit plain. Double cheese maybe average or a bit better. The veggie lovers would be good, meat lovers better, but mm., mm, mm. Kevin, He's a pepperoni lovers, stuffed crust with banana peppers. Oh, my gosh, he is the ultimate pizza. Wouldn't he be great as an all you can eat buffet. And I can eat! Especially when I'm really hungry; and I am starving! Hmm. What I wouldn't give to have just a taste of that man.*

(In the background, but loud enough for me to hear well). "Hey Mike, whatcha doin tonight?" Sheila flirts like her regular self. I knew that wouldn't last long.

"Hey, me and Steve and some of the guys are going to Trevors. You wanna come?"

"Sure, I got nothing better to do." Sheila smiles and sighs. "What time?" *She sure seems down.*

"I gotta go home and get outta these work clothes, get a bite to eat, then... I guess like 6? How's that sound."

"The time or the rest of it?" she laughs in her flirtatious way. *Now that sounds like Sheila.*

"Well honey, maybe I'll tell ya later. We'll see, but for now, just the time." Mike winks.

"Cool. I'll be there with bells on."

"Can't wait to see that." Mike hurries off and Sheila goes the opposite direction.

*I know I shouldn't be so put out. I love God and all but I wish I could find someone. Just one. Not the buffet line Sheila's pulled up to, but just someone.*

*This bra is driving me nuts. The strap slides down and the underwire pokes and hurts. I think bras should be outlawed. I would've put this one in a bra burning in the 60's.*

*I never understood the real reason for burning bras but I believe it had everything to do with the smart girls saying we are uncomfortable and we refuse to wear them and their equally smart boyfriends saying "Yay! I'd rather see you without them anyway". And if you're big you can't find a cute one that actually does the job and holds you up. Ridiculous! I don't know. I saw some in a magazine that supposedly work and were cute but they're like fifty dollars each. I can't spend fifty dollars on a bra. That pays for cable, or gas for the van for a week! Fifty dollars!! That's ridiculous. Is it really so bad not to wear one? If I wore a really big shirt, it should be O.K. Of course if it's too big it could get caught in a machine. Me trying to escape the grip of the machine could be quite enlightening about the whole bra thing.*

*But if I did get stuck, maintenance would be called. Kevin could come to my rescue. Good thing he wears a name tag. I'd need to call him by name when properly thanking my knight for rescuing me from the huge steel dragon. Hmm. Wonder what all a proper thanks would need to entail. A 'thank you' wouldn't be enough for saving me. A kiss? Yeah that would be good; a good kiss, not just a peck on the cheek, a meet me-later-kiss. In fact I could lean up and whisper that in his ear just in case he didn't get it, or to make sure he knew that's what I meant anyway.*

*Tony, now he is it and a bag of chips with chocolate cake for dessert.* Deep sigh.

*Chips and cake and pizza; geez, I am hungry. It's 8:50 a.m. I am so glad they put that clock right where I can see it. I love to keep track of time. Well, some days, like today. Time is flying but, some days time creeps by and, oh my gosh!*

*I gotta go to the bathroom. I'll do that then maybe the lines will be shorter by the food truck and the pop machines. Hmm. What do I want for lunch?*

Buzz, buzz, buzz. Good!

"Connie! What are you having?" *I don't get why Sheila has been so friendly lately. It's weird. I mean she's nice but it's like all of a sudden... friends? Hmm.*

"I guess a hot ham and cheese."

"Sorry we're out of sandwiches already." The woman standing by the mobile meals truck says.

"Already?"

"Yep."

*I'm still two people back so I guess I'll look when I get there.*

"I got a pizza. Wanna share?" Sheila offers and lifts her box in the air.

# Inside My Head

"Sure, thanks." *Easy choice.* We walk back to the cafeteria chatting and I don't even know about what. My mouth runs one direction and my mind another. *Calvin- he's kind of a plain pepperoni. Average, well, above average. Maybe a six; I guess average is 4 or 5; cheese pizza is a 3; double cheese 3 or 4. Calvin is one of those rare few black guys I think look good. Not that all black guys are ugly 'cause they most definitely are not. Just given a choice, I like long, soft hair and that, they don't have. As far as fine bodies go, well... that's easy. Calvin is pretty high on the list with his big arms and fine body. You know he may even be a 7. I wonder what he looks like outside of work, in a tank and shorts.* "Yep I'm guessing a 7."

"What are you thinking about?" I snap back to Sheila. She laughs. "Oh my God! You musta been really deep with that look." She laughs. "I could tell you must notta been really thinking about fall being here when you said something about a 7. I'm thinking a 7? What's a 7?"

I have to laugh just out of embarrassment. I roll my eyes, swallow hard and bite my lip, "Calvin."

Sheila laughs so hard I bet everyone will turn and look at us…A quick glance and…yep, they are. I just smile. Caught! I hate when I do that. I start thinking something then I start talking out loud. Not good. I guess my brain doesn't do two things at once for too long. "What were we talking about?" I hope to get into the conversation I was supposedly already a part of.

"Oh, no! I want to know more about what you were thinking." Her smile is huge.

"Umm…" *do I tell her? Surely she has to know the whole pizza thing anyway but that sure doesn't make me sound to Christian-like I don't guess.* (Sigh) "Well, I'm sure you've heard the whole sex is like pizza thing. Haven't you?"

"Yeah."

"So, then, well, I was thinking about that earlier for some reason and then when you offered me pizza it just came back to mind." I hope that's enough as I smile at her.

"And..."

*Oh shoot!* "And?"

"Calvin?"

"Umm, yeah let's see. I don't know how I got there. It seems my thoughts are wild some days. I have ADD in my head. I can go from dust on the floor to buying dinner with the kids and not know how I got there. It's weird!"

She laughs a little, but isn't appeased. "Calvin is a 7, huh? You like dark chocolate?"

"Not usually. In fact, no, only when it's with peppermint. I only eat milk chocolate. Funny enough I don't like white chocolate either. That Nutella; oh, my gosh! Have you tried that? I love it by the spoonfuls. It's like a hazelnut chocolate..." I look up and see her shaking her head and smiling.

"You are ADD!" She jokes.

"Why now?"

"Calvin? Dark chocolate? Men? Or are you teasing me?"

"Oh! Oh!" the light goes on *duh! I'm so stupid!* I rub my head and close my eyes. "Uh, men. No, I was thinking you were giving me a way out of the pizza/sex talk." I have to laugh. And so does she.

## Inside My Head

"Not a chance," Sheila says, shaking her head, "I want to hear more about you and Calvin."

"No, no," I wave my hand, "It's really, really not what you're thinking. I just happened to see him while I was thinking."

"So, who do you think about when you're not checking out Calvin?"

"Tony, Kevin. Definitely Kevin." *Oh, my gosh, I can't believe I just told her that!*

"Kevin, from maintenance?"

"I can't believe I just told you that." My eyes are bulging out of my head. What if she says something to him?

"What kind of pizza is he?" she smiles. Actually, I don't think she has stopped smiling since the '7' question.

Buzz, buzz, buzz.

"Oh, man! The bell, gotta get back to work. You know that line manager. She'll be all over me if I don't hurry." I give her an I-just-got-away smile.

"Yeah, I'll be all over you if we don't finish this chat later." It's good to be friends with the line manager; even if we're not like real close or anything.

*Look at him! Nice walk. I gotta quit. It's just one of those days. I need to get my mind on something other than men.*

*Let's see, church. I go to church tonight. I did that Bible study last night. That went good. Sarah plain and tall is going to give her testimony next week. We're supposed to invite friends. I'm the one that suggested it. Who in the world could I invite? I don't really do anything but work and church and I don't really have any friends I hang out with. Hmm. What to do, what to do. It's not right if I don't think of someone.*

"Kevin," Sheila mouths and points to a machine on the next aisle as she passes me. I smile and my eyebrow goes up. I shake my head and sigh as my whole torso melts.

*He is definitely a pepperoni-lovers-stuffed-crust-with-banana peppers pizza. I'd love to have him as an all you can eat buffet. Just him. I don't think I could ever get enough. Every time I see him I want him more. I'd turn into an oven. A preheated oven. Put him inside and let him bake. Oh, that is bad, Constance! Geez girl! Get it together. You are bad. How is God ever going to use you if you think like that? God, I need a man. I want Kevin but Tony, Sean from the gas station, Stephen at church, Calvin, definitely; well, Tony is a definite, too. Almost anybody will do. It's been ten years too many with no one. What do you say to that God?"*

Silence.

*10:45 O.K. I'll clear my mind. I'll listen; maybe God will talk.*

Silence.

*Xanadu, Xanadu-oo, oh, the headbands and workout clothes. That was fun. The eighties were a great time to be a teen. 10:50 nothing. God doesn't talk to me much. Oh, what's that other song she sang. Oh, I don't know, but, Grease! Now that was a good movie. I love it. I used to know every line. I haven't watched that in years. I want to do that. I don't know when. I never get to just relax and watch a movie.*

*That's what I'll plan for the weekend. Porter may object but in the end he'll love it ,too. We'll get pizza and popcorn, and we can all dance and just have fun. Oh, that is going to be so much fun.*

## Inside My Head

*I used to have an outfit like Sandra. O, man, did I look great. Now I couldn't pass for Sandra's pet cow. I don't know how I'll ever find a husband like this. I wish I could stop eating all together, but no, it seems like I can't stop at all. I never would have guessed I'd be in a size 20. I didn't believe them when they said 'wait till you have kids.' Your body will never be the same. Not only will it stretch but it never gets quite back to the original size. It's like a stretched out balloon. Now look at me, two kids and fifteen years later I look like a punching balloon. I've been blown up and punched, and put down over and over till I can't bear to look in the mirror anymore.*

*Man, this sucks, and I don't anymore. Life is just not fair.* Deep sigh.

My mind goes blank as I stare at the machine and allow my thoughts to be drowned out by the screeching of the saws and the pounding of the punches and drills in the background.

*Bzz, bzz, bzz. Afternoon break already? Good! I'm tired today. I wish I had time for a nap. Fifteen minutes isn't enough time. But it's worth laying my head down.*

"Hey girl!" Sheila calls out.

"Hello," I respond in my 'I'm trying to take a nap voice'.

"Oh, no you don't!" she's looking at me with a half grin and her arms crossed like she's waiting for something. "What?" *did I forget something?*

"I want inside your head."

I really know she wouldn't want that. I won't let anybody go there; I'm somebody totally different there and that has to stay far away from everyone else. "What?"

## Inside My Head

"Calvin, Kevin, Tony, sex and pizza." She smiles and raises both eyebrows. "What kind is Kevin?"

"Oh." *I can't believe I told anybody that, least of all her.*

"Well." I say with a deep breath slowly, wishing I could get out of this but here I go. "A pepperoni-lovers-stuffed-crust-with-banana-peppers."

"Hmm." She says as she nods and looks up and to the left. *She's trying to understand something or picture it or something. I learned that in psych 20 years ago. I loved that class. Getting into people's heads, I love that. Unless it was my head, then, no one is allowed there.* "I take it that's a great pizza."

"The ultimate." I grin.

"So, Kevin is the ultimate. Have you two had sex yet?" Only Sheila would say that so nonchalantly.

"No!" I blurt out as though that would be horrible instead of everything I could possibly ever want.

"Why not?"

"I don't even know him."

"I can fix that for you." She smiles mischievously.

"No, that's quite alright." I shake my head.

"Why?"

"Because." *She wouldn't understand. She doesn't have to consider the fact that a man may not want her. She also doesn't care if he's a Christian and I really do. I know sex would be phenomenal with him but it's not worth Hell.*

"Hmm?"

## Inside My Head

"What?"

"Why?"

"Sheila, it's complicated." I close my eyes and shake my head. *It's better to be able to fantasize than to come face to face with obvious rejection.* "He'd never want me anyway. Look at him! He's fantastic and I'm..." I lift my hands in resignation.

"You're what?"

"Sheila, I'm a cow. Please, he'd never go for me. Besides I really want a Christian."

"He's not one?"

"I don't know."

"Well, I can at least find that out, can't I?"

*Oh my gosh! What if she does?... What if he is?... What if he's not?*

Buzz, buzz, buzz.

"I will," she says as she gets up. "That would be cool, wouldn't it?" She leaves without an answer.

*Would it? I don't know. If he is a Christian, that may even be worse. Not only is he THE most fantastic, drop dead gorgeous, hottest man I've ever laid eyes on, but he'd also be a Christian and I wouldn't even stand a chance at the ultimate man. If he's not, I can at least reason with myself that he's off limits and not worth it.*

*I've tried a hundred zillion diets and I can't lose weight. I want to, but I don't want to bad enough I guess. I know how it should work but I look in the mirror everyday and want to puke. Just from the sight. I'd like to be bulimic, then I could eat*

## Inside My Head

*anyway, but I can't puke. I've tried over and over. I know I shouldn't but I hate the way I look.*

*I used to be so beautiful. I used to get compliments all the time. I knew girls hated me; well, at least didn't like me. They felt about me like I do about Sheila. I could get anybody. And I did; all the time. That was before. Now!* I shake my head in disgust.

I let my thoughts go with the sounds of the music. I can't stand to think about how disgusting and fat I am. I have to drift off into a better place. Music does that for me. I can be anyone, anywhere when I am in the music.

"Hey, Sheila, what are you doing tonight?" Joe calls out across the lines.

"Don't know yet." She smiles back. "Whatcha got in mind?"

"What I got in mind shouldn't be put out there right here. I am a gentleman. But I do plan to start at O'Malley's. You want to meet me there and I will fill you in later?" His devious grin makes him look cute.

"Well, Mike asked if I'd go to Trevor's. I gotta go home and check on the monsters and get outta these damn clothes first. What time were you thinking?"

"Well, if you're getting out of those clothes, we could start at your place

"Not a chance, buddy. You know I would need a few first anyway."

"O.K, how about we start at Trevor's and then hit up O'Malley's?...And don't eat anything." Again the deviance appears on his cute face.

## Inside My Head

"Sounds good. I don't know about the eating thing though. I don't need to get wasted tonight.

"Yeah, well it can end so much nicer if you are a little tipsy anyway."

She laughs. "For who? I don't forget what it's like just cause I lose my inhibitions." She teases. "See ya about six."

*Yeah, and I will be in church. You two kids have fun. I will think about you while I am reminding myself how great Heaven will be, and how I don't have to be in Hell with you.*

"Connie, wanna join us?" Sheila asks for the first time. *Are you serious?* I look across the line at her, and she is.

"No thanks." I say without explaining that I will be in church contemplating our eternities apart.

The day went by quickly and I rushed out trying to leave the parking lot without too much aggravation. *Yeah, me at a bar. I haven't done that in years. It would be so much fun to hang out with others, especially if those others have different parts that would fit into my puzzle perfectly. Just slide that piece into that piece and, Oh, Yeah! We could be perfect together.' We' who, you idiot? Who wants you anyway? No one! That is why you are going home alone to two kids who don't have a father at home. That is why it has been over ten years since anyone has tried to see what your puzzle looks like just to see if they want to work on it. Really? If anyone looked close enough, they would work a different puzzle anyway. I don't have a life or anything worth looking at anyway. I guess my puzzle would need to be appreciated by an art lover who likes Picasso. That way they can imagine it being something beautiful.*

"You Idiot! You just cut me off! What if my brakes didn't work? You need to slow down! Are you really in that big a hurry to get to Hell? What a moron! I hate when people drive like maniacs. Stupid men! They all just want to get where they are going before everyone else, like they are more special than everyone else." *I can't believe she asked me if I wanted to go to a bar. I am a Christian. Doesn't she get that? I just told her I didn't know if Kevin is a Christian. Duh, why would that matter if I wasn't one? She is kind of dumb it seems. But she does have people checking out her box to see if they want to work on her puzzle. She has a lot of people trying to put it together, too. What am I complaining for? So what if she's dumb. At least she has someone; someone different as often as she'd like, too. Look at me; I have no one! Maybe I am too smart! Yeah, right,* I nod. "More like too fat and ugly to get past the box top! Who wants to look inside?" *My pieces are more like the giant size that six-year-olds can put together; no one wants to do that anymore. Men want the tiny, thousand piece puzzles. Guess I can't blame 'em. That is what every movie, TV show, commercial, billboard and magazine show want. I can't compare to those stick people.* "I am more like a balloon person."

"A balloon person, Mom?" Jade questions as she reaches for her seatbelt. "What is that supposed to mean?"

I close my eyes, realizing that I was thinking out loud again. *Crap!* "Oh, I was just thinking about the differences between me and models."

She looks at me like I just said the stupidest thing ever. "You and models?"

"Yeah, I know, not much of a comparison really stick and the balloon at the end. They are the sticks and well..." I frown as I picture a clown holding a stick and lifting the balloon in the air away from itself in order to give away the prize to someone.

"Yeah! The sticks are the only way that some kid could hold onto the big beautiful balloon they are so excited about! You are right, Mom. You are the best prize."

"Well, I wasn't actually thinking of it like that but thanks." I smile at her perception.

"Church tonight!" Jade sings. "It is so much fun! I love to go and hear what pastor John has to say. He always puts a certain spin on things that I hadn't thought of. It's like he can read the same thing I am reading and understand it so much better. I want to get things like he does someday." She puts her ear buds in and pulls out a book without waiting for a response from me.

I shake my head. *I am pure evil. I was just thinking of puzzles, balloons and sex and just really not wanting to have to go sit in a church pew one more time and she put me right in my place. I don't guess I thought of it like that at all. I just want to go and warm a spot and not go to Hell. I am so bad! I don't even know what to say or think anyway.*

Porter gets in with little more than a grunt before putting in his ear buds and pulling out his Gameboy. We stop off at the golden arches I am supporting with all my money, individually keeping them open, and we order the same dollar menu meals we get a couple of times a week before going home to feed and walk the dog, wash dishes, change clothes and rush out to church. Life is one big thrill after another.

# CHAPTER THREE

*There's Maraschino looking like a '9' as usual. Man, that is just not fair. I'd give about anything to be as beautiful as she is and to afford her wardrobe. She must spend a mint on it. That dress! And those shoes, oh, my gosh! Of course with a husband like that, how could she ever be anything but happy. That man is incredible. She can wear make-up and hide any flaw, even though I can't imagine she has any, but he is plain ol' perfect with no way to hide anything. Perfect marries perfect. How can it be any better? I can't imagine how she said she was not happy. I can't stand her.*

*I'm a 5, tops. Wearing a dress I've had for at least four years several sizes larger than I ever wanted to be. I bet her house is spotless too. She doesn't even work! She's perfectly tanned all year and no kids. I bet they're both so selfish they don't want kids so that they don't have to spend money on anyone but themselves!* I shake my head in disgust for her beauty and selfishness.

"Connie!" *Oh crap, here she comes. Sigh!*

"Hi!" I smile to show how glad I am to see her like I always do. We hug. *Crap! She smells good too. I forgot about that. Well, I smell like strawberries.* I roll my eyes.

"I really enjoyed last night. You really got me thinking in an entirely new direction about myself and my role as Jay's wife and even as the betrothed of Jesus. You're amazing! Thank you so much. I will be bringing friends, I promise. And I want to give my testimony the next week after Sarah. Ok?"

"Sure, I'll put it on the calendar. And thank you so much for the encouragement. I really need it." *Oh, I hate that she is so nice. Man, couldn't she be nasty? There's gotta be something wrong with her.*

"Connie!" Fancy snaps my back into the realization that I am standing in a church.

"Hi, Fancy." I smile. *At least she is dumb. It's O.K. to be pretty if you're dumb as a stump. At least she's not perfect.*

"Oh my gosh! Last night was so sweet! I never thought of myself as a crown before. How cool! I'm gonna be the crown of my husband. Wow! Just thinking 'bout it again just now makes me get goose bumps. I love this bible study. Thank you for taking the time to study it all out so good. I'll be bringin' somebody with me next week for sure."

"Thanks. That really means a lot to me." *Man, I can't believe the reponse. OOH! I love those shoes. But those over there don't even go with that dress at all. Man, some people just shouldn't wear dresses. Look at that girl. I thought I was big! She must be related to Jo Ann. I don't even know where Jo Ann finds clothes to fit. She must be a five or six x at least, she's huge! She must not do anything but eat all day to maintain that weight.*

*I can't bend down to tie my shoes without being uncomfortable and I'm a 20. I can't imagine that she can do anything without being out of breath. How do people let themselves get that big? I'd rather die than be that gross.*

"Connie!" JoAnne calls out as she waddles up. She leans in to hug me. *She smells like sugar cookies. She's so sweet I do feel sorry for her.* "Connie, I am so thankful for that bible study group." She's more serious than I have ever seen her. "You all made me feel so smart and so important. Oh, my goodness, I will definitely be bringing friends. And you just wait till you taste those snacks next week!" Her eyes got big and her smile even bigger. "I love you, Connie. You're so special. Thank you for doing this study!" She smiles and hugs me again, and I return the smile.

"You're welcome, JoAnne. I am so glad you're getting so much out of it. Thank you for your encouragement."

*Wow, how cool is this!! I'm so glad everyone liked it so much. Oh, my gosh! Look at Fred! Man, he looks good tonight. He looks good every night. Well, I bet he would anyway. He is at least a '7'. Ya' know, I'd be more than happy with a '7'. His blond hair and blue eyes suit him fine. He is more serious than I'd like, but oh, well. He is kinda losing his hair but at least he doesn't do the comb-over. That is the most ridiculous style anybody can have. Someone said he'll be 53 next month. I guess that'd be O.K. A little old, but he still looks good and he's single and a Christian. Beggars can't be choosers.*

Shout to the Lord all the earth, let us sing. Power and majesty praise to the King...

*Oh, what I wouldn't give for her hair. Who is that? I think she's new. Man, long, thick black hair. I love it. I wish mine would grow. I have the worst hair ever. I can't get it past my shoulders and it breaks. It's flat and straight and ugly and fine. No style. Geez! Honestly, no man has to even look at my body to know he wouldn't want me.*

*I bet Sheila is having fun. I know, God, I shouldn't be jealous of her. She's on her way to Hell. I do get to go to Heaven but sometimes I wonder why I have to live a dull poor life and so many non-Christians live life to the fullest.*

"Tonight let's open our Bibles to John 10:10. The thief does not come except to steal and to kill and to destroy. I have come that they may have life and that they may have it more abundantly.

"What does this verse actually mean to us? What is abundant life? Is it simply wealth or is it something different? Let's pray and then we'll look into the abundance of life. Father, teach us tonight to more adequately understand the abundance you came to give. Teach us, Oh Lord, to hear your voice and to choose you. Thank you for your Word, your love, your grace, your mercy and most of all for the salvation offered through your Son's death and resurrection. Forgive us for our murmurings, oh Lord, I pray. Amen.

"O.K. folks, I had a friend tell me not too long ago that he had finally come to understand this verse better. He said that in life there is good and there is bad and when Jesus said we'd have life more abundantly, He obviously meant more good times but also more bad. You see, he found out he has cancer of the liver. It's untreatable and he will have six months or less to spend with his 6, 9, and 12-year-old children and his wife of 15 years. They were high school sweethearts and have already waded through the mire of two miscarriages, the sudden death of her father, the suicide death of his sister, a near fatal car accident involving their middle child and a bout with breast cancer in his wife. These of course, are the major traumatic events. I won't list the minor day-to-day troubles at work, school and in their finances.

"This man and his family understand abundance. But, on that note they have also been blessed with an extraordinary business that has pulled them out of financial straits, afforded them an annual family vacation to anywhere in the world and they have traveled extensively in Europe and Africa. He and his wife have come to understand the vitality of getting away alone and quarterly, the two of them run off for a romantic weekend alone. They've been blessed with three beautiful and healthy children whom he and his wife cherish tremendously.

"Abundance... This family is a fine example of abundance, both in good and bad. And they, like Paul, have learned contentment in each and every situation. They also have learned to hear their Shepherd's voice and to follow His lead knowing that He will take excellent care of them. As in Psalm 23, they do not want. They are at peace in the times of blessing as well as the times of trial. They are completely at peace with God's will and provision for their lives. They lie down in green pastures and follow God to still waters. They have allowed Him to restore their souls. They follow the path of righteousness sharing with everyone they meet, their faithfulness, trust and peace in their God.

"Several times they have walked through, key word here being "through", the valley of the shadow of death. Never have I seen them filled with fear. They call out to God for mercy and strength. They fully rest in the knowledge that He is with them. That His Word remains as true today as the very day it was written. They know that they know that they know that He will NEVER leave them nor forsake them. They are comforted by His presence.

"Abundance truly is a pregnant word. It is a word just waiting to break forth into new and unexpected directions. When Jesus said in this world you will have trouble back over in John 16:33, He also said 'be of good cheer, I have overcome the world.' And in John 14:27 He said 'Peace I leave with you, my peace I give to you...' In Matthew 6:33...well, let's back up to vs. 25 and I'm going to skip a bit here, but I suggest you read the whole thing for yourselves. 'Therefore, I say to you, do not worry about your life, what you will eat or what you will drink; not about your body, what you will put on.' He describes the birds and even the fields and His provision for their needs. Then in vs. 33, He says...'but seek first the kingdom of God and His righteousness and **ALL these things** shall be added unto you.' The emphasis there being mine.

"'ALL THESE THINGS.' Your life will be provided for abundantly. Your food and drink and clothes. Every single need will be met. He shows us back up here in vs. 28 the lilies of the field. My wife loves lilies; they are, in her words, beautiful and elegant. There are also a variety of lilies, not just the white ones we see at Easter. They are arrayed in a multitude of colors. And God likens our attire to them saying that King Solomon was not even arrayed as magnificently. God doesn't just give us a pair of pants and a shirt. If we are obedient, He provides us with an abundance of clothing. Many times I've gone to a store with my wife looking for a new shirt or pair of pants knowing I have only a certain amount of money to spend. We'd pray first and ask God for a sale and lo and behold I'd come home with exactly what I was looking for plus something for my wife without going over budget.

"God is truly a God of abundant provision. Not simply more money or clothes or a nicer car than your neighbor. It's not meant to be a way to keep up with the Jones' or to surpass them. His abundance is far more precious and valuable than that. God's abundance is in the everyday things; in the bad as well as the good. His abundance of peace allows us to endure far more than the Jones'; to sleep at night even during a fight with cancer or a fight with the Jones'.

"It rains on the just and the unjust. That will never change but the abundance of grace is incomprehensible and the abundance of mercy, when we find ourselves once again begging God for it, is mind-blowing. The abundance of His unconditional love is priceless. Especially to those who have known an abundance of hurt and rejection by others. The abundance of joy and strength in the midst of our darkest trials can only be described as super-natural.

"Some wicked people may appear to be living life to its fullest, but when you look deep they may be going down for the final count and those around them don't even know. The depths of hurt, fear, bitterness, anger, sadness, confusion, and even apathy may be the only abundance they feel. We need to ask God to allow us to see through His eyes. Then we need to be willing to offer them the hope and the abundant life only Jesus came to give.

"Let's pray. God, thank you for sending your one and only Son that we can have eternal life with you and so that we can have life here on Earth abundantly. Give us, this week, the opportunity to see others through your eyes, Lord. Make us willing to share our abundance with them.

"Lord, God for those here tonight without the abundant life you came to give I pray. Your Word says if we confess with our mouth, and believe in our hearts that you are faithful and just to forgive us and cleanse us from all unrighteousness. Pour into our hearts, God the desire to be cleansed from our sins and the willingness to confess them and turn from them so that our eternities will be spent with you.

"I love you, God. Thank you for abundant life. Teach us all week more because of Your Word tonight, Lord, Amen. You are dismissed and I will see you all, the Lord willing, on Sunday.

*That was weird. Good, but weird. I was just wondering about that to you, God and then Pastor John answered me. This is freaky, God. Lately you've been doing that. I'm guessing it's you since I know nobody can read my thoughts. Well, I hope not anyway. No, most people wouldn't talk to me any more if they knew. I guess that's a bad thing really.*

"Mom!" Jade calls out. I turn to find her holding onto Porter like some prize she won at a carnival several hours earlier. I raise my hand since I can be easily lost in a crowd.

"You two ready?"

"Yep" says Jade and Porter nods in agreement.

"Connie!" I look around to see Martina working her way through the crowd followed by her husband, Michael. Both are smiling. *I guess this is good.* I wave. "Connie! I'm so glad we caught you before you left. You know my husband Michael, don't you?"

"Yes." We exchange smiles and cordial nods.

"I don't know exactly what was said last night, but I do know that I appreciate it. Martina has not stopped smiling since she got home. She's been singing. I just wanted to say thank you. I hadn't really expected to see any change so quickly, thank you." Michael blurted out in a manner so uncommon to any I've experienced with him before.

"You're welcome, but it's really more of a group thing and God, of course is the real leader. It's just at my house, but I'm so glad you like it so much, Martina. Does this mean you'll be back?"

"Yes, definitely! I haven't felt this important in ages. I never fathomed how prodigious being a wife is. I am an asset to my husband and I never believed that before last night. I couldn't sleep from the exaltation of that very realization. I am Michael's crown! Not his trophy!"

"She keeps saying that!" Michael adds with the non-stop smile and his head moving back and forth in a mixture of joy and confusion. With that, they turn to leave.

*Wow! Martina likes me. I don't guess I ever expected that. She acts different than usual too. Lord, I know all this must be you.*

"Let's go guys."

"Mom, I'm so proud of you. You're letting God use you." Jade remarks casually as she and Porter make their way toward the van.

## CHAPTER FOUR

  *Oh, good, the machine is down, and there **he** is! Man, if there were any reason to get up excessively early it would be to see him! I'd rather see him next to me when I wake up after a full night of uncontrolled passion. Seeing him in the morning would no doubt make me want to start all over. I wonder if I could wear him out. I don't know if anybody could wear him out, he looks powerful! Those legs! Oh, my gosh! Long and strong! His arms! Oh, what I wouldn't give to have them wrapped around me, although they're so big he could crush me with 'em, but what a way to go! I can't even work for thinking about rolling around in a king-size bed with that king-size man! Just one time...NO WAY! That would be an appetizer. I'd just be hungry for more. A lot more! Like all night every night...what if he wore me out? What if I'm not that good? I mean mmm, look at that incredible beast of a man! I bet with all the practice he's surely gotten he must be perfect. Perfect? What's perfect in bed? Man, I'd sure like to find out.*

  *Shoot! The machine's up and running. Way too quick. Perfect would definitely be not too quick. What if I'm not good enough for him? How can I be? It's been ten years. It's not like I've forgotten, by any means, but it's been too long. I can't imagine him alone for a week. Although, no ring. But, he is maintenance and that would be bad for rings.*

  *Yeah, this is just the place to be thinking about his shirt coming off and watching him undress... boxers or whitey-tighties? Hmm...Whatever; doesn't matter because they wouldn't be on long anyway.*

  *He's what...six foot? Maybe, six-two or even six-four. I wonder if that has any bearing on his length. That would be something else I'd sure like to know. Porter was only five-nine and everyone else, well, all teens or young men and I was young*

## Inside My Head

*and I don't remember. Well, I do, remember some things...like the way it felt sliding in (deep breath) I've almost forgotten the way it really feels. My mind is only so good.*

*You know, God, it would be great if in Heaven I could get excited and then satisfied over and over for eternity. Maybe in Heaven we could each get whoever is the ideal mate for us, like...oh, I don't know...maybe KEVIN!*

*Just seeing him makes my blood pump faster, my heart race and my temp rise. Sometimes I wonder if anyone else hears my breathing change. He has got to be THE finest specimen of the entire male gender. He is scrumptious!*

*I wonder if he is nice at all. I mean, there's no way of knowing by watching him fix a machine. (sigh) I don't guess I will ever really know. But, I imagine that he's rough and strong and protective, and at other times gentle and sensual and maybe, since I can imagine anything I want for him to be...vulnerable and open and considerate and faithful and passionate, not just in an exciting yummy sexual passion but about ideals and things that matter to both of us.*

*OH! OH! OH! He likes to walk. Long slow walks through woods well, anywhere in nature. Oooh, and he loves to talk...about life, everyday things. He loves water and dogs; someone who loves to have fun but, can be serious when the need arises.*

Buzz, buzz, buzz. Break!

*Wow! Time goes by fast when you're having fun. I didn't realize...I just wish I were really having fun.*

"Hey, Sheila." *She drives me crazy. All she ever talks about are her kids... How they are in trouble and they went to this party or whatever. Geez, she needs to get a reign on those kids; her girl will probably be pregnant soon the way things go in their lives.*

"Hi, Connie." a frown envelops her countenance. *I knew it; here goes fifteen minutes of bad.* "Can I talk to you about something personal?" *Odd, she never bothered to ask before. This must be really bad.*

"Of course, Honey let's get this table back here."

"Connie," *tears already, oh gosh this is bad.* "Chuck is in the hospital."

"What happened?" I gasp, I didn't really expect that bad.

"He went to a party Wednesday night and a policeman called me about three yesterday morning." The sobs make her hard to understand. She sniffs and I hand her a napkin. "He said that Chuck was at the hospital and that I needed to get there quickly. So, I raced there thinking about what the problem could be. A fight, I decided must've been the answer. I expected broken bones, a black eye, whatever." She breaks again. I can't take it; my eyes fill up and I don't even know the problem. I glance at the clock; half the break is gone. "But when I got there he was all hooked up to machines and unconscious. The doctor said he had overdosed on alcohol. I didn't even know you could do that! I guess he and his friends were doing a shot contest and he did 15 shots in less than 15 minutes. He was already drunk on beer. No one seems to know how much beer he'd had. Then he began throwing up and everyone was laughing and getting buckets and he passed out. His buddy, Justin, tried waking him up 'cause he actually passed out in his own vomit. But he wouldn't wake up so he took him there. He told the doctor and the cops what happened. I don't know why the cop was even there. Some details are foggy, I don't know. But he could die!" Now the sobbing is uncontrollable and I'm hugging her, crying right along with her.

## Inside My Head

*Wow! I wish I knew what to say to her. Hey! H.R. I think they have counselors there or something.*

Buzz, buzz, buzz.

*Break is over.* "Sheila, let's go to H.R. and see if there's someone there that maybe knows what to do. I'll pray for you and Chuck." The walk is slow and long. I just shake my head. *What do you say to someone when things like this happen? I mean, it's horrible, but he brought it on himself. I mean, well, I don't know what I mean. It's horrible and she is devastated. What if he does die? Oh, my gosh! What if it were my Porter? Oh, my gosh!*

*God, help the person in H.R. know what to do. I think she should go home. I don't know why she's here. I wouldn't be.* "Sheila, I'd go home, or the hospital or somewhere, just not here."

"I can't face the house alone. I just sit and cry. And at the hospital I just keep staring at this nearly dead boy not knowing what to do. I want to pray, but I don't know how. What do I say? Will God even listen? This is all my fault. I should've done something before it got this far. I just don't know what. His dad has never been a part of his life. He was a partier anyway and so is Chuck. I guess I just figured that's the way it is, and Patty's dad didn't want him around because he wasn't his. We fought over it all the time and so Chuck blames himself for that breakup. I don't know. I'm so alone, Connie." She's bawling. *Whew! H.R. I don't know what to do but they will.*

"Sheila, I'll pray for him. Here," I take a pen and paper from the desk, "here's my phone number. Call me this evening. We'll get together and you don't have to be alone." I give the pen back to the woman at the desk. "Thanks," I say with a slight smile and nod. "She needs some counseling and I thought maybe you could help. Bye

## Inside My Head

Sheila." I wave as I head off to the line. *Wow, I don't even know her that well. I mean, sure she talks to me here some, but this? I don't get it. I don't know what to do. Why'd she tell me?*

"Ron, Sheila needed some help getting to the H.R. office. Did John come around asking about us?"

"No. is everything O.K. with her, or should I ask what's wrong?"

"Her son is in the hospital close to death. She just broke down and told me the whole story. I took her over to H.R. They can send her home. I don't know what to do for her. I feel terrible."

"What's her son's name?" Ron asks.

"Chuck."

"I'll pray for him." *What? Ronnie is a Christian? Maybe someone younger would be O.K. He's not bad looking, although he does look like the typical Christian man. I guess that doesn't matter. At least he's a good man. Well, little more than a boy, I bet. He's about 20 to 25 or so. That's ridiculous.* I can't help but roll my eyes at the thought of Ronnie and me together. *I don't want to have to raise someone. Of course, men do it all the time, 40 and 50 year olds picking up on girls 20 to 25.* My head shakes and I realize Ronnie is still looking at me. "Are you O.K.?" He asks.

"Oh, yeah. Just thinking of what Sheila's going through and is still here today. Not me. I'd be at the hospital. She's certainly committed to work. She needs prayer too."

"Of course, I'll be praying for them both." He turns back to his work.

"Here comes John. I'll let him know, thanks." I walk over to him expecting a question as to why I'm not working or why I'm talking or where Sheila is, but instead I get...

"Hey, Connie, thanks for helping Sheila out like that. I love to see my team help each other. You went above and beyond today. Good Job! She is going home." I nod, but my face has a questioning expression as I try to grasp the whole situation.

I sigh deeply as I ponder the chances of her calling me. *I hope she doesn't call. I don't want to go sit with her and watch her cry. I don't know if there are any words of comfort I can offer. Just sitting silently is boring and awkward. I just don't think I can do it. Hmm, well, if she calls maybe I'll be too busy to do anything.* I let my mind follow the music so I don't have to think.

It's a nice day for a white wedding. *Yeah, Billy Idol having a white wedding, right! Not a chance! He might have white hair at his wedding, but that is it. It doesn't seem to matter anymore. Everyone has a "white" wedding. The whole white gown to show virginity is a farce.* I'll tumble for you. *Boy George. I guess wearing those clothes and all that makeup he had to let people know he was a boy at one time. I bet the company thought they were making a good investment when they bought this c.d. but man, is it old. They should have at least two or three different ones or something. Not just the same songs day in and day out. Five years of* Xanadu, xanadu oo oo, *and* You don't have to be rich to be my girl, you don't have to be cool to rule my world, *or how about the oldy moldy or...no...golden oldie, yeah! Yeah golden oldie, umm,* Pink Cadillac. *Not that I don't like any of those or* Papa don't preach, I'm gonna keep my baby...*something like that anyway, but what if we heard...*Urgent, Hot Blooded, Back in Black *or maybe one day could be songs from like...The Doobie Brothers and Three Dog*

## Inside My Head

*Night. Hey! We could have a 70's day a disco day, an 80's day, a rock and roll day, and a country day. Break it up a bit.*

*Journey, John Denver, Randy Travis, The Judds, Foreigner, The Beach Boys, Peter Frampton, Captain and Tenille, Reba McEntire, Bee Gees, Andy Gibb, Hey! We could do a musical day. Songs from The King and I, Oklahoma, The Sound of Music.*

*Music is incredible! There are so many variations that are clean at least not so vulgar and violent. We could have different songs everyday for a month and it wouldn't have to be so monotonous.*

Buzz, buzz, buzz.

*"Lunch!" Oops! I said that out loud. Hmm, for lunch I brought a yogurt and a salad. Not too great, but I've got to do something. Sometimes I hate that I eat at all. I'm so far overweight now. I'll never find a husband.*

"Connie."

"Hey, Mark."

"So, what's up with Sheila?" He asks as he sits down across from me.

"She's got some personal problems going on. So she went home."

"But, like what's so bad that she'd leave her line?" He pushes for an answer.

"I can't really talk about it, Mark. I don't think she'd feel comfortable with me talking to anyone about her problems." I know how horrible gossip is, especially here. Tell, one person, and 1600 know. I can't do that to her. Not to anyone."

## Inside My Head

"But is she gonna be O.K.?"

"Yes, I think she will." *Now let me alone so I can eat, please.* A bite of yogurt. *He's still here.* Another bite and a sigh. Close my eyes as I take another bite. *He's pulling out his lunch? Oh, great.*

"Are you just having yogurt today?" He pulls out chips and cookies to go with his huge sandwich. *Great.*

"Yes, well that and a salad." I point to the bowl in the shopping bag.

"Hmm, I don't know how women eat like that and keep going all day. Ya know my ex-wife used to eat like a bird." He continues as he crams food in his mouth.

"Hmm." I barely make a sound as I nod, not wanting him to think I am interested. *Yeah, and how I stay so fat and eat like this. He must think that I eat like a cow at home and bring this here to make it look good.* I look around the cafeteria to keep him from seeing the sadness in my eyes. I see a very ugly man wearing a t-shirt that reads something about his twin. *Oh, my gosh, God, please tell me that you did not make two of those. You wouldn't do that to the world, would You? Man, I know I am not beautiful, but at least I am not butt-ugly either. Now, I'd rather be single till my dying day than to be stuck with someone that looks like that. ...Oh, my gosh! He is wearing a ring! He's married! And I'm not? What's that all about, God? Am I that ugly?* I close my eyes and shake my head.

I forgot Mark was across from me until he touched my arm. I jerk, as an automatic response. No one touches me. I look at him with such a look on my face that he apologizes. "It's O.K. I'm sorry I was just kinda in my own world, and didn't expect it."

"Oh, I was just asking what you are doing this weekend."

*You have got to be kidding! Mark?...No ring, ex-wife...God? Mark?* "Umm," I shrug. "I'm not sure yet. The kids usually make plans and I follow." *Humph, now he knows I've got kids. Maybe that'll deter him.*

"Cool! I'm taking my kids to see a movie. Maybe we could all go." He states as he shoves more food in his mouth.

I cock my head like Duke does when I ask him something. *I don't believe it. A man asking me out? Uhh...Hmm...Do I even want to go out with Mark? Hmm.* "Well, I have to see if they have plans yet. When are you going?"

"Tomorrow afternoon—to the matinee. It's the cheapest way to go, and when you have four kids you really gotta do what you can to save some dough, ya know." His eyebrows rise as he shovels even more food in. "Can I get your number and I'll call in the morning and see what's going on. What's a good time? I don't want to call too early, bein' as though it's the weekend an' all. Myself, I still get up early 'cause of work all week, ya know? But I know alotta people like to sleep in an' catch up, ya know?" More food goes in as he finishes his unwarranted explanation.

"Umm, hmm, well, I'll get a pen when we get back..."

"Oh, I got one right here." He cuts me off. "I always got one with me. It's good to be prepared, ya know." He nods and pulls a pen from his shirt pocket. "I was a boy scout." He holds three fingers up and begins quoting some pledge or something. "On my honor I will do my best to do my duty to God and my country, to help other people at all times, to keep myself physically fit mentally awake and morally straight."

"Mm." I smile. *A boy scout, huh?*

*Buzz buzz buzz. Saved by the bell.*

"Oh, shit! I didn't know it was that late. Talk to ya at break, O.K.?" He takes off with his pen.

*Shit. Humph, I hate cussing. I used to think it was cool. I was the biggest cusser of them all. I talked like a sailor. Then I grew up. I don't even know why I did it at all now. It is so vulgar and unnecessary. I don't know if I want to go out with someone who cusses. I guess it doesn't mean much anymore anyway. Everyone does it. I hear "Christians" cuss too. Around here that is all I hear. "F" this or "f" that. The "f" word can be used as a verb or an adjective, and it is, frequently. I think sometimes, "Man, I used to sound like that. I could add a cuss word to any sentence just to give it more... more...meaning, I guess.*

*I don't suppose that answers my question about whether or not Mark is a Christian. I know it doesn't honor God, but so many people do it. I don't suppose you'll go to Hell for it, so does that make it O.K.? I am sure the Bible says something about not having a dirty mouth or something; I'll have to look that up some time. So, God, if it's not a Heaven or Hell issue, is it a sin?*

**Does it glorify me?**

No.

**Then, yes, it's wrong. If you really love me you'll honor me with all you are, your everyday life.**

*Oh, God, be with Sheila and Chuck. Don't let him die, God, please.*

# Inside My Head

*I've only heard of o. d.ing on alcohol on a TV show. One of those C.S.I. type of shows. The kid was walking home throwing up and choked on his own vomit and died. I remember that was tough to get. I think maybe Cold Case, or something. I don't know. I like all those shows. Mysteries, cop shows, unsolved mysteries, good-guy vs. bad-guy things; so interesting, like, hooked in the first five minutes good. I nod in agreement with myself. As if I would disagree with me. I shake my head at the ridiculousness of that thought. You'd think I could at least not let the whole rest of the world know that I'm carrying on a conversation in my head. I wonder if everyone else does this too... I bet so. I wonder what everyone else thinks.*

Buzz buzz buzz, final break.

*After this the day should fly by. Of course if I were actually having fun it'd be much faster, which is probably why sex is so quick.*

"Hi Connie." *Oh, I forgot about him.*

"Hi Mark."

"Didja getcher number down for me?" *His English is atrocious.*

"Yeah, on this napkin here." I pull a crumpled napkin from my front pocket and out drop my ear plugs.

"Great! I'll call... what time did you say was good?"

"I don't think I did. But, nine is fine." *Nine is fine. I love to bowl. Like everything else, I am not good at it, but I do enjoy it.*

"Nine it is then. Look I'm going to get a drink. O.K.?" He smiles. *I don't recall paying any attention to his smile before. It's nice. Maybe this…Oh!* I notice he is still looking at me.

"Yes, of course." *He waited for me to answer. That's nice. I figured that it was a rhetorical question, more or less. What do I want? Diet Pepsi? Yep, That'll do. "At'll do donkey. At'll do." I love that movie. Oh, it's hilarious. Donkey cusses in it. I guess it is very common anymore. I didn't even pick up on it the first time I watched it, someone pointed it out to me. It's like it belongs there. Pop needs to be very cold, especially diet, but it is so good when it is.*

"Hi, Connie." I look around.

"Oh, hi Joe."

"Hey, what's up with Sheila? She never misses work or goes home early and she missed yesterday and went home early today. I saw you two talking at first break."

"Well, she's having some major problems at home. I'm sure she'll be back Monday."

"With Chuck?"

"Umm, I don't think it's my place…"

"Oh, no, of course not. I'm sorry to put you in that position. I just…I am really concerned about her. Listen, can I give you my number and you can give it to her?"

"Sure. I think she's going to call me this weekend." He takes a pen out of his shirt pocket and scribbles his number on a napkin. I fold it neatly and press it in where my number used to be. *He must've been a boy scout, prepared and all. He must have a thing for Sheila. I wonder if she knows.*

Buzz buzz buzz.

# Inside My Head

Back to the old grindstone. I wonder where that saying came from. Must've been like the wheat being ground or something. I should've gotten her number. I don't know what I was thinking. I just...I don't know. I don't know much today. I'm kind of afraid she will call and I'll have to go be with her. What about her family or other friends? I'm sure she'll call them instead. Whew! That's a relief. They'll probably know what to say. Good! I feel better now. Did I pray yet?

"Well, God, Sheila is so desperate right now and her son is close to death. They really need you. Stay close to them and heal Chuck, Lord, and keep him from drinking. Change his life, Lord. Help her to call someone else 'cause I don't know what to say. I don't really pray in front of people. I'd probably make a fool of myself. And what if You don't want to answer that prayer? Then I look stupid and you look weak. I don't want to mess up. You can heal him, God. I know you can. Please do it."

Boy, if it were Porter I'd be devastated. I don't know what I'd do. She must be frantic inside. I don't know her very well, but she did say today she doesn't know how to pray. She isn't a Christian. How does anyone go through something like this without God? I can't imagine. I wouldn't want to. What if he dies? He'll go to Hell! ...Does he know about you at all, God? Does she? She's pretty nice at work. But she cusses with the men and laughs at all those jokes. She seems like...I don't know...like she doesn't lack for company anyway. They're always talking about going out to the bars. Chuck probably watched his mom. She did say his dad was a 'partier'. Man, he gets it from all over. How could he not drink? What does she expect? Hmm.

I'm sure she must know the fault lies on her since his dad took off right away. I mean, I shake my head, once again letting the whole world know about my silent conversation. If his only parent goes out most weekends and Lord knows if she goes home alone or even goes home at all...She'll be lucky if her daughter doesn't get pregnant. She's like fifteen or so. If she's anything like her mom…two kids, two dads, and she still hasn't changed.

I guess if I hadn't have become a Christian when Porter left I'd be that way too. I was a wild thing, and boy did that seem fun at the time! I don't know, it was and it wasn't. When I finally hooked-up with Porter I never really thought anyone would keep me around for long. Thinking back I was constantly being rejected. I felt wanted far less often than I felt hurt and lonely. There was such a hole in my soul. Nothing seemed to fit it. I just kept thinking if I found the right man…ten years of thinking that because I was sleeping with this one he loved me and this could be it. Porter only married me because of my pregnancy. He still never wanted me long-term. Our marriage only lasted three years. That was the worst pain ever. I really thought he'd stick around. My heart felt literally like it had been ripped from my chest and shoved into a paper shredder and put back. The pain was truly physical.

Honestly, I never loved him either. I was just tired of one guy then another, but it was better than being alone. Sometimes I'm a little jealous of Sheila. She always sounds happy and all, but I bet deep down inside she feels like I did. Her life is in shambles and she's still alone come Monday morning.

**Constance,**

Yes, Lord?

**Talk to her.**

About what? I really don't know what to say and I can't watch her cry. It makes me cry.

**She needs that, a friend to cry with. And she needs to hear what you were just thinking.**

That she's a whore?

## Inside My Head

*No, Constance, that you understand her promiscuity and her loneliness. That you've felt rejected and alone. That I will fill that emptiness she has.*

*I don't want to shove religion down her throat.*

*Offer her the same opportunity you were given. Offer her hope and peace; Love that knows no end.*

*God, I'm alone. What hope is in that?*

*I'm with you always even to the end of the earth. I will never leave you or forsake you. You don't have sex, but for the first time in your life you have love; Real Love. What if that's what she wants?*

*I'm sorry, God. I love You and I'm so sorry I said that. You are better than any man has ever been to me. I know I'm not easy, even for You, at times. You are always, always here with me and for me. I guess I still have a hard time recognizing true love. I'm really, really sorry. If she calls me I'll tell her.*

Buzz, buzz, buzz

*Finally! I get to go home.*

"Have a great weekend, Ron."-*nie*

"Thanks, you too Connie."

"Connie!"

"Mark."

"Don't forget I'll call you in the morning."

"I won't forget."

"Connie!" *Geez I can't even leave today.* My head turns and turns till I see the one calling me. "Connie!"

"Joe."

"Please call if she calls you. If she okays it. Or have her call me. Just let her know I care." His face shows just how much he does care and again, I'm shocked.

"I promise, Joe." I touch his shoulder, he relaxes and smiles.

"Thanks."

Finally, I'm to the car. Wow, what a long day. Mark asks me out. Sheila tells me her son is close to death. Joe shows how much he cares for Sheila. Ooh! I love this song. (I begin to sing along) "I was made to love and to be loved by you. I was, I was made to adore you, made just for you, I was made to love you and be loved by You." *Yeah I gotta get this song. Well, the C.D. hey! I could see if I can download it, Toby Mac. He's great. I like that Jesus Freaks book too! Man, now those stories put me in my place. God I know I'm pathetic. Sometimes I think I'm not that bad, then I read stuff like that and I get a severe slap in the face. I don't know, God if I could be like those people. I'd like to think so, but I don't know. Am I that good? I try to live by all the rules. I go to church every Sunday and Wednesday I'm doing this Bible study. I don't cuss or drink or smoke. I pray all the time. Well, I talk to You anyway. I don't ask for much, only if there's something really important. I'm nice to everybody. I even go out of my way for others.*

**"Without complaints?"**

"*No, I don't complain to them at all.*"

**"You complain to me."**

"*But not to them. They don't know.*"

**"So then it's okay?"**

"Hey, Mom!"

## Inside My Head

"Hi, Jade! How was your day?"

"It was fine. I got a B in American Government; I forgot about the test and still got a B!"

"That's great."

"Hey! Mom! There's a group of kids from church going out tonight to dinner and bowling, can I go?"

"How much?"

Jade's face twists with a "please" look before she even says, "20 dollars should cover it all." She doesn't stop staring with a hopeful look. "Please!"

Sigh! "I guess."

"Thank you, Thank you!" She smiles that sweet smile and bites her bottom lip like I do.

"But... You have to help around the house tomorrow."

"Oh, I promise," and another smile. I just roll my eyes and smile back. I'm so thankful I can trust her. A church group. I bet Sheila's daughter never goes out with church groups. She probably worries her mother to death.

"Hey, Mom!" Porter climbs in the back seat with a huge grin.

"What's up, Porter?" I have to know the cause of such delight.

"Well, Jamie talked to Kale who was talking to Kate on the phone after she talked to Jeanie who's best friends with Sandy and she said she likes me!" That smile is priceless. He looks so much like his dad; no wonder I fell for him. I can't help but smile back. I shake my head, lick my lips and bite my bottom lip as I glance over at my baby boy.

"You're growing up too fast, Porter, I'm not ready for you to start liking girls yet. I smile a half smile and tilt my head like I'm hoping he'll say 'O.K. Mom I'll stop till you're ready,' knowing that will never happen. He just laughs.

"Mom! It's better than me likin' boys isn't it?" He laughs at that like it's the funniest thing ever and all I can say is "Porter!" I shake my head and smile.

*Man, these kids are growing up so fast. Where has my life gone? It's been such a waste. Except for these two, but they'll be gone and then what? I've let myself go. I've got 60 pounds to lose and my hair is graying. I never wear makeup any more. I just sit at home all weekend recouping from last week and getting ready for the next one to begin. My house isn't clean-clean, just straightened up. I don't work in the garden anymore, I don't run like I used to, heck! I don't even have a membership to the Y, let alone a gym. I haven't dated in years and will probably be alone forever. My life sucks! I'm a mess. I'm disgusted every time I pass a mirror; I avoid them like the plague. Boy, when I was a teenager...* (deep sigh) *I was 'it and a bag o' chips'. Everybody wanted to go out with me. I had the pick of the litter. I went out every weekend and always had a good time, sex all the time. Life was fun, to say the least. Now, life just sucks, and I look like a sewer rat. No one cares about me, but my kids. I spend every day working just to make bills and every night alone.* My head shakes and I sigh repeatedly trying not to cry. *I am so hollow inside. My life doesn't count for anything! I am such a loser!*

"Mom! Cassy is picking me up at 5:30 O.K.?" Jade interrupts my thoughts.

"Yeah, Honey that's fine, Porter what are you and I doing tonight?"

"Jamie asked if I could spend the night tonight, last weekend, remember?" His little face all scrunched with that questioning face.

"No, Honey I'm sorry I forgot. Am I supposed to take you?"

"Nope, his mom is picking me up at 4:30 so we can go out to eat and then to the movies."

"Oh, yeah, movies, I almost forgot! Mark, a man from work asked if we could all go to the movies tomorrow. When will you guys be home?"

"I don't know," Porter answers.

"Mom, I'll be back about midnight. Who's Mark anyway? We haven't heard about him before." Jade looks at me like I just told her a portion of some juicy secret. Porter stops everything and looks at me as though I'm about to reveal something of great importance.

"Just some guy at work."

"Just some guy at work?" Jade teases. "How long has this guy been around and you just happened to keep him a secret?" *She's loving this.*

I have to laugh. "It's not like that at all. He just sorta asked me out today, but with you guys also. He has four kids and he's taking them to a matinee and asked if we weren't busy if we'd like to go." I shrug like it's something that happens all the time instead of never, or at least not in the past decade. I smile as it hits me that I was asked out on a real, well sort of real, date. *He didn't even care that I have kids.* My eyebrows raise as I smile like a child and shrug.

"Well, we can't let you go out alone with just some guy." Porter says as though he's taking authority. "We'll have to go. What time do you need us, Mom?"

I shrug again, "Noon I guess. How's that sound?"

They look at each other and smile then simultaneously, as though rehearsed they say, "O.K., we'll be here."

My smile defines my pleasure. "O.K. then both of you get ready and get outta here so I can spend some quiet time tonight. Jade, got your phone?"

"Yep." Both head upstairs as the phone rings.

"Hello?" I say with a cheer in my tone.

"Connie, can we get together tonight still?" Sheila asks quietly, sounding like she's cried out every available tear.

*Oh, my gosh, I hoped she wouldn't call.* My eyes close as I shake my head. *Both kids are going out and I have no excuse.* "Of course." I answer in a tone that I use when I am trying to show concern; I don't want her to think I'm not. I am. I'm just not sure what to say or do. "Both of my kids are going out with friends, so I could come about six, is that O.K.?"

"That would be great." I don't hear 'great' in her voice, more like 'whatever'.

"I'll bring dinner. What sounds good?" Food always sounds good to me…any kind.

"I'm not hungry."

"Have you eaten today?"

"I don't know. I don't usually eat when I'm upset. But, you can eat here anyway." *That's kinda desperate sounding. She just wants me there and here I am thinking of food. How wrong is that? What a jerk. I'm so bad.*

"Listen, give me your address and I'll be there about six. I'll bring something little in case you change your mind, O.K.?"

"O.K. 5130 Lincoln Rd. I'm right by that old school house on the corner of Lincoln and Elm."

"I know right where you're talking about, 5130 right?" I repeat as I write the address on a receipt from the junk drawer.

"Yes, and thank you, Connie."

"Oh, no, you don't have to thank me, Sheila. We're friends. What are friends for?"

"Oh, I never knew you were so good. I'm so sorry." She starts to cry. "I don't deserve your friendship."

"Nonsense. Now, I'll be there shortly, so you try to rest till I get there, O.K.?"

"O.K.," she says, sniffing away her sobs. "Bye, Connie."

"See you in a little while." *I hate goodbye, it seems so final; like a forever kind of thing. And in this case I really don't want her thinking in finalities. This is going to be a loooong night! She sounds like a mess! What in the world am I going to say? What* **can** *I say? She's probably thinking I'm going to say something swift, like I'll have some kind of answer, but I don't.*

# Inside My Head

*Oh, hey! I'll take a movie so that we don't have to talk and maybe it'll get her mind off things. Nothing to cry at, no family thing. The King and I? No, the end is sad and he dies, oh, my gosh! No! Westside Story. Duh! No! The Godfather? Mm, no. Brigadoon? Yeah, that's good, there's music and love and no one dies...perfect.*

Jamie's mom honks and I make Porter hug and kiss me goodbye. "Have fun tonight." I smile as he runs out to the car. His smile is so sweet and his hugs are exceptional. I never realized how much volume hugs speak till I had kids.

"I love you, Honey. Be good for Mrs. Stewart tonight."

"I will, Mom. I love you. See ya by noon for that movie." *His smile could light up the midnight sky.* We wave and he's gone. *I miss him already. I know he wants to be with his friends, but I want him here. I know I'm selfish. I don't care. Life has flown by so fast and soon he'll be gone.*

"Jade! Are you nearly out of the bathroom?" *I thought she spent a lot of time in there before. Now that we put a radio in there that's where she spends all her time.*

"Be right out, Mom." *I'll change first, I'm sure I'll still beat her out of there... I was right; the door is still shut and the radio is blaring, I may have to remove the radio.*

I look in the mirror as I finish getting ready. I brush back my hair and am once again reminded of my ever-increasing age. "So many grey hairs, I hate this growing old thing. I like the longer hair just not the grey streak down the center. Get it any wider and I'll look like a skunk. Who am I kidding? I already look like a skunk. My hair color has got to be right for tomorrow." *Why'd I tell the kids about Mark? I guess I do wanna go. I don't know.*

*It never fails to surprise me, the things that get on the carpet up here. Looks like mud or chocolate. I gotta put that on the Saturday to-do list. Prioritize it before it begins to blend in. That's why I didn't want beige carpet in the first place.* "Well, what's done is done."

"Jade, you look beautiful! I mean, not that you don't always, but today you look exceptionally beautiful." *I love her long flowing, wavy hair, every girl's dream; and jet black, my dream. I hate my mousy brown mop. The light brown eye shadow setting off her gorgeous green eyes. I sigh and Jade smiles.* "I'm not just saying that either. You look fantastic! Is there a reason?"

"I'm going out?"

"You're going out with a group. So is there a certain someone in that group?" *I try, but there is no give. Her smile is almost one of embarrassment.*

"No, Mom, I'll tell you if I ever find Mr. Right."

"Yeah, but what about Mr. For Right Now?"

"Mom, you know that's not an issue. If he's not my husband then I am not cheating on the one that will be. You know that, Mom. But thanks. I should be back about midnight. I love you."

·········

*Sheila's house, Hmm, I could pick up pizza, getting back to the embarrassing conversation from work is still better than only talking about Chuck. It seems horrible to have her son near* death, but it's weird how we're becoming friends. I'd like to have some friends. It's so bad that I know the number to Pizza Hut by heart. An hour? What to do, what to do. Well, a shower and...I can't believe Mark asked me out. I can't believe I didn't jump at it. At least he's a man. It's been far too long since someone asked me out. I don't even know how to act. He's not a Christian, I don't think. What if we start to date and I like him? Then I'd be right in the middle of being unequally yoked and unhappy. It would be wrong and I don't know...but I do know I love this shampoo, strawberries, and that body spray to match, I may not look appetizing but I sure do smell good enough to make someone hungry for dessert.

I have to hurry. What to wear, what to wear? Geez, Constance you're going to a woman's house, who cares? Of course, she always looks great and I don't. But she is going through a crisis maybe she won't look so great. Who cares? I'll just wear my old chinos and a sweatshirt. Which one? Maybe my scarecrow one, yeah that's fall looking. Cool—and these boots. I love these boots. A great reason for fall and winter is boots. Don't look in the mirror, just look down. Oh yeah, this is good. Just a peek... Oh, crap! How now, brown cow? Man, could I just escape one time from having to look in that mirror? I hate it every time! I know it's a bad idea and I do it anyway. Then I feel like a slob the whole time.

I step on the scale—*One eighty-eight. I hate that! What did I think after looking in the mirror? Four more pounds? The boots! They are heavy, I'll take them off. Man, I'm getting later and later but, I need to know.* Deep sigh, close my eyes and get back on the scale. *Maybe...*open my eyes. *I know I don't want to do this.* "One eighty-six? No way! The boots only weigh two pounds?" Step off and back on. "One eighty-six. Oh, crap!" The boots go back on. *I get fatter and fatter everyday! Maybe I should be happy to go out with Mark; he's no prize, but look at me.* I shake my head and close my tear-filled eyes. *Who'd want me, anyway? No wonder I'm still alone.*

## Inside My Head

*I gotta get outta here.* I check my watch, *Oh, 45 minutes already? I gotta go. Pizza Hut and movies. Maybe it would be easier to exercise if I weren't so out of shape. I'm so tired all the time with work and kids and church and being so huge I can hardly bend over and tie my own shoes. Yet, here I go to get pizza. I love food, so I eat, and then I hate myself, so I eat food. It's a vicious cycle. What the heck?*

"Hello, order for Stone, please."

"That'll be 18.99. Debit or credit?"

"Credit."

"Have a good night."

"Thanks. You too." *I'm sure I will, I'm going to a beautiful woman's house of whom I'm completely jealous right after getting on a scale to find I've gained two more pounds. I look like a frickin' brown cow and I'm gonna pig out on the ultimate pizza while I watch some movie so I don't have to talk to her about her nearly dead son and I contemplate the total rejection that would be imminent from the ultimate man. Oh, yeah, my night's going to be fantastic!*

"You Jerk! I can't believe he cut me off like that! I'm going the speed limit and these idiots seem to think that's the minimum speed not the maximum speed." *Great, this night's already going well. Two more pounds, I shouldn't have taken my boots off. I thought they were at least four pounds maybe even five. I should've left it like that. Now I'm in a bad mood. I got to do something about this besides eat more. Pretty soon I could be sold off as food for a family of six for a month, or more. Maybe even six months. Well a month on the Atkins diet. I hated that diet. I want bread and pasta and potatoes. I can't even figure out what a main course is without one of those things. Meat's a good thing but it needs something to go with it.* Sniff, sigh.

## Inside My Head

"O.K., I'm here. Be nice, you big goon; who cares if you're the biggest cow ever? She needs you, and you need to be nice. God's watching you, remember. Don't mess this up like everything else you do."

"Who is it?" I can hear the continuous crying in her voice.

"Connie."

"Come in." *Oh, man, it's dark in here. I've got to get it brighter. This is no good.*

"Sheila, I brought pizza. How about we get some light on? Let there be light, and voila there is light. And look here, Pizza Hut's pepperoni lover's stuffed crust pizza with banana peppers. You don't get any better than that, huh?" She smiles, but it's not a real smile, more like an 'I-get-it' smile. *At least it's a start.* "Got any paper plates?"

"Yeah, in the cupboard above the stove." I rummage through the stark white cupboards even though the doors are glass. I scan the kitchen quickly to notice an updated and friendly place to cook and eat.

"Cool! Great place, I love the peaches-and-cream sort of color scheme. Man, you've got a great sense of décor. Did you do this all yourself?" I return to the living room with the paper plates and water I got from the automatic ice/water dispenser of her fridge.

"Some. Some was done when I moved in. I just kinda continued with the same ideas."

"When's the last time you ate something?" I ask, shoving a plate into her hand.

"Hmm, I don't know." Her eyes are all over the place, searching her brain to find the answer. *I should have been a counselor. Then I would know what to say. I love psych. I never finish anything. I have no idea what to do here. She needs someone who cares about her. I hardly know her, and to say I care might be pushing it. I mean, she's O.K. I just don't know how to act.* I take several bites before she finds the answer. "I don't know, I guess when I ate with you."

"You're kidding!" *I can't even imagine going days without food.*

"No, I don't eat when I'm upset and since I heard that cop tell me about Chuck and the hospital and saw him there. I haven't even thought about food." Her tears come again.

"Lucky you! All I do when I am upset is eat." *That's why I am the size of a hippo.* "Try to eat some anyway, Honey, it's important to keep up your strength for everyone's sake. Where's your daughter?" *What's her name again? I hate that! I can never remember names.*

"Patty? Uhh, she's at my sister's house. They're looking out for me...and her, I guess. My sister is so good to me. She's my only real friend...except you. She goes to church, too. You know, I didn't know what a good friend I had in you." She starts to cry again.

"Sheila, God knew just when to bring us together. Perfect timing, I'd say. Eat up, enjoy the ultimate pizza." I have to smile. I can't help but think of our conversation over lunch. *I wonder if she asked Kevin. I don't know if I want to know.* "Did you go to the hospital today?" I ask as I cram more food in.

She nods and takes another small bite. *I don't know how she can be away from him. If it were Porter I'd be there and not leave his side. It just looks like she doesn't even love him.*

"I know everyone's probably thinking what a bad mom I am, not being up there all the time..." she pauses.

"Oh no, I'm sure everyone realizes how hard it would be just to see him like that." *Man, it's like she read my mind, how weird!*

"Well," she sighs and continues slowly, "It's more than that, I guess." She stops and wipes her mouth and shrugs. She swallows hard and continues, "I guess they all are right. I am a terrible mom. If I hadn't've gone out Wednesday night I could've stopped him from going out with those friends...friends..." She shakes her head and rolls her eyes, swallows hard to hold back more tears and continues. "They've been nothin' but bad for him since they met. I knew that. I told him not to go but he's 18 and thinks he knows it all. He doesn't think he needs to listen to me anymore." She shakes her head and tears come despite her attempts to stop them.

*Really? Did he ever listen to you?*

"It's all my fault. I wasn't here to stop him."

"No, Honey, it's not your fault, like you said, he doesn't listen anyway. If you had been here he'd've found a way to do what he wanted to do." I hug her. *I can't stand to see her like this. This really isn't her fault. Although I did blame her earlier, it really isn't.* "Sheila, he made a choice...a wrong choice, of course, but it was his all the same." She nods and cries more. I hand her a tissue off of the stone end table, and look around the room. For the first time I notice the African wildlife theme. *This place really does look nice. I wish my place was this beautiful. She's barely eaten. I*

## Inside My Head

*can't eat when she won't. How bad would that look, my eating and her bawling? She's hurting so much. I don't know what to say. This is why I didn't want to be here. It's so sad. She's so alone. This is how I'd be if something happened to my kids; I don't have any friends either. Of course my kids are good and I wouldn't go through this at all, but I can't let her go through it alone.*

"Connie," she looks straight at me with red tear-filled eyes.

"Yes, Sweetie?"

"Will you pray for me and Chuck?"

"Of course." *Oh man, I can't pray out loud! Oh, man, what in the world do I say? I haven't had time to think up some good words. I am going to sound like a dummy! God, what if he dies? Do You even want to heal him?* "God, I ask You to hear our cries tonight, Lord. I lift Sheila and Chuck up to You. Umm, I pray that … You'd spare his life and make Yourself real to this family. And…hmm, give Sheila that peace that passes understanding. Help her to know that Your hand is on her and Chuck right now. I pray that when he wakes up that You'd change his mind about drinking, Lord…And, umm, uhh, that you'd change his life forever. Bring him out of this coma right now, God I pray with all that is in me I ask that You do this. Yeah, Thank you, Amen." *Oh, my gosh, I hope that didn't sound too dumb. Umm, uhh duh! You're so duhh-dumb! Oh, my gosh, I hate praying out loud.*

Sheila answers the phone that was obviously ringing while I beat myself up. "Hello," silence… "Really? When? Awesome! I'll be right there! Thank you, thank you so much!!!" She jumps up and down hugging me. "That was the nurse beside Chuck's bed. She said that he just woke up and asked for me!"

## Inside My Head

"Wow!" *I can't believe it! Is that because of my prayer, Lord?*

**Yes.**

*I wonder if that's just me thinking that or if that's really God answering me.*

**It's really me, Constance.**

*Wow! I didn't think You'd answer that quick. Most the time you don't even answer my prayers at all.'*

**I do, you don't listen. And if the answer is 'no' or 'not now,' you reject that answer.**

"Will you go to the hospital with me?" Sheila asks.

"If you want me to, of course." *Why would she want me to? She doesn't even know me that well. I want to take some pizza to eat on the way. I wonder if that would offend her.*

"Would you mind driving? I don't think I can concentrate on the road right now. All I can think about is Chuck."

"Not a problem." *I'll eat later. I'll take it with us in case I don't come back. Movies! I didn't even get them out yet.* "I'll leave some pizza here for you."

"No thanks, I don't eat meat so it would just sit there. Besides, you like it a lot. Thanks anyway." She smiles. *That explains the cheese pizza at lunch.*

"I'm sorry."

"For what?" She looks confused.

"For bringing meat for dinner. I just thought it'd be kind of funny to have my version of the ultimate pizza.

## Inside My Head

You know the whole pizza, sex, Kevin thing?" I grin and shrug, she's the only one that knows that and it seems cool that someone does. Maybe we can be friends. She laughs through her nose like I do. That laugh that I do when something really isn't funny. *I don't know why she would laugh. She's got so much on her mind and Kevin and I are probably pretty far down the list. I wonder if she asked him. Should I ask? How insensitive is that?* I shake my head.

"How could you know?" Her voice snaps me back to the moment.

"Know what?" Now she does laugh.

"You are so A.D.D. The meat thing, how could you know I don't eat it? No big deal, for real."

"Oh, yeah, but now I do, so I'll remember it." She smiles. "By the way, I'm headed toward St. Joe's, but is that the hospital I should be going to?" I glance over.

"Umm, yeah, St. Joes is the closest, so that's where his friend took him."

"Good. I figured, but wanted to be sure."

"I asked, ya know."

My forehead wrinkles as I try to think of what she means by that comment. *Oh, I hate that! I get older every time I do it. I need to think without aging! What the heck is she talking about? She is so confusing sometimes.* "Asked what?"

"I asked Kevin." Her eyes haven't left me, I'm sure. I've only glanced over, but I feel her watching me. My eyes are bulging out of my head and my mouth hangs open like the dork I am can no longer hide. *Why can't I do anything without looking like a dork?*

## Inside My Head

"Well, you wanna know?"

*I'm not sure. Do I want to know? What if he is a Christian? I shake my head. That would make him even more perfect, if that's possible, but I'd have even less of a chance. I'd never get the chance to be with someone as incredible as him. Especially the even more perfect, him as a Christian? Oh!!! A huge sigh sneaks out as I shake my head again.*

"No?"

"No?" *What is she talking about now?*

"No, you keep shaking your head no."

"No, I mean..." sigh, "I want to know but...I'm afraid."

"Why?"

"Well," *I can't believe I'm going to tell her this too. She'll never get it.* "well," *deep breath and let it out slow, concentrate maybe she will understand.* "See, if he is not a Christian then I can reason that I shouldn't be with him no matter how incredible he looks. But, if he is a Christian it would make me feel even worse about the rejection of another man."

"Another man?"

*What? Did I really just say 'another man'? Crap! Why do I say some things? Another man?*

"How many have rejected you? And why?" *She actually sounds concerned, not fake. I glance over and she looks concerned.*

"Here we are." *I try to get out of it.*

"Just because we're at the hospital doesn't get you out of this. You always try to get out of things. Besides, who am I gonna tell?"

*How should I know? Maybe all your friends, maybe I'll be the loser of the day one day when you're out with them. Or maybe the guys you're out having fun with. Maybe I'll be the joke of the week at some bar.* I shrug as if I don't have any ideas. I wouldn't tell her that for sure.

"Nobody! I don't have too many friends...well, to be honest, I don't really have any friends except you. I know it looks like I do, but I don't. Those guys...they're not friends."

*Yeah, but lovers don't necessarily need to be friends.*

"They aren't even lovers. I suppose most people think I'm quite the whore, but I'm really not." *You've got to be kidding! Can she read minds? I better watch it, that's freaky!* "Maybe you even thought that." She looks over at me as we enter the hospital.

"I don't know you, how could I think anything about you?"

**Yes, how could you think ANYTHING about her?**

*Biting my lip, a dead giveaway that I'm lying. Man, I hope she doesn't read people like I do. Seems like she's already in my head anyway.*

"Well, to be honest, Connie, I go out a lot so that I don't have to be home alone. I feel so lonely even when my kids are there. Listen, I'll tell you more later. I don't want Chuck to be hearing me, O.K.?"

"Uh huh."

## Inside My Head

"Hi, Honey! I'm so happy to see you awake. Oh, my gosh, Honey you scared the begeebees outta me!"

"Sorry, Mom, I love you." He can barely talk, but he is talking, *amazing, God!*

"Honey, Honey, don't talk. I love you. I was so scared I'd lost you. But, Connie. Oh! This is Connie, my friend from work." She turns toward me with a nervous smile.

"Hi." He breathes out.

"Hi, Chuck."

Well, Connie came over to help me get through the night and she brought pizza and movies and then we ended up just talking and she prayed for us...both of us. And she had just barely gotten done prayin' and the phone rang and it was your nurse and she said you were awake. Lord, have mercy! I was so excited! I couldn't even drive for bein' so happy, so Connie drove me here. And we talked all the way here, so how ya feelin' Honey?"

*Mile a minute like me. She's so happy. Maybe we're not all that different after all. Maybe she's me without God. Maybe she just needs God. Maybe she's not really as happy as I thought. She seems happy at work, but she seemed different when she was opening up. I'm different inside, maybe she's like me. Do I stay in the room or do I step out? Oh, this is awkward. Well, better than I expected though. I know they have so much to say to each other and I don't want it to seem like I'm eavesdropping. It sounded like he just said he saw an angel or something.*

"Really?" Sheila asks, not sounding too sure about whatever he just said.

*Did he really just say he saw an angel?*

"And what did this angel look like and what did he say?"

*Sounds more like she's challenging him rather than believing the possibility.*

"Mom, I'm serious! He was massive! He looked like a warrior, kinda, but I wasn't afraid. He had a..." he shakes his head and looks like he's thinking. He's been moving his hands and now his pulse is racing according to the machine's nearly constant beeping. "...a...I don't know, almost a softness somehow."

"Hmm." Sheila isn't sure if she believes that this massive, soft, warrior angel is real. "Honey, you've been in a coma for two days. Maybe, this was a..." she fishes through her thoughts for a suitable word. "hallucination."

"Mom! I'm telling you he is as real as you and me!" His machines go wild.

"O.K., Honey."

The nurse rushes in. "Ma'am, if you'd like to stay in this room you'll have to keep him still and comfortable. He's just woken up from a coma and he needs stillness, calmness." She snips as she checks his arm and the machines attached to them. Finding nothing wrong she leaves with another quick warning. Sheila and I raise our brows and roll our eyes in synch. We are so much alike it's scary.

"Mom, I have a guardian angel, for real!" Chuck gets right back to his former conversation as though there were no break at all. "Remember when me and Patty were little and you used to tell us we had guardian angels?"

"Yes."

"We do. I asked the angel if Patty had one too, and he said 'yes.'" Excitement oozes out of every word.

"So, he talked to you, this soft warrior angel?" Her curiosity was now getting the better of her.

"Yes, Mom."

"What else did he say?"

"He told me it's not time for me to die, but I have the choice to live or die. Then he said that there is still something I need to do. And, that God cares about me and you and Patty. That He never stops watching us or loving us." He shakes his head and furrows his brow. "I can't remember it all and that wasn't exactly like he put it, but he talked to me just like I talk to my buddies. Not all holy and that, just…normal. But the last thing he said is, 'You'll be waking up soon because someone is praying for you, and don't forget, the choice is yours. I set before you today life and death, choose life.' And I did."

*O.K., now that's incredible! I was the one praying. My prayers were heard by an angel and answered? My prayers? I wonder sometimes if they even get past the ceiling and…Oh my gosh, God! I can't believe it! God, I didn't know you really hear my prayers.*

**Constance, I understand your thoughts from afar and I know every word on your tongue before you speak it.**

*Isn't that in the Bible somewhere? It sounds familiar.*

**Yes, Psalm 139. My Word is living. I Am the same yesterday, today and forever and I am no respecter of persons. My words to David are the same to you, my dear.**

*But, David was the apple of your eye, of course you listened to him, he was special.*

*Constance, David loved me wholeheartedly, but he was a disobedient, adulterous murderer who didn't even control his own children, yet he repented. He poured himself out before me humbly and turned from his wickedness each time he failed, and then he went on with the realization that his forgiveness was complete. He didn't take his sins back. He worshipped me from the depths of his soul. I love him for that.*

Hmm, hmm, David was all those things. I never thought of that. I read his Psalms and they are beautiful. It's like he had an inside look at who You are and who he was.

*And he accepted that. You are my daughter, my treasure. I delight in you, the same way that I did David. You just need to accept that for yourself.*

"Connie?" Sheila breaks in.

"Huh? Oh, sorry I was lost in thought."

"Connie, I was just telling Chuck that you were the one praying."

"Thanks." Chuck says looking at me with clear eyes. There's a simple smile on his gentle young face that I can't explain.

"No, no, of course, no, I umm, you're welcome. It was truly nothing."

"Connie is MY guardian angel, I think." Sheila says nodding and looking from me to Chuck.

"Oh, I definitely wouldn't say that about me. No, huh-uh."

"Of course you wouldn't, you're so humble." Sheila says with a half-laugh.

## Inside My Head

"Thank you," Chuck starts, "my life will be totally different because of this. I should've died, but you prayed. I don't think anybody has ever prayed for me before. And, you didn't even know me. How awesome! Thank you!" Chuck finished before closing his eyes.

"You rest, Honey. Mom's going to be in the hall." Sheila pats him on the arm before we walk out into the hall. She gives me the biggest hug and starts to cry again. "It's joy this time," she says, wiping away a cheek full of tears. "You really are my guardian angel." She hugs me again. "Can I ask you for one more favor?"

"Sure."

"Would you mind taking me home to pick up my car?"

"Tonight?"

"Yes, I want to stay here with him." Her eyes fall on her sleeping son beyond the cracked door.

"How about if you stay here tonight, and I come get you in the morning. You both could use the rest and the time together."

"Do you mind coming all the way back out here tomorrow?" She wipes tears as she asks.

"No, no. You know what? That would be an honor, to help you two. I'm glad to do it. Honest." And to my own surprise, I am.

"Thank you, so much," she hugs me again "You are too much! I don't know what I'd've done tonight if not for you. You're great." Her tears wet my shoulder. "Oh, I'm sorry." She tries wiping them off as though it would immediately dry my shirt. But somehow I don't mind.

"Don't worry, about it. You try to rest, and I'll be back in the morning about...hmm, what time would be good for you?"

"Uh, how about..." She wrings her hands and her eyes shift left; thinking. "Ten?"

"Perfect. I'll be here. Would you mind if I brought my kids?"

"Oh, no, that would be great. I think Chuck could use some new friends."

"Cool, we'll be here then, about ten. See you in the morning."

*She really isn't that different from me. I mean, except for being thin and beautiful and sweet as sugar. I can't believe she'd think I could be her guardian angel. Did I turn left here? Where are the elevators? Restrooms, telephones, cafeteria, gift shop, elevators, good! I get lost so easy. I get to thinking and forget where I am.*

*First floor lobby. I wonder if people really do have sex in elevators. Like stop 'em or something, like on TV Oh, how ridiculous, just because it's on TV doesn't mean it's real. Constance, people don't just go around blowing each other up. Well, terrorists do, but not normal people. O.K., people don't really cut people up with chainsaws anyway. I know movies aren't real, but I still think about the sex on an elevator thing. Maybe like doctors and nurses late at night or something. Probably not.*

*I'm glad parking lots are well lit. No one ever knows who could attack while tryin' ta get in the car. Geez, Constance! Even if someone would attack, they wouldn't choose you! Besides, you're sounding more like Connie tonight.*

## Inside My Head

*I want some of that Pizza. What time is it? Only ten? Hmmph! I've got two hours before Jade gets home. I could turn on some good music and take a hot bath and think about Kevin and turn myself on. I love to do that. Yeah, how far is it home? I wonder, I guess probably only ten or twelve miles. This could be a very interesting ten to twelve miles with the right music. What's a good station?* I flip through several. "Oh yeah, this sounds good." *I can almost feel the hot tub. Me and Kevin...I bet he looks amazing in nothing but a hot tub. The lights would be very low so he wouldn't have to see me, that'd be better for him. Candles! Yeah, all around the edge. Some cold wine and this song. Man, this is great. I wonder who this is, 'cause I want it.*

Mmm, me and Kevin in a hot tub. What a way to spend an evening. Sex there, then in the shower, I could...

Crap! How fast was I going? Sixty-five, that's not too bad. Did that cop see me?" I check the rearview, right side, rearview, left side, rearview. "Whew! Guess not." *Everyone else is probably going faster. I wasn't really paying attention. I gotta pay attention. I'll be home soon. I can think a lot better there anyway. Well, actually thinking is not the problem it's the acting on the thinking. Sure, I can do that while driving, I have before, but it's better at home anyway. I don't have to think about anything else but that. It's sooo much better then.*

# CHAPTER FIVE

I was so glad to see Chuck doing so well this morning. Sheila looked like she'd gotten some rest. She talked so much on the way home. I can't believe Chuck will be going home today or tomorrow. I never see God work so quick, especially not for me. I forgot to ask her about Kevin, well not really but I am scared to know. Mark is plain, but at least he is a man. He likes spending time with his kids, and his kids seem good. I wonder why he and his wife aren't together. Was he a jerk? Was she a whore? Was he a whore? How long have they been apart?

Good movie choice. I didn't know they played old movies at noon here. Spiderman, action, family, romance, a little bit of everything. He's not ugly. I guess I never paid attention to him before. I do kinda focus on Kevin most of the time. I'd never get him, but I can dream. Wow, he's great. I'd love to kiss him, not just like a kiss but a KISS! A long hot kiss. A kiss that takes you further. A kiss that makes you never want to stop, to feel his body, to feel his temperature rise, to feel him start to undo my shirt one button at a time so he can touch my skin. Our breathing getting deeper like our tongues. His tongue on my ear, his breath and moans in my ear. He'd whisper to me what he really wants to be doing and I can't even speak, just...

"Mom!" Jade whispers in my ear. Not exactly what I wanted to hear in my ear right now.

"Huh?" I shake my head reminding myself of the dark theater, Mark and six kids watching Spiderman.

"Are you sleeping, for real?" She sounds irritated.

"What? No." I whisper back.

"Your eyes are closed and your breathing changed. You were to asleep. How embarrassing for Mark, Mom. At least stay awake."

"Yeah, sorry." What can I say? No, I'm horny and all I can think about is the most incredibly sexy man I've ever seen talking dirty in my ear? Guess not. "I'll pay better attention. I do like this movie just as much now as the first time we saw it." I offer an 'I'm sorry' smile and she smiles back.

*It's about over, I wonder what he'll want to do. Hmm, just go home? A late lunch? Should I be ready to say no? What excuse can I use? Sheila may need me, or I could go with him somewhere and find out more about him. Maybe we could meet again later…alone. I mean, at least he's a man, he's not really ugly, but hmm, he is single…so why is that? Is he a jerk? Hard to live with? Controlling? Was she just not happy? Did she want more freedom? Did he? This is all important stuff.*

The credits begin to roll and the lights slowly come up so that eyes can adjust painlessly. Mark stands up and the kids follow. "Good choice," I offer as I stretch.

"Is anyone hungry?" Mark looks around and his four are nodding and smiling. 'Yes' seems to be the consensus. I look at my two with a questioning look and they return the look. I nod slightly to approve, hoping he doesn't catch it and they both smile and nod.

"What sounds good then?" Mark asks.

"Pizza," suggest a couple and "Chinese," suggest his other two. My two shrug and give up a quiet 'whatever.' *They are so good and polite. This is all new; we've never really gone out with strangers before. I haven't actually gone out since that couple of guys right after Porter left. I don't know how to act, either. Is this really even considered a date?*

## Inside My Head

"Is Chinese O.K. with you all?" Mark finally decides with a smile. It's a nice smile. *He reminds me of a teenage boy, not a grown man with four kids.*

"Sure," Jade and Porter ring out simultaneously.

"Chinese it is," I say, returning his smile.

"So you want to meet us at the Chinatown over on First?" Mark asks, rather than demanding.

*Well, he doesn't seem to be controlling. Of course, that could be because this is our first date or whatever.* I nod.

"O.K., see you all shortly." They walk off toward a silver Kia mini-van. *Nice car, not overpriced, but fairly new. You don't see too many single men driving a mini-van, it's a refreshing change.*

"Well, Mom, what do you think?" Jade begins her interrogation the second the doors are all shut.

"Well, he seems nice enough, and his kids seem well behaved. What do you two think?"

"I agree. It seems very gentlemanly to ask you out for a first date with all you guys' kids. You know he's not going to try anything." She adds in her motherly tone.

"I like him too." I look in the rearview to catch Porter's grin.

"What do you like?" I turn the interrogation tables.

"Well, I got to come, and they all like Chinese…And it would be nice to have brothers and sisters." His afterthought faded to barely audible.

"Yeah, that's not exactly what I was thinking, but his kids were on my mind. Blended families are tough.

What if we all didn't get along?" Jade; always the philosopher. "Well, that is an important issue when a single parent begins dating again. However, you know that's why this should be a long process. This was just a first date. Most importantly, the two of you would have to take time to know if you'd get along with each other's kids. What about beliefs? What about both of your parenting ideas? Backgrounds, families, why is he divorced? These are all very important issues that would need to be discussed privately," she pauses briefly, "possibly before you could proceed with a dating relationship." I look at her as though she were an alien. *Are you serious, Dr. Laura? My gosh, where did my 15 year old gain such extraordinary wisdom?*

"Well...don't you agree?" she queries after waiting only two seconds for my response and not getting one.

"Yes, of course. I would just have expected that type of response from someone 30, not 15. I am continuously reminded of how I don't have to worry about you."

"There it is!" Porter excitedly points out the restaurant just ahead.

"Thanks, I had gotten sidetracked by Dr. Laura here." He smiles, thinking he is also helpful.

.........

"Hey! We're kinda the Brady Bunch!" Frank observes. "Three girls and three boys and a mom and a dad, now all we need is a maid." He turns toward me and Mark ruffles his hair.

"He is eight." Mark tries to defend him but I don't think it's necessary. So I smile and nod at Frank.

## Inside My Head

"A maid would be quite the luxury." I try to show my alliance with Frank and he smiles. *Why in the heck would anyone name their son Frank? What a gawd-awful name. Frank...well maybe one of their relatives was named Frank. Reminds me of Franklin the Turtle. In fact with that turtleneck and those glasses he kinda looks like Franklin the Turtle.*

Everyone gets plates and chooses a seat and starts to eat. No prayer, so my kids and I bow our heads slightly and pray silently not to make a statement but just because that is what we do.

"Oh! Sorry, Umm, we didn't think of that. Uhh, I mean...I didn't know that you'd want to pray first. I'm sorry." Mark stammers.

"No big deal." I smile. *What can I expect? He may not even believe in God, I wouldn't know. Why did I say I'd go out with this guy...this is so weird. But I did just tell God again that I hadn't had a date in years and I wanted one. At least he's a man. You know, I could've been selective when I was 20 but... well, I could've been selective from 14-24 and I was...well, I wasn't really selective per se. I took on anyone. I slept with a lot of guys. I guess technically I was selective – I selected everyone. It was fun while it lasted.* "Nice smile, I don't get to see that very often at work." Mark was still looking at me. His eyes are so clear and his face soft. *I wonder if he'll kiss me with all our kids here. I haven't had a kiss in so long. I miss kissing.*

"Thank you." I look down at my plate, embarrassed to think he might ask why the smile. What would I say? Lie? Tell him it's because of today. *Maybe we could get together later.* I smile at the thought. *Oh, my gosh, it's been so long. I really want it and evidently no one else does...not with me anyway. Just to feel that way again. He's just as good as anyone.*

"So, do you like this place?" His daughter is looking straight at me, well at least straight at the side of me.

"Yes, I do like this place. The kids and I come here every so often. We really like Chinese food. Do you like this place?" I smile at this very cute little girl, so sweet, but I can't remember her name. She just smiles back.

"Yes, we all do. Dad doesn't cook so we get to come here a lot, but sometimes we have pizza, but Johnny only likes bacon, so we have to order one with bacon for him. We usually order four or five. I like veggie pizza because meat is not good for me. My mom told me that. She's a vegetarian." She rambles.

My smile envelops my face. Jade used to chatter like that. I bet she's around nine or ten. "Kayla's seven, and she loves to talk…about everything." Mark said with an 'enough-is-enough' look in her direction, and they exchange smiles.

"You don't cook, huh?"

"Nope, never learned; I always expected my wife would be there to take care of dinner. But that's just not the way it is nowadays. Divorce is so frequent it almost seems like marriage is a fraudulent contract. It takes far less effort to divorce than to end a business, legally." His eyes shoot down at the table toward his children. They don't act like they heard him. He didn't expound upon that, but my guess is that it wasn't his idea.

"Mom doesn't like Daddy anymore. She likes Susie." Kayla perks up again. I look at Mark and see the shock and embarrassment in his eyes.

"Kayla, Honey, just eat, please."

## Inside My Head

*What do you say about that? She chose a woman over him? How embarrassing and hurtful. I knew this girl once whose husband left her for a man while she was pregnant. There was nothing she could do to compete for him. Mark is right; marriage does seem to be a faulty contract. That does answer some of my questions.* I continue to look at Mark. He swallows hard.

"I did say she likes to talk about everything." He tries to offer, I just smile. The rest of lunch was quiet. We only talked a little and it was very shallow. *Not likely will he try to kiss me and may not even ask me out again, surely not for a quiet time later.*

"Mark, I'll see you Monday, thank you for today." I stand close in hopes that he'd kiss my cheek or something, but no. There are six kids watching and all.

"Yeah, thank you for coming would you mind if I call you again sometime?"

"Sure, you can call. I'll be spending the evening with Sheila, but, yeah, call me." *Maybe I'll get a kiss later. If he doesn't kiss me next time, maybe I'll kiss his cheek.*

"It was cool that he brought us and paid and that he talked to me so much." Porter says as he wiggles into his seatbelt.

"You really had a good time, huh?"

"Yeah" he barely gets out before popping in his earbuds.

"I like him too," Jade starts with deep thought, "what do you think, Mom?"

"Well, I like him. He isn't really cute but he isn't ugly. He's nice...but six kids?"

# Inside My Head

"Yeah, six kids would be hard. But not fair that he has to be a single dad for that reason," she adds and glances at me to let me know that she heard Kayla's explanation of the divorce.

"Yeah, that was a surprise. Four kids and then she decides that? I don't get it at all." We ride the rest of the way home in silence.

## CHAPTER SIX

*I don't think I've ever brought a friend to church before, this is kinda cool. With Sheila looking so hot I'm sure every single man here will present himself. Well, maybe if they don't get her, I could be a second choice. Maybe sticking close to her will invite new friendships or something better. I wish sexy could rub off. I'd get extra close. I'd like to not lack for company as a change of pace.*

*I hope she likes it. I bet she feels so out of place in that mini-skirt. Everyone's looking at her. You'd think people would just know not to dress trashy for church, for goodness sake.*

"Do you think I look alright?" Sheila asks nervously pulling at the hem of her skirt.

"Yeah," *I wish I looked half as good. People don't look at me at all anymore, especially men.*

"So many people are looking at me." Her eyes are looking everywhere apprehensively.

"They're just surprised to see me bring someone new."

"I wore my best outfit. I tried on a bunch of other stuff, but this is my only skirt and I wasn't sure if this was one of those churches where you have to wear a dress, so I chose this." She continues to look everywhere and is fidgeting with her clothes. "But, everyone is dressed up so nice and all."

"Hey, Connie!" JoAnne waddles up with a wave. *You know she's jealous of Ms. Hot Body here. I am, and she's got even more reason to be.* "Oh, my gosh! Great study the other night. I can't get over the whole crown thing. I thought about making a crown and setting it on my dresser to remind me...is this a friend of yours?" *The real reason for you to waddle my direction. I know that smile is not real, she doesn't give a darn about Sheila; she just needed an excuse to see her. The crown thing was a good one though. At least it was relative to something.*

"Yes, this is Sheila, my friend from work." Sheila and JoAnne shake hands and smile at each other. *Sheila must be grossed out by her size.*

"Are you the friend Connie's bringing to the Bible study Tuesday?" JoAnne asks, and Sheila looks at me then back at her.

"Well, if my son is out of the hospital by then I will be there." The two of them discuss Chuck and the last few days quickly before JoAnne gets back to the crown.

"Oh, my goodness, I knew Connie's prayers reached Heaven and now there is proof." JoAnne smiles at me, "Well, Fancy and I would like to put together a craft thing for Tuesday so that all of us can make crowns and put them out to remind us daily of who we are. Would it be O.K. with you if we bring everything and create while we listen? We don't want to step on your toes or anything but you know Fancy and her creative juices and I could certainly use the daily reminder."

"Sure, no problem." *Fancy is creative, huh?*

"Sheila, I look forward to getting to know you better also." JoAnne waddled off back into the crowd.

"I didn't know you did a Bible study," Sheila commented.

## Inside My Head

"Yeah, I just started one last week. It's at my house on Tuesday evenings. We're studying the Proverbs 31 woman. You're welcome to come if you want." *I'm sure this morning will get her out of her indebted feeling and she will not repeat this. She isn't the type to go to church stuff. She always finds other ways or other people to occupy her time. It's not fair that she is skinny and nice and even kinda pretty. Why can't I be any of those things? Well, besides nice. At least I'm nice.*

**Are you?**

*Nice?*

**Yes, are you nice?**

*Well, yeah.*

**You don't sound very nice to me.**

*But God, that's only inside my head. No one knows that stuff, only you and me. I'd never say that stuff out loud. It doesn't count.*

**It does count and it isn't O.K. with me.**

*Why? I don't hurt anyone.*

**You hurt me.**

*How?* My forehead furrows and my wrinkles deepen and I know I'm looking older by the second.

**Each person you belittle and degrade in your head is my baby. My child. Including you, and that hurts Me. How do you feel when you hear that someone called Porter 'Portly' or 'Portky the Pig' or 'Porter Potty'?**

*Angry. But he's my baby.*

**Spiritually speaking JoAnne, Sheila, Martina, Maraschino, Fancy and Sarah are all my babies. So when**

*you think bad things about them you're talking about my babies, and it makes me angry and very sad.*

*But I do say that they are beautiful.* I try hopelessly to defend myself."

*Some of them, then you condemn them for their beauty, and for the "flaws" you perceive.*

*But, only inside my head.* I whine.

"Connie," the whisper comes soft but urgent. I look around to see who it could be. *Oh my gosh, I almost forgot that Sheila was here.*

"Yeah?" I whisper back.

"Your church is beautiful."

"Thanks." I reply, still curious about the urgency in her voice.

"I liked the songs," she continued.

"Good." I smile back. *She's like a kid. Has she never been in a church?*

"How much am I supposed to give? The bag will be here soon." *She looks lost and of course she is. God, she needs you.*

"Honey, you don't have to give anything. You can give whatever you'd like but first timers don't usually give anything." I try to console her.

"But after what God did for Chuck, I gotta give something." Even in a whisper the distress is evident.

"Give anything you'd like." I say hoping to soothe her.

"But how much do you give to have your son back? Isn't there a...like some kind of ...I don't know..."

"Price list?" I finish for her. *I can't believe I just let that come out of my mouth.*

"Yeah! At least a suggested price?"

*She's serious.* There she sits with her hands in her open purse as her face changes from anxious to excited, or something on that order, as she waits for my answer.

"No." I shake my head. "Everything God does is free." *Wow! Look at her face. Anger? Confusion? What kind of reaction is that?* "You can give whatever you'd like. God loves a cheerful giver." I try to smile hoping to make up for whatever I just said to cause that reaction.

The purple velvet bag reaches us and she throws in a ten. I put my tithe envelope in and send the bag down the row.

"Where did you get the envelope? I didn't get one. Are you supposed to have them? Oh, my gosh, I feel so stupid now."

My eyes must be as big as UFO's. I explain the envelope and the tithe and the taxes realizing that it's a good thing we sat in the back. We missed the announcements and I missed the singing. Sometimes I get so lost in my thoughts. *I am sooo A.D.D. I wish I could go back to school and study psychology. I would love to know why I do this. I was on my way to a degree when I got married. When was that? I wonder if I can count those credits. Oh, you dummy! Fifteen years ago, it was the night after finals. I was six months pregnant and I was stressed so badly. I'm sure those are too old to count for anything. I should've never quit. That stupid excuse for a man told me he would support me. How did I ever trust him?* I shake my head slightly then roll my eyes, realizing that Sheila is watching me.

"You don't agree?"

O.K., UFO eyes again. "Agree with what?" *I can't believe she's talking to me again, won't she ever shut up? How is she going to learn about being a Christian if she won't shut up long enough to listen to the preacher?*

"The preacher just said we can't out give God."

*Oh, crap!* My shoulders go down and my eyes go up. *I am so stupid! I really need to shut up and listen.*

"Yes, yes I do agree with him. Why?" I nod and roll my eyes.

"You were shaking your head."

"Oh," I say barely above a breath. "I was thinking about something else," I admit.

"Oh, O.K." she faces the front again, listening intently to Pastor John.

*Geez! I am so stupid! Stupid, fat and ugly. No wonder I am so lo...so lonely and low sometimes. I don't think I'll ever pull out of this nose dive I call my life. God's right, I am mean. I wouldn't have any friends if they knew what I was thinking. Good thing they can't get inside my head.*

*I don't really have any friends anyway. I don't call anyone just to chat. I never just go out for coffee. I get up I go to work, I pick up kids and dinner and run around taking them where they go. I have no life. I do the Bible study and church and that's it. Good thing they have friends. No wonder I live in my past. My present is non-existent. Who'd be my friend anyway? I don't do anything. I don't go anywhere. Yeah, how will I find a husband? How could I? I look like a cow. No one would want* me. I am doomed to live my life alone, going to work and home…alone all day and all night forever! Life sucks!

The clapping snaps me back to the present and I clap along with everyone else.

"I like this guy. He's down to earth. He doesn't act like he's better than anyone else," Sheila reports as she smiles and claps.

*I think he's stuffy. Well, I'm guessing he is anyway, I've never seen him or his wife outside of the church. Of course he's better than us, he's a pastor; he has to be better. He doesn't know what we go through. He hides away in his little office all day doing whatever a pastor does while I slave away in a factory just to make ends meet. His wife…I don't even know what she does. I know she thinks she's better than all of us.*

After the service Sheila leaves right away to get up to the hospital. The sun warms the crisp fall afternoon so Jade, Porter and I decide to eat our burgers and fries on the back deck. Duke runs through the back yard chasing a neighborhood cat, his paws crunching every leaf, drawing me back to the fall of my 16th year.

"What do you mean she's pregnant?" I question Tommy.

"She's pregnant. That can only mean so much." He looks at me as if I've lost my mind.

"So what are you going to do?" I cling to the hope that he'll dump Tawny and want me back all the time instead of just sometimes.

"I'm going to marry her. That's the right thing to do." He put his head down and shook it slowly like he had no option and regretted this one. "She's due in June, so we will get married before Christmas."

# Inside My Head

*I knew our friendship and our sex was not going to continue. It didn't seem fair that I wouldn't get to be with him at least sometimes. Maybe...*

"You know this means we can't talk any more, right?" *He could read my thoughts. He had always been able to do that. It was like he understood who I was from the beginning.*

"We're soul mates! How can you marry her?" *I refused to believe this was happening.*

"Connie, we're not soul mates. It's been fun and all, but both of us have been sleeping around for a long time. That's not what soul mates do. I'm not in love with anybody, but I'm going to have a baby so I need to be there for her. I don't want to be like my dad...gone." *He had tears in his eyes but I realized it was more for him than us. My tears were for us. I ran away, every step crunching the leaves.*

I look around and find myself alone in the backyard.

## CHAPTER SEVEN

"Last week was short and sweet. I am so thankful for all of your encouragement this week, and that you invited friends. I invited Sheila," I point with my whole hand like a Price is Right model showing off my only friend. "So let's go around the room and introduce ourselves and our guests. For those that don't know me, my name is Connie and I lead this study. We only covered the first two verses last week so you didn't miss much. This study is supposed to go for six weeks and each week one person will give their testimony, they'll tell about themselves and what God has done in their life. Please ask questions and invite friends. We do ask that anything said here stays here. Our goals are to learn through God's Word and from each other as we open up."

"I invited my friend, Sheila. Oh, yeah, let's also tell your favorite thing about you."

"'I'm Sheila and am so glad I could come here tonight. I look forward to getting to know each of you. And, Uhh, I'm not sure about my favorite thing about me...I guess since I get complimented most on my smile that would be my favorite thing." She shrugs and turns her head to the left and nods.

*Her smile? Interesting she's beautiful. I guess there's too much to choose from.*

"I am Martina, and I like my hair. It's thick and naturally curly and has never had any sort of chemical treatment. I simply have it trimmed every six weeks. It is also quite long, though I wear it up most of the time; I am able to wear it in many different styles." She smiles as she looks left.

*Wow! I have to perm my hair and I have it touched up every month, it costs me a mint! She's so lucky, she has the money to do her hair and I don't that is not fair at all! I wish my hair was nice instead of this fine yucky graying mess.*

"Hey! My name's Fancy and that is also my favorite thing about me. I was a little girl when Reba McEntire sang that song, Fancy. Ya'll know it?" She looks around and some nod. "Well, anyway I thought it was my song. I loved it. Everybody useta say it's your song, Fancy! But later I found out the words and I was shocked! I didn't like it as much but by that time it was a part of who I am. And I brought my friend here." She says as she looks at her neighbor. "I've known her forever."

"Hi, I am Patty." She smiles with the same simplicity as Fancy. "And I guess my favorite part of me is my eyes, most people say that they can tell a lot about me 'cause of 'em. So..." she's nodding "I like that they express who I am." She just looks around so JoAnne begins.

"Well, since I'm on her left I'll go next. I'm JoAnne. I'm a good cook. I made chocolate chip pecan cookies with whipped chocolate frosting for tonight, and for drinks I brought Pepsi, lemonade, and Hawaiian Punch." Everyone claps after Fancy starts and JoAnne beams.

The silence settles for only a moment before Sarah begins. "Sarah, and I'm tall so I played basketball and was pretty good in high school." She rolls her eyes and head to the left.

"I'm also Sarah" she smiles "that's how we became friends. We've been friends since third grade." *How is that possible? I don't have any friends and these two have been friends forever; probably because they don't have anyone else to be friends with. I guess if you find someone and hold on forever you at least have one friend.*

"And what's your favorite part of you Sarah two?" I smile and she returns the gesture.

"Well," she looks at the floor.

*She's probably like Sarah Plain and Tall. That's why they can be friends forever; they don't talk to anyone else.*

She takes a deep breath before continuing slowly. "Well, I'm short, very short and small so I can fit into small spots. Actually, we're always called the odd couple because of our heights. But, I think we complement each other." She looks at her friend and they smile.

"O.K. that's great, Maraschino?" *Could she find one thing? Watch it's her perfection in every area of life that is her best point.*

"Yes, umm, I have to say my eyes also. Although sometimes they give away too much about me, I like them best."

*Yeah, how could she say everything? I am beautiful and have a great job and a fantastic gorgeous husband. I have a perfect figure and hair that won't quit. Eyes? Whatever! For one person to have so much good is not fair in any way. I can't stand her. She's just too perfect for me, it's disgusting. I could only imagine half of her perfection and my mind would literally explode from an overactive imagination.*

"Well, thank you all. Tonight is the night for Sarah to give her testimony and Fancy and JoAnne have put together a craft for all of us to do while we study the Proverbs 31 woman. So, Sarah, you're up."

## Inside My Head

*She is so nervous. She's twisting her hands and biting her lip. If it were me that would mean I was lying, but I doubt she's ever lied.*

"...So... we went to church on Sunday morning and night and Wednesday night as a family..."

*Geez, you've got to be kidding! First of all, we all know her, how can she be so nervous? Big deal. She won't even look up off the floor. That only shows what a loser she really is. No confidence. No self-esteem. I feel sorry for her. I hope I'm not really shaking my head and rolling my eyes. I hate when I don't know...*

"So, umm, I never dated and uhh, decided to wait to kiss till I marry. Umm, I think it would be like so umm, romantic umm, for our first kiss to be when, you know, the preacher says 'you may kiss the bride'." She laughs slightly.

*Everyone is smiling. Yeah right! No kissing till you're married? How? That's impossible, isn't it? I mean, how do you even know if you want to be with someone if you don't even know what they kiss like?*

"Yeah, so uhh, I thought this study would be good for me to learn how to be a good and godly wife... so, yeah, that's it, I guess." She lets out a deep breath.

*No way, you've got to be kidding! That's not even a testimony!*

"Phenomenal testimony!"

My head spins like the girl from the Exorcist to find Fancy smiling at Sarah. *Fancy, you can't be serious! That shows how dumb you really are.*

"Wow! You are truly an example of how God can spare us from hurtin' emotionally and physically. How many people have been that blessed all their lives like that? What a tremendous heritage. I grew up in the church and still made bad choices in my teen years. You're amazin'!"

*Well, I guess that shows how stupid I am. I guess I hadn't thought of that. God, you spared her from being in a pit and having to dig her way out. But how can she help others?*

"You know..." JoAnne starts, "you should consider talking to the tweens and teens about your life. So many need to know that it's possible and even cool to stay pure. I'll tell you, raising kids nowadays is scary. Every movie, song, newspaper, TV show all say that it's normal and O.K. to have sex early. You should even experiment with a lot of people because that's how you know you want to be with them. But, honestly, whether they're a good kisser or good in bed is not what makes them a good life long marriage partner. You have a gift to give. I mean it."

*O.K., God that's getting freaky!*

**You asked.**

Everyone is nodding. I have to agree. Sarah's smiling so big, she looks almost pretty when she smiles. "I have to agree, Sarah, you would be someone I'd want Jade and Porter to talk to."

"Really?" She smiles and looks down at her wringing hands some more.

"We'll see if you can talk at church one night." Fancy urges.

"Oh, I couldn't do that!" she remarks showing her fear.

*I don't get it, she grew up in that church. Everyone knows her and she knows them. She's not hideous or anything. At least she's skinny. I wonder what she thinks is so scary about talking to people she knows. How stupid.*

"Yeah, I understand your super-shy an' all but maybe ya could jus' talk to the girls 8-15 or something like that. In fact, maybe ya could sit and talk to 'em. That's a trick I learnt a long time ago. It puts ya atta same level as ever'body else and then ya don't feel like yer in the spotlight. It worked for me in high school speech class. Best thing I learnt, well, one of the best anyways." Fancy continues the conversation while I check out mentally. "...so anyways y'all just glue any o' these here gems on these B.K. crowns. This is something ya'll can put out an' remind ya that yer the crown o' your husband, not that y'all are cheap imitations 'cause we know now that we're not that at all but beautiful emblems of our virtue and nobility. So do your best to make 'em beautiful."

All the women are giggling and passing around the cardboard replicas and JoAnne is dumping gems of every shape and color on the coffee table.

"Well while you start that I will go over last week quickly for those who have no idea why were making crowns. Proverbs 31 is the place in the Bible where the king's mother is telling him what a good wife is. It is impossible to be everything but this is something to work toward. I'll start with verse 10, 'a wife of noble character or a virtuous wife who can find? She is worth far more than rubies.' Now to expand on this I looked up the words virtuous and noble character in my concordance then re-presented the verse like this…" I look through my notes quickly and find the exact explanation. "Who can find a strong, able, moral, high quality woman with fine character? For her value is far above rubies. So as wives with this one verse we are more valuable to our husbands than diamonds since rubies are even more costly than diamonds."

Another verse I referred to was Proverbs 12:4. "A virtuous woman is the crown of her husband. A virtuous, moral, chaste woman is his crown. Or nobility found in a woman is a fine character, a high quality. The crown of a prince or a king is a point of pride and shows immediately their authority and power. We are those crowns for our husbands." I smile and look around at everyone enjoying themselves. "Thus, the crown project tonight." *Oooh! A huge emerald a rectangular citrine and a pink heart, this could be a lot of fun!* "By the way I heard a commercial on the radio for the Proverbs 31 woman the other day. It may be something we could look into. It's like proverbs31.org, or something. I will listen better and have that for next week.

These 21 verses will help us to aim at perfection in our personal lives be it mother, wife or wannabes."

"Yeah, I ain't never been married, like Sarah, but I wannabe the best I can be when I do get married so this class is kinda like a marriage prep class for us that ain't married yet." Fancy interjects with all her slang.

"Yes, well," I smile but I really want to gag. *I can't stand to be around stupid people and she tops the list. Poor beautiful hick. I wish I was as smart as I am and as beautiful as she is.* "I'd definitely be able to find a husband then." *Did that just come out?*

"When?" Martina asks.

"When, what?" I ask hoping beyond hope that I didn't just say all of that out loud.

"You said, 'I'd definitely be able to find a husband then.' What did you mean?"

*Oh crap!* "Well, if I was the perfect Proverbs 31 woman…" I start to lie.

"Oh, look at this diamond! I'm putting a few of these on my crown to make it like the ultimate crown. This is a very creative idea. I wish I was creative like this. Thank you both." Martina goes on like that answer was acceptable.

*Whew!*

"We're all creative in our own ways," says Fancy. "God created us in His own image. He created us to be creators. We all got ideas, hopes, dreams, plans etc. Some create new foods and cook good, some do crafts, some paint or sculpt. Some people make up new inventions while others come up with new ideas on how to be organized or clean quicker an' more efficient. In whatever ways we improve things an' situations around us we create."

*She didn't even look up from her crown while she said that. Sometimes she blows me away. I don't get how she can sometimes sound so smart. Oh that would be horrible! Two Maraschino's! Smart and beautiful, completely unfair!*

"O.K. let's get started on this week's verses. Verse 12 says, 'she does him good and not evil all the days of her life. Emphasis on all. This is perfect for all of us, those of us that are not married; this suits us as well as those that have been married for years. I was running the kids to school one day a long while back and heard an interview with one of the Barlow Girls or someone from Superchick I can't remember but anyway, this verse was one of their favorites. They were saying how they have spent time praying for their husband since they were young. They think about things in such a way that says would this action be good for my husband.

I'm saying as unmarried women we need to pray for whomever God has planned for us to marry. Lift him up in prayer for strength to stay pure and godly. That God would build him up emotionally, spiritually, and even financially. That God would give him the power to get wealth to establish His covenant like it says in Deuteronomy 8:18. Pray that God will help you to remain pure and faithful to your husband. Another suggestion I heard once was to begin writing letters to him. Love letters explaining your hopes and prayers, your thoughts, desires, and dreams, then wrap them with ribbon etc. and give them to him as a wedding gift."

"Aww! How Sweet!" Fancy couldn't stand it anymore. This whole time I thought she'd bounce off her chair. "I love those ideas! I am so glad I came tonight, Constance, how beautiful! That's so great! I knew this Bible study would be for me."

"From now on that is going to be my mantra." Sarah, plain and tall, blurts out boldly, not loud just bold and confident.

*That's new.* She and Fancy seem to bond in that moment. They continue to create crowns and contemplate their future husbands.

"For the two of you, and anyone else who's not married, your song to him could be 'Wait for Me' by Rebecca St. James. If you haven't heard it, look it up and begin to sing it around the house." *I'm so happy that they are getting so much from this.* "I want to remind you that she does him good ALL the days of her life. Key word again is all, every day, from childhood to her death, meaning after marriage she continues to do him good. We need to pray continuously that we would learn to be good with money, and that we would be experts at keeping house, raising children, and excellent lovers. We want to do him good in every way. For us who have experience at being a wife we need to pray that we would learn how to be a better wife. Ask God to show you what it is that would make your husband truly happy. Maybe it's something as simple as being able to save an extra ten dollars each week or to put makeup on daily and have your hair and nails done. It may be just snuggling close on his hard days to take his mind off of a hard day out in the cruel and unforgiving world. Whatever that extra something maybe it's worth it for us to do that for him.

Last week we discussed the trust issue; an issue that will cement any relationship. It goes both ways of course; however, we need to remember we can only work on ourselves. We can't change anyone else.

For those who are not married I want you to go home this week and look up that song, 'Wait for Me' by Rebecca St. James, and pray for your husband, who he is and that he will wait for you. Make a list privately of the virtues that are important to you. These need to include looks, age, height, etc., but also his relationship with God. Maybe you want to meet an evangelist and travel and minister together, or someone who is going on the mission field or possibly someone who works in a factory but loves God. You may want a hard worker or someone who can make you laugh. You may decide anyone with a diploma is fair game." Everyone laughs and continues with the crown project.

"For those who are married, go home and write a list of all the reasons why you're glad you are married to him. Things that are simple, like 'he kills bugs for me' or 'he opens jars that are too tight.' Maybe because he is still the most incredible looking man in the world or he brings home good money. Maybe he is amazing in bed or makes a great cup of hot cocoa and watches a chick flick on a rainy night. Whatever that list is, start telling him about those things one or two every day, things that make you smile. See what a difference that will make. Do him good this week, ladies. Next week we will get into what she does. You may be surprised at how much she does. The perfect wife is not one kept by her man but one who works tirelessly for her family and others. She buys property and makes clothes and cooks. She is an amazing woman that any man would die for. Now I want to make a crown while we enjoy JoAnne's snacks and discuss anything you'd like."

# Chapter Eight

Beep, beep, beep, beep, "Oh, my gosh! I hate that horrible noise! I meant to put it on radio. Oh, what a miserable way to start a day. Jade, Honey, get up." I gently open her door to be on the safe side but she is already up as usual.

"Just finishing my Bible study, Mom; how did yours go last night?"

It went well; did I tell you lately how proud I am to have the best girl ever born as my very own daughter?" She smiles that perfect smile.

"Porter, Honey, up, up!" I open his door to find him asleep with the pillow over his head so that I'm easier to ignore. "Porter, my dear, you need to get up now so we don't run late. Did you get a shower last night?"

"Yes, Mom, and I am getting up. I wish we didn't have to get up so early, none of my friends have to get up until a half an hour before they leave for school."

"O.K., Honey, thanks." I ignore his complaints as usual. "Your lunch is on the counter and there is a breakfast bar there or you can get some cereal while I get a shower." I turn toward the bathroom before allowing him to answer.

I check my face in the small oval mirror covering the nearly empty medicine chest. *It never changes. Plain as it was yesterday. Fuzzy dark brown hair and chubby cheeks, solid boring brown eyes and freckles always the same. I don't know why I look. It's as if someday I hope to wake up to find*

## Inside My Head

*Maraschino's face…and body for that matter!* I look down, but it is very clear I didn't get that wish either.

"Mom, are you almost done?" Porter whines.

"Done enough for you to get in and out quickly." I rush off to my room to pick out the same jeans and t-shirt type of ensemble I wear every day. They go so well with the pony tail and safety glasses; no style whatsoever. (sigh)

*Rush, rush, rush, everyday, I wish I could relax with a hot cup of tea in a warm fuzzy robe and watch the rain hit the window while I listen to some good music. Instead I'm shoving my children into a minivan racing across town to drop them at Bonnie's house extra early so I can race further down the road to the factory I call home more often than I do my real home.*

"Got your lunches?"

"Yep! Love ya," Porter slams the door and runs.

"Yes, Mom. I love you." Jade smiles and turns to walk away in her typical bubbly way.

*I love you both so much you can't imagine. Nothing keeps me going more than you two. The greatest joy in life is you. I can't imagine my life without you. I can however imagine my body and my social life, but you two are worth everything. God, it's so true all of it, thank you for my children. Help Porter today, he takes right after his dad so chubby and so cute. The doctor says he'll thin down some once he hits puberty and has a growth spurt. That will probably help with his basketball, he gets made fun of so much. I'm sorry I let his dad talk me into naming him Porter.*

"Hi, Connie!"

"Hi, Shelly." I moan as I pass her.

"Great weather, huh?"

"Uhh, yeah, well it's not snow." I answer optimistically in order to brighten her day.

"Yeah, see ya at lunch." Shelly shuffles down the aisle to her line and I go the opposite direction to the place I've known for so long I could run the machines in my sleep. And technically I do some times. The same monotonous music begins to play as the machines are turned on.

*This was definitely not supposed to be a career but at least the bills are paid and I have insurance. That is important. Like when the school called and Porter had been pushed off the swing. Well, the school said he had fallen, but I know better. I feel so sorry for him – the kids tease him all the time, calling him Portly and Porta Potty. How horrible is that?*

*God, how were You able to sit there and watch and listen as people made fun of and beat up Your Son and killed him! How, God?*

**For my other children.**

*What?*

**You, my daughter, and Porter and Jade and...**

*I get it, but it was more a rhetorical question. I mean I knew what You'd say but didn't You just want to zap them or something?"*

**It had to be done.**

"Yeah, I guess, but, ohh, I don't know. *Is it wrong of me to be angry for my son when others hurt him? I mean he's not saving the world.*

**How do you know?**

*Know what?*

## Inside My Head

*How do you know who he may lead to me?*

My head shakes at that.

"What's wrong with you? You're shaking your head and frowning," Ron questions.

"Oh, just thinking kind of in my own world, ya' know?"

"Yep" he chuckles.

*I had no idea he'd been watching me. Maybe he likes me. I hadn't thought about him lately. I heard he was engaged this summer. He's certainly not married, and he really seems nice. I almost forgot he sat at my table for lunch the other day. Hmm, maybe he is checking me out. Yeah, Connie he's checking you out. Right! 'What size jeans you think she wears?' and 'where do you suppose she found that wide load sign to fit just across her butt like that? Nice hair, brown and fuzzy like a poodle. Cute boots, yeah as though anyone is checking me out anymore.*

*What was I thinking about before that? Oh, oh, oh, there's Kevin! My eyes close and I sigh. I wish he'd check me out. Like a library book. Open me up and read me from cover to cover and start again! Man, is he fine! He's a mustang that I'd like to ride. Whew, what I wouldn't give to watch him for hours. He could do anything or nothing. Crap! That was a quick fix, and off he goes into the wild blue yonder! Like a wild stallion. Maybe someday I can try to tame him. Maybe I don't want to tame him...just ride him for awhile.*

*O.K., Constance, back to the real world. You know the one you belong to, the one that doesn't have any prospects; the real one, where men see you and turn the other way to run. Actually, I should turn and run. If I had any brains at all, I would have long ago.*

## Inside My Head

*Look at Tommy. Oooh, Tommy and that first time! I've always heard the first time should be special, and it was. It was so exciting. He was slow and gentle and so exciting. I still look at that day as if it were a movie playing over and over. I love to watch it. I couldn't believe after giving him my virginity, him, my best friend, he would end up sleeping with at least three other girls during that same time period. He was a man whore. Of course, he was gorgeous and so sexy. Sexy and seventeen, yeah that song was about him. Even at fourteen I couldn't resist him, and he sensed that somehow. But I didn't see the reality. I trusted him so completely with everything that was me. The lifetime I expected was a year and a half. Then there had been Francine, Charlotte, and Sonya, and Lord knows how many others. And worse yet, he told all the guys about me. He played me! I was so dumb, even at sixteen when guys asked me out, I didn't get that it was because they just wanted to sleep with Tommy's leftovers. Hmph!* I shake my head again this time in pure disgust.

"Must not be a very good world you're in right now, huh?"

*Ron again.* I look up to acknowledge him and see a smile. It makes me smile.

*He does have a kind face. What is he, about 30 maybe. What a shame. A younger man? Nope, can't do it. Aunt Marge married a man, ten years her junior and that was a disaster. He took her to the cleaners and then skipped with a guy! How awful!* I close my eyes and open them to look at Ron who is still looking at me.

"It's almost lunch; want to break free from your world for a while? We can chat over our meal."

*What? Is he wanting to sit with me at lunch? Does he like me? Wow! I mean he's not Kevin but he is a man. Two in a week? Oh, my gosh, maybe I should go with my first instinct.*

## Inside My Head

"O.K." What? What did I just say? Not my first instinct. Oh boy, I hope I'm not sorry. I never can tell if it's right to talk to someone or sit with them at lunch; what's the big deal? Constance, you're so dumb.

I snap back to this world as the lunch alarm goes off. I feel like a kid as we walk to the cafeteria. *I brought a p.b. and j. with chips and an apple, exactly what I packed for my kids, and now I am going to sit next to a boy, oh brother. Are you really still twelve, Constance?*

"Connie, I've noticed lately that you seem to be a bit stressed. Is everything O.K. at home?"

*Well, nothing like being straight forward. At least it didn't start with 'hey howabout goin' out Saturday and getting home Sunday' or 'how about breakfast... at my place?'*

"Umm, everything is cool."

"Do you go to church anywhere?"

*That was totally unexpected.* "Yes, I've been going to the same church for almost ten years."

"Oh, that's awesome!" His face lights up like a Christmas tree.

*Is this like Jason, Tim and Steve? They all went to church too, but after listening to Tommy's stories of us, each one lost his interest in church. Things never change, and neither do men. Church or no church, they're all the same...*

"Connie?" Ron is looking at me as though he had lost me again.

"Oh, yeah, sorry."

"Do you know Jesus as your savior?"

## Inside My Head

"Yes, I've been a Christian for nearly eleven years. After my husband left, my life was a shambles and I hit bottom. A friend asked me to attend a Bible study group with her and I found Jesus there. My life has truly never been the same." *That sounded well rehearsed, even to me.*

"Incredible! Then this is just a reminder. Jesus is the Prince of Peace. He says to come to him if you are heavy laden and He will give you rest. He loves you and wants the best for His children. Connie, my wife and I attend that big full gospel non-denominational church just down the street on Oak. If you ever would like to visit, we have church on Saturday evening so you don't have to miss your own church service. We'd love to have you and your family."

"Thank you. I may do that some time. That's really nice. Is that what you wanted to talk about?" I look up to see that lunch is only half over and swallow hard.

"Yes, the Lord has laid you on my heart and I needed to know that you know Him also. That has just made my day!" His smile reveals his honesty. "Would you like a pop or something I noticed you don't have anything to drink with that peanut butter. My mouth is always sticky with p.b. and j."

"Uhh, yeah that would be great. I forgot a drink this morning."

"What's your pleasure?"

"Diet Pepsi." *I'll just leave it at that, I'm now sure you have no interest in my real pleasure. That's it? He's so pleased with himself. All that misguided thought of sitting with a boy at lunch and for what? I'm so stupid! Why did I think that he'd be interested in anything more than a chat with me? Geez!*

## Inside My Head

"Here you go. Do you have any kids?"

"Yes. Jade, who is 15, nearly 30 and Porter, who is 12."

"Cool! My wife and I are expecting our first in May. It's so exciting!"

I nod as I take a bite of the apple so that I don't have to talk.

"We're hoping for a boy, but want to be surprised, so we're not going to find out the sex. My wife, Mia, is already redoing a room at the house as a nursery. We're..."

*His childlike excitement reminds me of when I was pregnant with Jade. Everything going so fast. Porter acted like he was excited, but that ended abruptly when I found out we would have another baby. A storm had come quick and I was running through puddles to find him. He was at the gas station talking with Gerald about his new life. Married with children seemed to be the hot topic among all the twenty-somethings around town. Gerald had just had a baby girl also, and the stories the two of them shared were hilarious. When they saw me they stopped everything as though I had intruded on their secret conversation. I told Porter with all the excitement I could muster, knowing that he would be thrilled. He was anything but. His eyes filled with tears and he turned away from me. I was sure he was overcome with joy. He hugged me without a word and looked at Gerald. No congratulations, no wows; no nothing. I didn't understand. It took until he told me he was leaving for me to actually get that moment.*

*He and Gerald had been discussing Porter's affair and how he would be telling me goodbye. That next year was a nightmare. He was sad all the time and late coming home most of the time. I cried as I held Jade and felt the new baby moving and growing. I couldn't understand what was going on.*

"Connie?" Ron's voice brings me back. "I was just saying that Mia and I have big plans for our future and you muttered something about crying and feeling the baby move. Are you sure you're O.K.?"

"Yes. I'm sorry. What was it you were telling me?" The alarm sounded and we both began trudging back to the line.

"Well, I went to college for business but the economy is slow and this job has benefits and pays well enough for Mia to stay home with the baby."

*The love in his eyes for her blows me away. It's like a child talking about his mother. How she's the most beautiful, perfect girl in the world. I wonder what that feels like. I smile and thank him for the lunch conversation and get back to work.*

*Great! Put this old mare just outside the door of the glue factory! I used to know what guys wanted. I wasn't always glad, but by the same token, I still knew I was wanted. Now they don't want anything. I think that's worse.*

*It's not enough that Porter never loved me and neither did Tommy, John, Jason, Kyle, Steve, Tim, Tony, Nathan, or Bill. No one ever loved me. But at least they wanted me for something. I'd give my eye teeth for someone to want me now.*

**Constance, Why do you want that?**

*God, you gave that to us as one of the first gifts. You know how good it is. I just want to be loved again.*

**Constance didn't you just say that none of them loved you?**

*Yes, but it felt like they did at the time. They were nice and they put me at the center of attention when we were* together. They wanted me. They saw me differently than men do now. I want to be wanted.

**I love you for real; with a love that never ends.**

Yeah, I know, but you love everyone. I'm no more special than anyone else.

**I didn't choose everyone. I chose you. I adore you. You are very precious to me.**

That's true…out of millions, even billions you chose me. Me! Why? I'm no good. My heart is wild and my mind is uncontrollable. Plus, if you loved me so much why have I never felt loved?

**None of the men you chose were the right one. You chose to go in the wrong direction.**

But, God, I have been single for eleven years, three months and eleven days. The entire time I have been a Christian. I've had no dates. None. Zero. Hello!? Why?

**Do you really want to know?**

Yes.

**What are you looking for?**

What, my standards are too high?

**What are you looking for?**

I take a deep sigh. A Christian man who will love you first, then me; someone who will love who I am, not just what I look like. But that man doesn't exist. Men don't think outside of the bedroom.

**All men?**

*Yes! I haven't met one yet that isn't interested only in sex. They say stuff like 'look at that piece of ...well, you know...what I wouldn't give to be with her for awhile'. Or they say, 'Yeah she's nice and all, but I don't think so; she's not my type.' Why? Because she's not a size five? Because her hair isn't blowing with a fan and her shirt isn't open to her belly button? God, men think of only one thing. I've been with enough of them to know. I've heard what they've said. What they whispered in my ears. I've seen their reaction to women on TV and in movies and even on the street, and especially on the beach. I was good enough for a while but only a while then... later, 'I'm off to find some fresh meat.'*

**Who are you talking about?**

*Tommy, Jason, everybody. You know all the guys I have been with.*

**Was that before you asked me to come in and forgive you?**

*Yes, God, of course; you know that.*

**Huh! That's why I have no idea what you're talking about.**

*What? What do you mean? You know about all the years of sleeping around, living as wild child. Wanting and being wanted.*

**Actually, I do hear your thoughts about them all the time, but as you recall, I am the same yesterday, today and forever. I change not. I am not a man that I can change, my Word clearly states that when you ask for forgiveness I willingly cleanse you of all unrighteousness and throw your sins into the depths of the sea as far as the east is from the west, and they will be remembered by me no more. So past your spiritual birthday April 2, 1998 I only know what you think about.**

My mind can't wrap itself around that. Wow! Silence even in my mind, for a moment. *You honestly don't think about that; or wait till I get to Heaven to embarrass me by playing my life out in front of everyone? You aren't just waiting to hit me with a 2x4 or something spiritually equivalent for being so terrible?*

**Honey, I don't even know what you're talking about. All I know is that you live in your past and don't trust anyone, especially men. So, how can you marry someone when you won't trust him? Trust is a two-way street and marriage won't work without it. I know you've got a lot of wounds on your spirit. Wounds I'd like to heal for you, but each time I apply a healing balm you reach inside your mind and rip your wounds open again. I ask, do you want to be healed?**

I'm stunned. *Do I want to be healed? Well, yes, but what does that mean?*

**Healed, not hurting. Your spirit doesn't have to be a bleeding ulcer all the time. Your mind doesn't have to relive every past hurt, every past betrayal, and every rejection. You can be free from all that.**

*But, how? It still happened.*

**But you don't have to live in it anymore.**

*Then do I just not think about it? What about the good parts like late nights at the drive-in, the sex in the back seat instead of watching the movie. What about the way it felt to have a guy touch me or kiss me or want me or love me? Do I never get to think about those things either?*

**Are they really that precious that you'd hold on to them, instead of me?**

## Inside My Head

Our conversation ends as the alarm sounds for the end of the day. It amazes me how I can be in this world doing all that is required of me and still involved in my thoughts so fully.

"Bye, Connie!" Ron says as he rushes past.

"Bye, Ron. Hey, Sheila, you coming tonight?"

"Wouldn't miss it!"

Joe looks at me and then Sheila" Where you two goin'?"

"Church." Sheila grins.

"Yeah, right.' Joe looks with a smirk at Sheila who's always at a bar on Wednesday.

'No, I mean it. I'm going to church now."

"Why?"

"Come with me tonight and I'll tell ya." She smiles a sly smile

"Really?" he answers like he just won the lottery.

*She did not just ask a man to church! And Joe her sometimes...lots of times, bar pal. How can she do that? What the heck! It's church, not a party, for crying out loud.*

"Yep, pick me up about six and I'll show ya where, O.K.?"

"I'll be there for sure. Five-thirty would be even cooler and we can have some dinner."

*Are you serious? A church date? Dinner and a service, there ya go!*

"Well, I don't mind, but Chuck and Patty are comin' too, so maybe dinner is a bit much."

"No, I don't mind, we can all go. How about that new Chipotle that just opened. I know you like that natural organic stuff. I really do know how important it is to you to eat healthy." *He looks like a kid shrugging his shoulders and looking at the floor.*

"Really? I didn't know you knew that about me." *Surprise overtakes her face. She has no idea that he likes her so much.*

"Yeah, well..." *Yeah, well, come on guys, really?* "How about it?"

"Sounds great! See ya in a little while." They finalize the plans as we get into our cars.

*I can't believe it! A date for church! I can't even get someone to ask me out to a bar and she has a date... to church.*

**Constance, how do you know you can't get a date?**

*I just know. Where would we go? No one ever asks me out, except Mark asked me out last weekend, but I don't know. He hasn't asked me out since.*

**You could ask. Maybe you could ask them to go to church.**

*Yeah, who would I ask?*

**Mark, or Tony or Kevin or... should I go on?**

*God, are you serious right now? How could I ask any of them? I mean Mark maybe, because he asked me out, maybe that means he'd say yes, but those other guys? They don't even know I'm alive. So how could I just go up to them and say 'hey ya* wanna go to church with me?' Should I twirl my hair and turn kinda cutsie-like too?

**Constance, I'm just saying you don't know unless you ask. And for that matter fear of rejection will send you into old age alone.**

Geez, thanks, God!

**I am not man that I would lie.**

Yeah well could you be less straight forward?

**You haven't gotten me in ten years; it's time to be a little bit more blunt. You have to stop living in fear. I didn't give you the spirit of fear but of power, strength, a sound mind, and self-control.**

Isn't that in the Bible somewhere?

"Hi, Mom." Jade gets in the van and flashes her amazing smile.

"How was your day?"

"Incredible! I asked Keith if he'd go to church with me tonight and he said he'd see if his mom will let him. Wouldn't that be a perfect first date? Well, that and dinner, that would be cool, but this is a good start. It's O.K. that I asked him, isn't it Mom?"

"Absolutely, today it doesn't seem to matter who asks whom." *Very funny God!*

"Hi, Mom." Porter crawls in like every other day. "Guess what, Mom."

"What, son?"

"Well this girl at school asked me if I go to church."

"Really?" *I can't believe You, God. Do you run on themes or what?*

"Yeah, I told her yes and she asked which one and I told her and she told me that she goes to the really big one down on Oak Street. Can we go there sometime?"

"I guess so. Tonight Sheila is coming and bringing her kids and a friend from work, so I feel I need to be there. Plus, Jade invited a boy from school so it'll have to be another time. Maybe she can come with us."

"Cool, Mom, thanks!" He beams.

**Hmm, that big one on Oak. Ron goes there too.**

*Yeah, God. Is there a point?*

**Oh, I don't know. I was just reminding you that you'll know someone there.**

*You want me to change churches?*

**Not necessarily, but a visit isn't a bad thing.**

*I guess not, sometime, I guess.*

Both kids settle into their own worlds as do I, all the way home.

# CHAPTER NINE

"Hi, Sheila, hi, Joe." Their smiles speak volumes. "Where's Chuck and Patty?"

"They saw someone from school and they all went to some class or something."

"Great, Patty will see Jade then."

"This is more comfortable tonight," Sheila remarks while wiping her cords and sweater. "I am so glad you told me I could wear pants tonight."

We pick out a seat near the middle and settle in.

"Perfect," Joe and Sheila say simultaneously. "You owe me a coke!" they also say at the same time and laugh like a couple of kids.

*Ughh! That's not fair! It's so wrong that she can get saved and get a man all within two weeks. Although he's not saved, maybe I should tell her about the whole unequally yoked thing. If she really wants to be a Christian she'll dump him before he drags her back into the blackness with him. He probably thinks she'll sleep with him as soon as they leave tonight. She might, she probably doesn't even know it's wrong. How do I tell her? If you're a Christian you can only date other Christians and you can't have sex until you marry him. And you should always dress modestly. She'll understand that she needs to see life differently. Dating around, the bar life, and sex are not allowed and are not really fun even though it seems like fun at the time. It's not worth Hell, so she'll need to think up new things to do.*

"I like this song," Sheila whispers in my ear. I'm clapping with everyone else, but I didn't even realize we were singing yet. *Man, I don't know how I do that; must be a habit or something.* I nod and smile. I've heard it so many times.

*...I lift your name on high, Lord; I love to sing your praises. I'm so glad you're in my life, I'm so glad you came to save us...Kendra introduced me to this song and Petra when I first got saved. I loved rock and roll and this was the perfect way to blend my love of music with my new found religion. They have so many great songs. I remember listening to them for hours.*

"Tonight we want to remind you of the rummage sale we're having the first weekend in December..."

*Wow, I can't believe she wore that, knowing she'd be getting up in front of people. Yellow is not her color, and black shoes do not go with that yellow dress. I guess she doesn't care.*

"Yeah, so the rummage sales and the pictures for the new church directory and the teen Christmas break missions trip fundraiser, that's it, but if you have any questions I'll be in the back after service to answer any questions."

"Thank you, Tana, now we'll take up our tithes and offerings. O.K., Father, bless us, Your children and bless this body of believers as we give to Your kingdom our tithes and offerings. Give us wisdom in its usage and help us to bless others, thank You, Lord. Amen."

*The same basic prayer, week after week. Church is boring and predictable: three songs, announcements tithes and offerings his sermon and goodbye. Everything is same ol' same ol'.*

"Now how much should I give?" Sheila questions in my ear.

"Whatever you feel you should give."

## Inside My Head

"Five dollars? Is that enough?"

"It's fine. You don't have to give anything, I'm not."

"I want to."

"O.K." *Give, give, give, I don't always have something to give. What if someone were to give to me for a change? I know there are bills for a church, but I've got bills too. God, I don't get it. I work all the time, I have very little saved, I only go on vacation three days a year and that's to visit my sister in Albuquerque with the kids. No hotel or anything fancy. I have a '92 mini-van and two kids who always need something. Sometimes I just can't give. I tithe, but offering? I just can't.*

"With Christmas coming before we know it I want to remind you all that many people will be flooding in for their bi-annual visit. So over the next few weeks I want us to prepare our hearts for welcoming these people as well as others who wander in to get warm. Tonight we'll talk about Jesus' call to his first disciples. We will talk later about giving and receiving. We'll also touch on forgiveness of ourselves and others, as well as gathering together as friends and family, and as a church body.

"Together we stand, divided we fall, to repeat an old adage. We need unity in the full body of Christ. This church is not meant to be the box God dwells in. This building is meant to be a place where God's people join together to gain wisdom, understanding, and training to go out into their everyday lives and be the church body. So to start this series we will look at Matthew 4 starting with verse 18...

"As Jesus was walking beside the Sea of Galilee, He saw two brothers, Simon, called Peter and his brother Andrew. They were casting a net into the lake, for they were fishermen. 'Come, follow me' Jesus said, 'and I will make you fishers of men'. At once they left their nets and followed him.

"Going on from there, he saw two other brothers, James son of Zebedee and his brother, John. They were in a boat with their father, Zebedee, preparing their nets. Jesus called them and immediately they left the boat and their father and followed him."

"I'd like to make an observation here. Jesus, the Almighty son of the Most High God, the One that all things were made by, according to John 1:3, He could've done anything anyway he wanted by himself, But!!! He called men to follow him closely and to learn from Him. He desired to have leadership taught right, for the new church. Jesus was a radical! He went outside the four walls of the synagogue and preached. He even went to the quote unquote enemy. The Samaritans and a woman, at that! He preached, he taught, he prayed, he healed, he led, he loved all outside of the "box", per se.

Still, today we try to put God in a box. A building, or a box of rules. We wrap them up nicely like a Christmas present. Then we try to ask people to get in that little box and stay there. But, what about the multitudes who don't fit in the box? What about those that have piercings and tattoos, like so many have today? What about those who enjoy the bar scene?"

*Oh, good, Sheila and Joe may get something out of this tonight.*

"What about the ones who are wild at heart? The kind that everyone sees as plain and dependable, solid, and yet on the inside dream of the bar scene and wild nights or going to Vegas where what happens there stays there and no one will ever know? What about those people? Let's go back to that second verse and read it again. 'Come, follow me,' Jesus said, 'and I will make you fishers of men.'

"I will make you fishers of men. I am a fisherman. I love to go out on a hot summer day and relax on a boat, so if any of you wanted to know what he could do for his pastor…" everyone laughs with him. "Anyway, I put the bait on the hook first, and as any good fisherman can tell you, this is an important step. The type of bait depends on the type of fish, and without bait nothing will be caught.

"I like to dig through my lures and find just the right one. After putting bait on my hook I cast. I don't want to just drop the line in beside the boat. Now, sometimes that may be effective, however, the majority of the time, it is not. I want to cast my line out as far as I can." He demonstrates his technique as he talks and several of the men are nodding and a couple are casting with him.

"I draw the line in slowly and then recast, repeating this action till I catch something. A pro has highly sophisticated sonar and such to find exactly where the fish are and then he casts that direction, attempting to lure them with that perfect bait. Then once he's on the line Snap! I hook him, and reel him in, now that's the most exciting part, because then I can see what I've got!

"To me all fish are beautiful. I don't care what kind it is, just so long as I get one. Once I get pictures, I put it in a water bucket and keep it till I get back to shore when I make a buzz line to the fish market to let them have their way with it, magically transforming it into something my wife and I can enjoy for a fantastic dinner one night soon.

See, Sam over at the fish market I have been going to for years, doesn't mind the mess and smell of cleaning up the fish. He goes about his work quickly too. All I do is catch 'em and eat 'em. My beautiful wife, Trula, is a whiz at cooking and she can make a meal out of the scrawniest fish you've ever seen." Everyone looks over at her and laughs with her.

"My point, yes I do have one. Jesus told his new disciples to follow him and He would make them fishers of men. At that time those men would pull in nets full of fish and turn them into a local fish market where they would be sold.

"When Jesus said 'fishers of men,' He meant you'll be trained and skilled at how to find people who need to know God, then you'll draw them in and catch them, so to speak. He didn't say anything about cleaning them up or finding a particular home in which that fish would be dinner.

"Our call is the same today; we are called to find the people and lead them to Christ. To draw them in with our kindness, compassion, concern, friendliness, love, mercy, joy, strength, gentleness, the fruits of the Spirit. Then catch them with the simple gift of grace that God offers to every man, woman or child. He didn't call us to clean them up or even find a spot in the body for them. Why? Because that is God's job.

"God knows which fish need to be scaled and beheaded and which need to be left whole. He knows how to debone them as well. He knows which are best fried, broiled or grilled. He is The Master Fisherman. We simply catch them.

"We don't lead a friend from work, say, to the Lord then tell them the 'rules' of what they can or cannot do. We're not here to give them a list of rules to live by. God is plenty capable of cleaning anyone up. He sees the inside and knows where to start.

## Inside My Head

"If someone would have seen me before I got saved the job of cleaning me up would've been quite overwhelming. I was a mess. Not on the outside. No, on the outside I was a hard worker, with Straight A's in school. A few late night parties, but not often; a long-time girlfriend with whom I was careful not to have any unwanted babies. Everyone knew me as the good guy.

"But, inside I wanted to party like a rock star! I was very proud of what everyone else thought of me. I began thinking better of me than everyone else did. Once I went away to college I began to live the wild life I had only dreamed of. I had a string of girlfriends and I drank every day. I smoked a little weed on the weekends; I tried acid a couple of times as well. But, when I came home I was the good boy everyone thought I was. I lived a double life. Don't be deceived your 'insides' (all those thoughts and actions only done internally) will come out at some point.

"On my trip home after graduating from college my sister invited her high school friend to my party. I decided to show her who I really was; the 'fun' me, the party animal that I had let loose at school. We got wasted and then went to find a quiet place in the woods. I showed off the tree house I'd built when I was an Eagle Scout. We had a good time then I passed out. Apparently she got up at some point and decided to leave, but she was still so high she walked right off the edge of the tree house." Everyone gasps and some begin to cry.

"I woke up the next morning to my sister screaming and crying. She came looking for me and found her best friend lying at the foot of the tree with a broken neck.

"From there my 'insides' were torn out and laying out there for all the world to see. It was decided that her death was not my fault in a court, but I couldn't let go of the guilt. I began to, well I guess I continued to, drink. I was caught in a downward spiral of drinking, drugs and depression. I attempted suicide and was placed in the hospital for my own safety.

"A nurse at the hospital led me to Christ. She saw my filthy, self-loathing, unforgiving, heart and showed me kindness. I'd never understood that before. I believed everyone was nice to me because of whom they thought I was. But, she tended to me specially. She would come into my room in the morning and tell me about God. She'd explain that God had always loved me. The real me. She taught me that He had created me and written out each day of my life before I lived it. That He understands my frustrations and desires and dreams.

"She threw out the right bait and began to reel me in. I gave my life to Christ and have never looked back. It took a lot of cleaning me up. But, because I am so wild and boundless I would have jumped out of the boat if she would have given me a list of rules I had to follow. I began searching scripture and seeking God. He cleaned me up. He, and only He, knows the plans He has for each individual.

"As we go into our own worlds this fall and winter we need to look for people. We need to invite them to church or a Bible study. There are several small groups led by people in our own body. Invite them to dinner in your home, pray and let God give you the perfect 'bait' then cast it out and reel it in until your job is done. Then let God take over. You still are expected to help teach and direct but not to place them in a box.

"Let's pray. Oh, just a minute! I almost forgot a very important part of my story. The woman that led me to Christ through her gentle loving kindness was the mother of the girl that walked out of my tree house and into eternity."

Silence except for the sobs and sniffling.

"God, you are so beautiful. You are so creative, and artistic. How you could ever design so many billions of people and give each of us a uniqueness is beyond me; such a one-of-a-kind desire and ability for each of us. You not only form us in our mothers' wombs, but You also lay out a plan for our lives. You order our footsteps and draw us to You so that we find You when we are not even looking for You. You call us by name. You delight in us. Father, oh Father, as we go out this week, lead us to the cool, clear water of the fish you've intended for us to catch. Help us to pull in the fish for You and help us to refrain from every attempt to clean them up. Give us wisdom and patience and self-control.

"Folks, if there is anyone who has yet to pray and ask God to clean up their life come forward and let's pray together. God already know your heart. If there's anyone who looks good on the outside but is wild on the inside we can pray together as well."

*Sheila go, go Sheila, go up front. I have to peek. Oh, yay! Joe and Sheila are going up front. God, clean 'em up, change em.*

**Constance, what about you?**

*I'm not supposed to clean them, right?*

**Right, but what about you?**

*What do you mean, me?*

**What if you go up so I can clean you up?**

*Me?*

**Your wild side.**

*Yeah, well you can clean me up from here.*

**But then you're still holding onto your pride. You are in control. I can't clean you up till you let me.**

*Pride? Are you serious? I'm fat. I have thin fuzzy brown hair that I wear in a ponytail everyday at a job that I hate. I am alone with no potential of ever having anyone. Pride? How can You say that? I don't even like me. How can You say I am prideful?*

**You're too proud to be seen going up front for prayer. You're too proud to act like you need help. You're still trying to portray the 'good girl' image others have of you. But I know the real you.**

*Humph! I'm not that bad, God. You act like I'm Sheila.*

**Not a Sheila?**

*No*

**She has humbled herself and come before my throne. She is praying right now in front of a group of people that don't know her and a man she cares about a great deal. Sheila is covered by the blood of my Son. And I see her, who she really is, as in right standing with me, completely forgiven of whatever her past has been. Sheila is pure before me.**

*God? Are you serious? Look at that top. It's so low you see half of her chest. She parties at least two or three times a week. I can't even guess at how many men she's slept with. And...*

**Constance. I'm looking at Sheila right now and I see purity of heart. I see humility and honesty. You're right, you are no Sheila. And you're no Jesus.**

*What is that supposed to mean?*

**If you don't think you need to humble yourself then you must think you're as perfect as Jesus.**

*No. But I'm just human; I can't be like Jesus. He is perfect. And he is God.*

**Well, on earth he was fully man. He struggled with temptation and hunger and anger and hurt and frustration. He faced fear and pride and still did not sin. As a human he understood that he had to completely depend on Me for strength and hope. And He humbled Himself and was obedient, even unto death.**

*He struggled? Struggled? I thought he didn't struggle at all. He just said 'go away' and it did.*

**Well, Satan tempted Jesus. Tempted. When you don't eat for one day, or even one meal, you say 'I'm starving!' yet Jesus, all the way human, did not eat for 40 days. He came to save the world and Satan promised him power to rule the multitudes; to change history forever. He challenged Him to prove His word. He was a man after all, and how do most men react to a challenge. It would have taken just a step and He would have been proven right and in the same moment would've given in to the tempter and accuser. He spent those 40 days in prayer to prepare for the hardest moments spiritually as well as physically and emotionally. He remained sinless and obedient even as He was betrayed by a close friend, left 100 percent alone to face His torture and even I had to turn my face from Him at His death. Jesus knew the secret: I was, and always will be there for anyone to lean on. He never thought evil thoughts. He didn't waste His time on those wasted**

*moments. His heart and mind remained steadfast on His mission.*

*Well, I don't have all those things, but I do deal with eating.*

**Why?**

*I don't know?*

"Connie?"

"Hmm," opening my eyes for the first time since the call to prayer.

"Connie?" The whisper again but now I know it's to my left.

"Oh, sorry I was praying and I got lost a bit I guess. What's up?"

"Well, the preacher said we could go a couple of minutes ago so Joe and I are going to leave, but not without telling you first."

"Oh, Sheila, I'm so excited for the two of you. While I was praying I was praying for you and God said He sees you as pure of heart, humble, and in right standing with Him. You got saved! I'm so happy!" I can't believe how excited I really am. A week ago I barely knew her and didn't really want to sit with her at lunch, now she's next to me at church, all saved and everything. This really is exciting! I had always heard it was exciting to lead someone to God, but I don't guess I ever expected it to be.

Sheila's crying. *She must be happy.* I am compelled to hug her. "You're happy too, huh?"

"I can't believe what you just said."

"That you're happy or that I'm happy?" I'm so confused.

"How God said to you that He sees me with a pure heart and humble and in right standing before Him. You know me. I'm none of those things."

"You prayed, right?"

"Yeah." Her eyes search the floor.

"You asked forgiveness, right?"

"Yeah," she answers through tears.

"For everything?"

"Yeah, but..."

"Well, First John 1:9 says if we confess our sins He is faithful and just to forgive us our sins and cleanse us from all unrighteousness. All! All! Everything! You've been cleansed of all your past. He promises to never remember it again, to throw all your sins into the depths of the sea. I don't know how, but God says He'll never remember them again. That's what being saved means. Saved from living a life without God. Saved from going to Hell forever. Saved from living with regret."

Speechless, she hugs me. Tears wet my shoulder. Our friendship seems to be based on tears.

"I think I understand." She looks at me and Joe and again at me, "But I think it'll take time to really get it. How 'bout you Joe, how do you feel?"

"Like a weight has been lifted from my shoulders. I'm so happy." He's crying, and they hug.

*She's so lucky. She got Joe and they got saved together. I know it's awesome, but I don't think it's fair.*

"Hey, kids, I'm so glad you're all together."

"Chuck, are you ready to go?" Sheila asks as she turns.

"Yes, Mom, Patty is over there by the door." He says pointing to the furthest set of glass doors.

"O.K., Connie, we'll go. Thank you for all you've done. I'll see you at work tomorrow, O.K.?" She smiles and waves.

"Yep, see ya then. Joe, I'll see you too."

He waves and they all walk out together.

"Mom," Jade began as we got into the van. "Patty didn't act like she liked being here."

"Why do you say that?"

"She just kept checking her phone for the time, and texting. She never smiled or talked to anyone. I tried to stay close to her but she just kinda moved off by herself."

"Well, Honey there are some people that don't want to be in church."

"Yeah, I guess." She doesn't understand that concept, she has always loved church. She puts her ear buds in and turns on her music for the ride home.

# CHAPTER TEN

'Another day anther dollar', I wonder where that got started. Oh, my gosh, these wrinkles are worse every day. A wrinkled up cow, no wonder I am still alone. Who'd want something that looks this? Man, life sucks. I used to think I'd fit into a six again but over the last year or so I have had reality slap me in the face. I never thought I'd wear clothes with two digits. I remember... "Jade, Honey, get up."

"Mom, I don't feel good."

"What's wrong?"

"My head hurts and I feel like I need to puke. I feel terrible."

"You don't have a fever." I kiss her forehead like my mother always did. "But if you feel that bad go back to bed. I'll be right back." *Hmm, she's never sick. Maybe I should stay home with her. Bonnie doesn't need sick kids and I would love to have a day off.*

After calling in and talking to the machine I give Jade medicine and lay back down. *I will miss out on Kevin today, if there is ever a good reason to get up in the morning it would be to see him.*

*Pancakes would be a treat, with extra butter and syrup, mmm. I'll surprise Porter. I bet the first person to come up with the idea of 'just add water' was a super hero. I wish I had some blueberries. I miss the days of buying fresh fruit and eating it before it went bad. If it's not canned it's not here.*

"Porter, time to get up. I made pancakes for us with extra butter and syrup. How's that sound?" *At least he and I share a love for food. I could sell any food out there. I'm a regular commercial. Until the people see what that food has made me look like. You know it's so stupid to sell food and be skinny. Well, not really, it seems like you could actually eat and be skinny. It's all lies but we buy into the idea and then buy the food. I, for example, would look like I had eaten everyone's pancakes for the past year.*

"Pancakes?" I hear him rustling the sheets. *That's the fastest he's gotten up in ages. I knew pancakes would be a good idea.*

After checking on Jade I meet Porter in the kitchen. *It's so nice to wear comfy clothes and chat with my son before taking him to school. This must be what it would be like to be a stay at home mom. Although in this outfit, all big and baggy, I look bigger and baggier; and I thought I looked bad for work. It's no wonder I haven't gone out on a date in over ten years. What a slob. Ponytail, yeah I'll do something else with it later. A hot shower and a clean house, hmm it could turn out to be a great day after all.*

I lean over to kiss Porter goodbye as he gets out of the van and he leans over to offer his cheek. "Bye, Mom." He ambles off to the doors with a couple of other boys.

*It's been such a long time since I've had a day off. What do I really want to do? Well… I'll get home and get a shower first thing. Wish Kevin were with me today, we'd get a shower together. We'd need one since I'd have to have him first thing every morning. Oh, my gosh! Those arms! He has the strongest arms. I love to get close to him so I can breathe in deep the scent of a man. It's not even cologne, just man. I wish he could come to work with no shirt. I could watch every muscle in his upper body work. Even in t-shirts in the summer his arms turn me on quickly. So big it looks like the seams are gonna rip while he works.*

*Just thinkin' about his arms, Oh, my gosh! When he's pullin' on some part tryin' to get it to move… sweaty, and all I* can think about is touching that massive sweaty chest. Our bodies sliding together, those strong hands touching me, I could go on and on, whew! Don't guess I'll ever get enough of thinking about him. Although, I'd rather take action, actions do speak louder than words. Slow steady rhythmic actions, repeated over and over for days. We would stop to shower together and feed each other so that we have enough energy to keep up the passion that doesn't want to stop. Sleep would be brief and filled with dreams of us together.

I wouldn't mind just laying in his arms listening to his heart beat and resting my hand on his chest feeling it rise and fall with each breath; that would relax every part of me. I know he could take care of everything. I'd never have to worry about anything. He can fix anything…including me.

After checking on Jade, I'll get started on the house. Poor baby, I hate to see her sick. She was sick so much when she was little. It seemed like one thing after another with her. We were at the doctor so often I felt like the nurses were my best friends. I remember one time when we hadn't been in for a couple of months and that one nurse, hmm, what was her name? Sandy? Sherrie? Sheila? Sarah? Sonny? I know it started with an S… Selah, yeah Selah. I remember now it was a biblical name. Selah, yeah, anyways, she called to make sure we hadn't moved or something. We laughed. All of those nurses were so nice. I wonder how they're doing. I cried when Dr. Phillips retired. He'd been my doctor since I was born. It's so hard to get to know and trust a new doctor.

Jade got better shortly after his retirement and Porter has always been strong and healthy like his father. He is amazing and so adorable and smart. I can hardly believe he is so interested in sports since I am the one raising him and since he's so chunky. Maybe someday some fat desperate, lonely, aging woman will be fantasizing about their rendezvous. I shake my head as I finish pulling out the cleaning supplies. "What first? Laundry," I decide. "That can be going while I do other things. I can start in the basement and work my way up finishing at the upstairs bathroom. Then I could get a shower and do my hair and look as nice as a cow can look. I don't know why I really try; it's so rare that I even attempt to look nice it's such a waste of time."

"What's for supper? Hot dogs, hamburger, three pork chops, cubed ham left over from something, bologna... well, let's see, if I have cheese, we could have mac-n-cheese with any of those. Or, I could bake it with the ham in it like Mom used to make. Or, scalloped potatoes! Oh, it has been so long since I had scalloped potatoes. That sounds really good. Even fried potatoes and hamburgers or meat loaf and homemade mashed potatoes sound good. I used to love to cook. I wish I had more time, I love food! Which, of course, is why I look like this," I pinch my side and roll my eyes.

"Yes, cheese, well Velveeta, that's not great for baked mac-n-cheese but I could make creamy mac-n-cheese and pork chops. We haven't had pork chops in ages. O.K., these can thaw while I get my list done." I turn to see Jade in her pink fluffy slippers and pajamas; she's so pale.

"You're so funny, Mom." She says quietly with a smile.

"Why?"

"Well, you talk to yourself all the time; you even ask and answer your own questions."

"Oh, yeah, well at least I know I'll listen." I say with a smile. "How are you feeling?" I walk over and instinctively kiss her forehead again.

"Not great, but I am thirsty."

## Inside My Head

"What would you like? You don't have a fever so you can have pretty much anything."

"Do we have ginger ale?"

"Yes, I got some this morning when I dropped off Porter." I explain as I pour half a glass and hand it to her. "Look, I'm a the-glass-is-half-full kinda girl." I smile and she reaches for it as she snuggles into the corner of the old brown couch. She looks up miserably and manages a smile as she suggests TV

"Sure, I have no idea what's on but we can check." I pick up the remote and begin the surf from the other end of the couch. "Lifetime, there's always something mushy on there, what do ya think?" I glance over to find she's almost asleep with the glass tilting toward the couch, ginger ale nearly to the rim. I rush over startling Jade and causing the drink to complete its mission.

"Oh, I'm sorry, Mom." Jade gets up slower than I would have with cold liquid approaching my leg.

"It's O.K., I needed to clean in here anyway. Are you all wet?"

"Some," She says, wiping at her thigh and heading back toward the stairs. "I think I'll just go back to bed."

"Think you need some medicine? Are you in any pain?" I call out as I return from putting the glass in the sink.

I begin dabbing the brown and blue plaid couch with a hand towel and spot remover. I just had to have this couch for my first place, since it was used and I could afford it. I showed off my garage sale find to everyone with pride. The stains from years of kids and animals will never come out, but each time, I attempt to remove them. I smile as I remember the decision to get rid of it after years of use and how the kids cried. "It's our couch! What if we get sick? We'll have nowhere to lay. It's perfect!" I couldn't bear to put it out for the garbage men.

Jade had already fallen asleep. *I hate to see her sick. God, please help her. I wonder if Jesus ever got sick. Since He was fully human it seems like He would've. But He was fully God and healed everyone of every disease. So hmm, that's a good question. I'll go ahead and get my bed changed and do some laundry.*

*These sheets should need changing every other day. Someone should be sharing them with me. Now I just change places on the bed and change sheets once a month. 'Sleepin' single in a double bed thinkin' of all the things I wish I'd said,' I can find a song for just about everything. Yeah that would be bad but for heaven's sake this is a king size bed meant for a king size man. The two of us could be all over it in a night, not a month. I had such big dreams when I bought this house; A master bath to replace the walk-in closet now used for storage of all my too small clothes, a collection which is getting bigger all the time. After forty you just gain weight every year for the heck of it, and I started that early. I'm going to be a blimp by the time I reach fifty. God, how is that a part of your plan? Men age gracefully and only look at thin young girls and no one wants fat old women like me. I'd have to find a sixty year old just to have someone old enough to think I'm the younger model. How sick is that? But at least I'd have someone.*

*Vacuuming and dusting and dishes and... laundry to the basement first, I'm hungry must be lunch time at work. O.K., a sandwich and then laundry. Well, maybe I can start the washer first.* Shoot! No laundry detergent. I forgot. Softener sheets, 1, 2, 3 yep need those too. I'll make a list. I can make my sandwich and then eat and make the list. Bologna and cheese with mustard and catsup in front of the TV Wow that will be so relaxing. Wonder what's on in the middle of the day?

........

*That was such a good movie, I wish life were more like a movie then I'd have a chance at something wonderful. Of course that would mean that I was thin and young forever since there is no such thing as a fat girl in the movies that ever wins the heart of the man. Plus, all the women look as if they've never had to work for anything. Even if they work in the movie they look like they don't. No exhaustion, no bags under their eyes, makeup perfect, even first thing in the morning; always skinny, never on the rag, no reality at all. I can expect to be alone forever at this size. I raise my arms and stare into the door mirror in the coat closet revealing my apple shape. Now back to work at... 1:00. Crap! I haven't accomplished anything. I'm so lazy! What a loser! Nothing! How stupid! I just sat around watching TV My list only has two things on it.*

*Porter will need to be picked up soon and the house looks the same. Will I ever do anything right? Probably not, I always make the wrong choices in every area, sitting, working, food, men everything. I would go to the store but I have to get Porter soon anyway. Well, I could get the dishes done. I wish I had help around here. He wouldn't have to be the ultimate man, just... a man. I need music so I don't focus on how alone I am. It's just not fair; I used to be the one everyone wanted. I would've never dreamed I'd be fat, tired, ugly, and alone.*

*I hate Porter for what he did. This really is his fault. All of it. If I hadn't gotten pregnant I wouldn't have married that loser! I wouldn't have gotten fat. I wouldn't have had to raise two kids alone so I wouldn't eat junk and work 40 to 50 hours a week and never work out. I wouldn't be so tired and ugly. I wouldn't have bags under my eyes and I wouldn't hate everything about my life. I could've found a real man, one that*

## Inside My Head

*would've taken care of me; one that would've really loved me and the kids; one that would've stayed. I hate him. I don't know how he got another wife or why she has stayed with him... or why he has stayed with her. Of course she stayed skinny. They have no children, they travel all over the world and I'm sure she looks great in a bikini. If I put a bikini on and went to a beach a news crew would be on the scene right away trying to find help to save the poor beached whale! Groups of people would be out there trying to shove me back in the water.*

*God! Why am I so fat and ugly? Why does life suck so much? Why am I alone? Why is he not alone? He has someone to sleep with every night and to travel with and clean up after him and I have no one. Why do my kids not have a father? What is wrong with me? Don't You care? Is this part of some sick plan of Yours? What good does it do me to be a Christian? I hate my life!*

My hands swing up and the glass on the counter shatters. "You O.K. Mom?" Jade asks from the doorway. I hadn't even noticed her there.

"Yes, Honey, but don't come in yet. I just knocked a glass off the counter. How are you feeling?" I ask with my back toward her reaching for the dollar store broom dustpan combo. "Well, I planned to sweep and mop anyway." I smile in her direction.

"I'm ok I guess but my tummy is still upset." She turns back toward the couch as I ask about the cure all, ginger ale and crackers. She sits on the dry end of the couch and I finish the clean-up and prepare her snack. *I can't ever get anything done.* I reach down and 'kiss' her forehead noting a temp of about 100. You feel a bit warm so let me get you some medicine. We sit in silence for a while and she eats crackers slowly, intermittently sipping on the ginger ale.

## Inside My Head

"How's work, Mom?"

"It's the same as always, I guess." I welcome the conversation.

"What about Mark?" She continues.

"What about him?"

"Well, are you guys talking? Are you going to go out again?"

"I guess he's a good catch, but I don't know. We haven't really talked much. I'm not sure if he's a Christian. And I'm not sure how I feel about being the Brady Bunch." The interaction is not exactly the direction I would have chosen but it's nice to talk to her.

"Well, he does seem to be nice but of course you would need to know if he's a Christian. Why haven't you asked?"

"I don't know." *What do I say, he's not Kevin? He doesn't turn me on? I want someone and I'm being picky. You've got to be kidding! What am I waiting for?*

"Well, is there someone else you like more?"

I swallow hard, "well… yes, but I don't know that much about him either. Just that he is gorgeous and strong and…" I breathe deep and open my eyes to her grin. I can't believe I just said those things to my daughter.

"A-n-n-d?" she extends that short word longer as she looks at me. She raises her eyebrows like I do and smiles again.

"And, I don't know if he'd ever consider going out with me. I don't know if he's single. I don't know anything."

"Find out." She says matter-of-factly.

"And how do you suppose I do that?"

"Ask around. Someone must know something. What's he look like?"

I close my eyes again and picture him. I can't help but smile as I begin. "He's got the most beautiful green eyes and hair almost all the way down his back that he wears in a ponytail. He's about six feet tall and his arms are huge and strong. He's not too skinny. He looks like he could win any fight. He just looks strong and still sweet in his face." I shake my head. "He's everything I could ever imagine wanting in a man. I imagine him being kind, thoughtful, generous, talkative and willing to share his day with me, willing to share his dreams with me. I could easily love him."

"Mom, you need to find out what he's like. Ask him out."

My eyes pop open at the same time as my jaw hit the floor. "What? I can't ask him out."

"And why not?" She, in her youthful beauty and innocence, can't begin to comprehend the magnitude of that idea.

*Me? My fat, ugly, tired, stupid self, ask out the man the gods created with excellence? Really? How absurd!*

"He's perfect." That should be enough of an explanation. Just one look at me and anyone would understand.

"Exactly why you should ask him out."

"Jade, it's different for you. You're young and beautiful. Except for Mark, I haven't dated in like 10 years or more. He's completely out of my league. I can't just go up to this Greek god and ask him to lower himself to a date with the likes of me."

"Oh my gosh! Mom! You've got to be kidding me!" She looks at me and realizes that I am most definitely not joking. "Mom, you are beautiful! You are smart and strong and kind and thoughtful. You'd do anything for anyone. What are you thinking? This man may be a real loser with good looks." She looks me square in my eyes and tries to make me contemplate the impossible. I can't help but stare and shake my head. She's unbelievable.

"Thanks, Sweetheart, I really appreciate your pep talk but I don't know. Maybe I will ask around at work. Jade, I have to go to the store before I pick up Porter. Is there anything you want while I'm out?"

"No thanks. I think I'm going back to bed, if that's O.K."

"Of course, Honey, sleep well. I'm going to straighten up a little more before leaving. I'll check in on you before I go." I give a quick kiss on her forehead as she passes. "You feel a bit cooler anyway."

"Thanks Mom. I love you and I meant every word. You aren't getting off that easy. We will return to this conversation at a later time."

"Thanks, I love you too." She heads off to bed and I take her snack to the kitchen and eat a few crackers while I clean up a bit more before heading to the store.

………

# Inside My Head

*She's so sick. I can hardly believe how much she's been sleeping. I want some more ginger ale. While I'm here, I'll get some tissues and soup. That might be good for her for dinner; chicken noodle and tomato so she has a choice. I've got plenty of crackers. O.K., we need bread and something else... hmm... can't think. What else did we need? I know there was something else. Cheese slices would be a good idea since I ate the last one for lunch. Hmm, mustard, mayo, meat veggies, fruit? We could use some apples and they're on sale. Bananas would be nice. BRAT bananas, rice, apples, and toast; I think that is for anytime you're sick. O.K. let's see... I can't think. What else was there? Oh, my gosh! Who is it that smells so good? Someone has some amazing cologne on.* My eyes dart around trying to distinguish the man and his scent. *I bet Kevin smells like that when he's not at work.* I give up and check out and drive on toward Porter's school.

*I didn't get half of the things on my list done. I certainly didn't get a shower, let alone do my hair and make-up. I can be so lazy. I don't really guess it makes much of a difference. I'm still the same plain, lazy so-and-so. I even went through my "to smalls" today in hopes to kick myself into the diet mode again. I do want to lose weight but it's so pointless. I'd just fail again. I can never stick with any diet for long enough to see a difference. I guess I really just don't want it bad enough. I need to lose a little anyway so that I don't have to keep switching between 3 pair of work pants. I only wear sweats at home now since I can't fit into anything else. I don't know why I do this to myself. I'll probably never be skinny again.*

*I have 10's, 12's, 14's and 16's and my 18's are getting tight. I gave up my dream of being skinny and got rid of my 6's and 8's last year and I still can't give up the dream of wearing a 10 again someday. How stupid! I really do know better. I am such a failure when it comes to my weight. The only thing I lose is my grip on reality. I go into every diet with the hope of losing enough weight within a month to fit the next size down or better and walk away defeated.*

## Inside My Head

*I found that one dress that I wore on my last real date... yeah, like I could ever wear that again; and I'm not exactly sure why I'd want to. I came home the next day not able to remember who I'd been with, only that I woke up next to that horrible, ugly thug. I can't begin to imagine what ever convinced me to go home with him. He had to have put something in my drink. I had never and have never since been that wasted. I always knew when to stop. Even Kate told me by the time she came off the dance floor, we were gone. I never understood that. Then he tried calling the next day and accusing me of stealing something. What was that?* I shake my head outwardly showing anyone watching that I'm conversing with myself. *People must think I'm nuts. And I guess I am. What was that? A vase or a statue or something, and how did he get my number? He harassed me for weeks. I had to call the phone company and change my number and everything. Oh, that was such a nightmare. No wonder I didn't date for a while. Well, ever. I went to church with Kendra and got saved and found out I wasn't allowed to date anyone who wasn't a Christian.*

*Then there wasn't anyone interesting and now there's no one interested in me. It's awful.*

"Hi Porter, how was your day?" I look at him with hopes of a better response than usual.

"Great!" He smiles and continues to my surprise. "I heard that some girl likes me but no one will tell me who. But, they said she might ask me out." He is nothing but smile.

"Who wouldn't want to ask you out? You're adorable. So, who told you?"

"Jessica. But she won't tell me who it is. She just wanted to know if its O.K. for someone to ask me out."

"And what did you say?"

"I said 'yeah', kinda like that." He shrugged like it is no big deal. "Kinda like, 'whatever'. But, I was so excited! I almost said 'way cool' but I don't want it to seem like I'm too desperate. Ya' know?" His smile just got bigger and bigger.

"Playin' it cool, huh?" I smiled back at my little 'Joe Cool', already playing the games of dating. "Just a reminder that she's someone's little girl and you need to be a gentleman."

"Mo-o-o-m," he sighed, "I know." And he smiled again. "What if she tries to kiss me? Is it alright then?" He looked at me with his father's grin and for a moment I only saw his father. I wanted to cry at the realization that I had kissed first. Maybe this was all my fault. I simply ruffled his hair and smiled remorsefully.

*How could I have resisted? He was funny and popular. His eyes were soft and green and sweet. How could he resist me? I certainly knew what I was doing. Tommy had taught me well. What I didn't learn from him I learned from one of the many that came after him. Porter was just one more trophy for my 'shelf'. I should've known he'd leave like everyone else. Maybe I did. Maybe I missed a couple of pills on purpose. Maybe I didn't want to be alone again. Maybe somewhere deep inside I thought a baby would keep him. Wow! Where did that come from?*

"Mom?" Porter was looking at me and again I saw his father. I knew right away why I had wanted him to stay.

"Yes, Honey?" *He definitely has his father's eyes.*

"What do you do on a date? I don't know where to go or what to do or what to talk about. What if it's a girl I don't really like? Should I still go out with her so that I don't hurt her feelings? I don't know anything. I'm so nervous. I am 13 and I should know something, but I don't. Do you think I'm a nerd?"

"No," I say as tenderly as I can and shake my head as I see into his heart for the first time. "Honey, you shouldn't necessarily know any of that. It isn't a must to go out with a girl you don't like but it would be nice, and I can't imagine you as anything but nice. Every date is different. If she asks you out, she will probably want to plan it. It could be a movie, dinner, skating, a picnic and a walk, rock climbing, cave exploring, the art museum, the zoo or a play…virtually anything. It would be wise to suggest a group date or at least another couple to go with you so that if either of you feel uncomfortable there are others to talk to. Also it takes the pressure off. Neither of you have to feel like you're supposed to kiss, or do or say anything in particular; just enjoy the time together." His eyebrows rise like he's absorbing it all.

Silence.

"How's Jade?"

"She'll be O.K. but she's still not feeling very good. We're going to have pork chops and mac-n-cheese for dinner but she's having soup."

"Yay! Pork chops; we haven't had that in a long time. Cool. Creamy mac-n-cheese or boxed?"

"Creamy."

"Cool, Mom, thanks. I'm so glad I can talk to you. All the other guys say their parents are stupid and they don't like 'em much, but you're cool."

"Thanks, Porter. I'm proud of you, too." We work together to get groceries in the house. "Shoot!" I shout as I walk in and see the basket in front of the basement door. "I forgot the detergent and fabric softener and that is why I originally went to the store." Sigh. "Porter, will you please put away the fridge foods and take Duke for a walk? I'll check on Jade and go back to the store, I guess." I walk away without waiting for a response.

"I got a' lotta homework, Mom," he whines.

"Thanks", I call down. Jade is still sleeping so I adjust her pillow and cover her shoulder before turning to leave.

"Mom," she whispers.

"Yes, Honey?"

"I feel terrible." I scarcely hear her weak voice.

"Like throw-up sick?"

"I don't know". She's so pale. I kiss her forehead and she is burning up. "I'll get a bucket just in case." I rush off to the bathroom grabbing the cleaning bucket and tossing everything under the sink. "Here, Honey."

"Mom, will you pray for me?"

"Of course, Honey, I've been praying all afternoon." *I can't believe I didn't think of that.* "God, when You sent Your Son He took 39 stripes on His back before His death so that all of our illnesses would be healed. You said that by His stripes we were healed, past tense. Jesus said in His final words, it is finished. It's a done deal. Jade needs a healing and we are asking for You to do just that. Heal her, Lord, please. I ask You to reach down and make her well. Thank You, Amen." *I know that never works for me, but she is amazing and loves You, God. And You healed Chuck and he isn't even nice. So please do something for her. Please just listen, for her sake, this once.*

## Inside My Head

*I always listen.*

"Jade, I'm going back to the store to get detergent and softener and I'll be right back, O.K.? Porter will be here if you need anything."

"O.K."

"You rest till I get back. Do you want anything before I go? Or from the store?"

"Hm-mm. Thanks," she whispers.

"I'll be right back I promise." *She's already asleep.*

Back in the kitchen I realize Porter must be out with Duke. *Should I leave her alone? Oh, it'll be O.K., he'll be right back in and I wanna hurry.*

..........

*Start laundry, then dinner; check on Jade, then clean kitchen while I cook.*

"Mom, how long before dinner?" Porter looks up from his homework. *I swear that boy is always hungry.*

"About 45 min or so, you want a snack?"

"Like what?"

"How about a couple of cookies?" I say waving the package enticingly.

"O.K. I'm really hungry."

"I'll try to hurry with dinner. Let me throw in a load of laundry real quick." I hurry off to the basement. "How's Jade?" I yell up the stairs to silence. I wipe down the washer and dryer before heading back up the stairs.

## Inside My Head

Immediately I see Jade in the doorway on the floor with Porter hovering over her. "What happened?" I scream! She's so pale!" I brush the hair from her face and pick her up. "I'm going to take her to the hospital, get your homework and you can come along or call your Aunt Bonnie."

"No way! I'm going with you, she's my sister!" He demands as he gets everything shoved into his back pack. "Can I take a snack?"

"Of course, just hurry." He grabbed the entire package of cookies, some pop and locked the door behind us.

*God, I prayed and you did nothing. She's still sick. I may not be very good but Jade is great. Why? Every time someone in the Bible asked to be healed you healed them. Why do you never listen to me? Or at least answer me? What about when I prayed for Chuck? You listened then. What's wrong now? Heal her, Lord, please! I'm scared, what if she gets sicker? What if she dies? I couldn't take that, God. Please help her! Help us, God!*

# CHAPTER ELEVEN

"Sheila, I know it's two in the morning, and I'm sorry. We just got back from the H.R. and they said it was some form of virus and it should be gone in 24-72 hours...I guess she was dehydrated but I was scared." My eyes well up as I try to conceal my emotions. "I know, but she's never been this sick before and I don't know what I'd do if I lost her, or Porter for that matter. I knew you'd understand after that whole thing with Chuck. I mean, I know it's not the same but I mean, well, you know what I mean."

A smile brightens my face momentarily as she empathizes with me. *She really is a neat person. I'm so glad we're friends. I miss having a best friend. Since Kendra left I've just kinda lost touch with the idea of a best friend...or any real friend. Thank you, God.*

"Is Sheila at work already?" I turn to see Jade amble down the last couple of stairs.

"No, but I called her on the way to the hospital and thought I would update her before going to bed. I already called off work and plan to sleep in tomorrow. I called both schools too." I brush her hair off her face. "I was pretty worried about you, babe."

Jade sinks into that old worn out sofa like a luxurious feather bed. "I'm so glad you kept this couch, Mom. I love it. It fits just right, especially when you're sick. I can just sink all the way in." She closes her eyes and moans softly. I cover her with Grandma's afghan.

"Would you like some ginger ale or crackers or anything?"

"Not really."

"Well, you need extra liquids so how about a popsicle?" I tempt.

"O.K." she relents.

*I've already eaten enough for the both of us. I hate that I eat when I'm upset, but I guess that's who I am. Hmm, I'm also the one that eats when I'm sad, alone, scared, angry, happy or bored. Heck! I eat all the time. No wonder I'm alone. Who wants someone who can and will eat them under the table? Well, actually, I've found several in my time that love to be eaten under the table, but of course that's the old me. Well, not really, that was the young me, the old me isn't even given that opportunity.*

*I could have been the model for the Hungry-Hungry Hippo game. I could just lay on the edge of something with my mouth hanging open waiting for someone to throw food in and hope they make my huge mouth. I sure am looking like that humongous mammal. I sure wish I could lay around all day doing nothing. Might as well have a popsicle with Jade, one isn't going to make me any fatter. Mmm! Grape, my favorite.*

"Here, Honey, I picked a red one for you. Remember when you were little and you and Porter would fight over them?" She takes it slowly and promptly begins to coat her tongue with red.

"Yeah, we would do this and see who could get their tongue the reddest quickest." We sit in silence for several minutes attempting to be the one to have the most colorful mouth. "Look," she turns and sticks her tongue out revealing a tongue that matches the popsicle's bright hue. I stick my tongue out showing off the deep purple I had achieved and we laugh.

# Inside My Head

"I think I want to sleep right here," Jade decides after snuggling deep into the cushions and wrapping herself in the crocheted love of my family heritage. So I kiss her cheek and head off to bed.

.........

"She is doing very well," I reply to Sheila on the phone. "She has slept for the past three days waking only minutes at a time to have something to drink and go to the bathroom, but this last time, we watched an entire movie before she drifted back off.

"Sure, you're welcome over if you don't mind a mess. I have done very little but sit beside her and eat. The doctor said that she probably wouldn't be contagious after the fever was gone." I look around unable to believe I just agreed for someone to enter this disaster area I consider home. "O.K., I'll see you in a little while."

I start to frantically pick up the big stuff. *I bet her house is never this dirty.*

The knock came all too soon and I had not even thought about getting dressed. "Sheila, come on in. I am going to run upstairs and get dressed real quick. I did warn you about the mess, sorry."

As I descend from my quick change, I see Sheila cleaning the living room. "Oh, my gosh, you don't need to do that." I am so embarrassed.

"I know but, it's what I do when I'm bored or upset." Great! *She cleans and I eat. That's why everyone wants to be with her. She's a clean freak and doesn't eat. I eat and make a mess. I'm such a loser. I hate people like her. Oh, yeah, that's why I don't have friends. Pretty much everyone is better than me. I am fat and alone. No man and no friends. Who wants to be around someone who can't even get her own self together. I am so lame. She comes over and feels like she has to clean my house because I won't even do that. Man! She must think I'm so lazy. Yep, and my size plays into that whole scene. I wish I cleaned when I'm upset. I never have. I've always eaten. I used to be thin. I used to be her; well, not really. I used to eat all the time. I just didn't worry about gaining weight till after Porter left. I hate him. He sent me into such a steep downward spiral that I've never been able to come out of this nose dive.*

"Connie?" I suddenly hear her and it seems like it's not her first time saying my name.

"Yeah?" *Hopefully I wasn't talking out loud. I hate when I do that. No one needs to know I'm basically insane as well.* I try to sound casual as my entire life focuses on my inadequacies.

"Are you sure you're good? I called you several times. You're not getting sick, too, are you?"

*Yeah, I'm sick, but not like you're thinking.* "No, I'm fine. I'm just a little pre-occupied."

"What can I do to help?" I look at her curiously. *Why does she feel like she needs to help me?* "Did I say something that made it sound like I needed your help?"

"No, but I know you were there for me when Chuck was in the hospital. I just want to be able to do something for you. I am so glad we're friends. I am so thankful that God made us friends. He knows what He's doing, I guess. I'm still getting used to that whole idea. I look forward to hearing Maraschino's testimony Tuesday, don't you?" She, talks while she picks up papers and arranges them in a neat pile and runs a cloth underneath dusting my coffee table and end tables.

"Uh, yes, I do. I can't imagine having a life like hers. She is so beautiful and is married to a gorgeous man. She doesn't work and always has time to look nice. I just seem to crawl out of bed in time to get to work and then run kids everywhere, not taking time to ever look nice anymore." She looks surprised.

*Yeah, I know you always look good, too, and you have two kids. Seems like I'm the only woman in the world who can't do it all. Well, except for JoAnne who obviously doesn't take care of herself at all. So, I guess I am better than her anyways. She must wear like a 30 or something if they even make that size. I do get away with an 18 or so. Still...*

"Well, I don't know about any of the women at the prayer group but I love to hear people's stories. It kind of gives a glimpse of them, who they are and what they are like for real. It's just cool I think."

"Yeah, I agree. How was work yesterday?" *Of course she would see it that way. I hadn't even thought of it like that. I don't guess I really thought of it at all. Maybe talking about work is something so I won't look like an idiot.*

"Well, it was the same as every day. The same songs at the same time and the same people, Mark asked about you." I must have smiled and then looked disappointed. "Sorry, Kevin didn't make it over to our side of the plant. There were a lot of problems on the other side." I smiled and nodded but didn't respond. "I knew there was a reason to ask about the most boring place on the planet." She smiled and we worked together in the kitchen. *It is nice to have a friend again.*

As Jade wakes, we all settle into a chick-flick and some lunch.

## CHAPTER TWELVE

"Tonight Maraschino will be sharing her testimony after our study." *That shouldn't take more than five minutes. 'Look at me, I'm perfect, my husband is perfect, and my whole life is perfect'.* "While I studied for tonight I used a different version of the Bible. I used the Life Application Study Bible which has study notes. Before continuing with this amazing, impossible-to-live-up-to woman, I want to read this note I found in that Bible:

> 'Some people have the mistaken idea that the ideal woman in the Bible is retiring, servile, and entirely domestic. Not so! This woman is an excellent wife and mother. She is also a manufacturer, importer, manager, realtor, farmer, seamstress, upholsterer, and merchant. Her strength and dignity do not come from her amazing achievements, however. They are a result of her reverence for God. In our society where physical appearance counts for so much, it may surprise us to realize that her appearance is never mentioned. Her attractiveness comes entirely from her character.

> The woman described in this chapter has outstanding abilities. Her family's social position is high. In fact, she may not be one woman at all – she may be a composite portrait of ideal womanhood. Do not see her as a model to imitate in every detail; your days are not long enough to do everything she does! See her instead as an inspiration to be all you can be. We can't be just like her, but we can learn from her industry, integrity, and resourcefulness.'

"I read this so that we can rest in the knowledge that God does not expect each of us to become all of these things. This has always been an overwhelming thought for me. It's nearly enough to cause depression, seeing how far away from this 'ideal' woman I am, and how impossible it is to achieve.

"So with that in mind, I do want to continue, but kind of in a slightly different direction. I want to encourage each one here tonight to begin right away to determine our gifts and talents as well as our likes and dislikes. Not every woman can be a seamstress, or a realtor, or even an entrepreneur. Some women are happiest being an at-home-mom and home-schooling their children, while others long to choke their children to death instead of fighting them over homework." Everyone laughs.

## Inside My Head

"Many do great at bargain-shopping while others grow their family's dinner in a garden. So tonight I want to review then go over a few short verses; then take a quick test and finish with Maraschino's testimony, O.K.?"

O.K.'s and nods throughout the group let me know that at least they were listening. "We have several new ladies here tonight. I am so excited and apologetic for not having a larger place to meet. I will ask at the church if we can have a classroom made available to us next week. Now in verses 10-12 'A wife of noble character who can find? She is worth far more than rubies. Her husband has full confidence in her and lacks nothing of value. She brings him good and not evil or harm all the days of her life.'" I look around and see everyone's eyes on me.

"This started us off with the realization of just how valuable we are to our husbands. I explained that real rubies are extremely rare and very valuable. They are a part of the sapphire family and are typically very small. Either way, they can easily be more expensive than diamonds. Also these verses show that even as a young woman, we need to look ahead to the day we will marry and choose to do our future husband good by staying pure and lifting him up in prayer before we even know him. Sarah brought this to life with her testimony last week. She has stayed pure and is looking forward to God revealing her husband to her.

"The next verses begin to paint a picture of her willingness, and ability to take on all tasks necessary to support her husband and help provide for her entire household. Starting at verse 13, 'she selects wool and flax and works with eager hands. She is like the merchant ships bringing her food from afar. She gets up while it is still dark; she provides food for her family and portions for her servant girls.'

"These two verses show a wealthy woman who was a leader and a servant, like Jesus. She was a diligent, hard worker who provided only the best for her family. Her wealth did not cause her to become lazy or use excuses to refrain from developing her skills in every area of her life.

"Verse 16: 'She considers a field and buys it; out of her earnings, she plants a vineyard. 17: 'She sets about her work vigorously; Her arms are strong for her work. 18: 'She sees that her trading is profitable, and her lamp does not go out at night. 19: 'In her hand she holds the distaff and grasps the spindles with her fingers.' We will pause here for the night. Here, we understand that she is an intelligent entrepreneur and investor. She considers a field and buys it… this speaks of her ability to know the difference between a good field and a bad one. She would have to look at the soil, the layout of the land, and which types of plants would best grow there. Then she buys it… this doesn't indicate in any way that she needed anyone else's approval. Meaning, to me that as it says in verse 11, her husband completely trusts her; her ability, her intelligence, and wisdom in their finances. He trusts that she wouldn't waste their money. Also, others that she dealt with knew that she had full authority to purchase land. They didn't require a co-signer, so-to-speak. It doesn't say that anyone checked with her husband for credentials.

"Next, she planted the vineyard. More than likely, because of verse 15 stating that she had servant girls, she probably hired the planting to be done, but she must have overseen the work. Because verse 17 says she set about the work vigorously; and that her arms are strong, I believe she helped plant. She got in and got her hands dirty thus showing those that worked for her that she didn't look down on them just across at them. They were equal and yet she was superior; the ultimate servant/leader, symbolic of Jesus.

"I want to remind you here that in the New Testament Jesus said... wait, let me find it here and read it real quick." I speed through my Bible's concordance for the right verse. "Ok, here it is, Luke 22:26: 'But you are not to be like that. Instead, the greatest among you should be like the youngest, and **the one who rules like the one who serves.** Verse 27: 'for who is greater, the one who is at the table or the one who serves? But **I am among you as one who serves.**'

"So, like the Old Testament says of the ultimate woman, she prepared food for her servant girls. And she sets about her work vigorously and her arms are strong, meaning she works hard, she doesn't just order things to be done. Also, her lamp does not go out at night. She stays up late and gets up early; verse 15 says while it is still dark, to do her work.

"Her trading is profitable in verse 18, so she brings money into the house not just spends it. JoAnne told us she buys stock and trades on the stock market. She is like this ultimate woman. She also brings food home and prepares dinners from scratch for her family.

"So this is where we will stop for this evening. We will start at verse 19 next week. But I hope you have all been thinking about your best qualities and your talents and gifts. Anybody have questions?" I take a breather and look around.

"Do we have to tell everybody our answers?" Sarah asks sheepishly.

*As if we'd all want to know. Most of them will probably lie to make themselves look good anyway.*

"No, this is for your own understanding. In fact, I'll have you do this at home this week. And next week we will start with some if you would like to share or have questions. I pass out the tests that I had gotten from lifeway.com.

"Ok." Sarah replied quietly.

"Maraschino, would you like to start while I pass these out? Are there any more questions?" I look around but no one says anything. *Typical of women. Like they all think they're so smart they don't need help.* "Well, ok then. Maraschino, the floor is yours."

She takes a deep breath and begins with a strength in her voice I only dream about. She is confident and poised. "When I was very young, like three or four, I remember my dad explaining the "real" reason my name is Maraschino; he said 'I wanted the best cherry ever had so I created it myself.'" Everyone gasped, some covered their mouths and some shook their heads. "He said that over and over. I had no idea what he meant, but felt very proud that I was the best cherry out there. I'm not sure how old I was when the touching started. My guess has been about five. At that time, he'd show me porn magazines. I'd see these women with all their clothes off touching themselves and revealing every part of themselves and my dad would say to me, 'Let's see you do that, whatever that was at the time and he'd "help me". 'That's perfect.' He'd encourage and make me feel proud that I could do that." She takes another deep breath before continuing.

"Eventually, the touching and kissing progressed. He told me that that is what women did. He told me that mom did it, too. He told me that mom understood and even knew what we were doing and that it was ok with her. 'In fact,' he'd tell me, 'that's why mom goes away so much.' So I believed that mom's church meetings and Bible studies were her way of letting daddy and me spend those "special times" together.

"By the time I was eight, we were having sex on a regular basis. I didn't like it because of the pain, but eventually, it didn't hurt so bad and I accepted that it was normal. By the time I was ten, Dad and I would watch child porn together so that I could get new ideas from the other girls." Every woman in the room has a dropped jaw and a wet face. How could anyone do that to a child? And their own child at that? What kind of sick freak would even consider such acts? Hate developed inside me instantly, and I wanted to hurt her father. Not kill, just long periods of horrible torture.

"When I went to sixth grade, boys began to notice how I was filling out and I soaked it up. I was proud that I was the finest cherry available. Junior high and high school boys asked me out all the time. I had no idea that the other girls weren't doing the same things I was doing. I just thought I was better. I'd watched a lot of videos to learn the best ways to please men. I can't tell you how many boys I had sex with between the ages of 12 and 14 but I can say it was lots and ages ranged from 13 -25." Eyes are wider and wider; wider than I thought possible. Anger and disbelief embrace each of us as we sit in uneasy silence listening intently to the most horrifying story we've ever heard. And it's true!

"When I was 14, it all came to a head. One night I was at a party with the football team from my high school after an important win. We were all drinking. It was snowing and there was a couple inches on the ground already. Three of the boys decided they wanted "a cherry on top of their ice cream" and pulled me out into the snow where each of them raped me. I was scared and cold. I felt sick as I ran home crying. I just wanted to get a long hot shower and climb into a warm bed. It was the first time I had felt dirty for any sexual act. I didn't understand why they hurt me. I'd been with each of them before and no one had ever hurt me. When I got home, mom was out with some ladies for a meeting or something and there was my father. 'What's wrong with you?' I still hear his gruff voice clearly." She looked away with tears, shaking her head. "I told him all about the party and the three boys and all he had to say was 'hmm, that sounds good!' He warmed me up then took me outside in the snow and raped me. He repeated those actions several times until I wouldn't stop crying and begging him to stop. It was maybe two or three a.m. before I got my hot shower and warm bed. I woke up sick as a dog the next day and the next and the next and finally went to the doctor after nearly two weeks of flu like symptoms.

"My mother was horrified to find out I was pregnant, but even more outraged to learn that I had no idea who the father was. The next several months were spent in solitude for the most part. Dad wouldn't come near me in fear that I would tell my mom, but I took that to mean that he was mad at me and feared that he didn't love me anymore. Mom cried a lot and began to force me to go to church where people ignored me or gave me dirty looks and talked about me. She told all of the church ladies about the rape incident but nothing more.

"I made a list as best as I could recall of all the boys and men that I'd been with. This only disgusted my mother further. When she saw that my dad was at the top of the list, she was enraged at me and then at him. I explained that I was sorry if she was jealous but... and I went on to explain what we'd been doing for a year; the books, movies, everything. She broke down for the first time understanding my close relationship with my father as well as his urging for her to get involved more and more with the church.

"She took all the blame on herself for being gone so much and allowing him to do this to me. She made sure he went to jail, but to this day I really believe she wanted to kill him.

"The baby came; a beautiful baby girl. Immediately, testing was done in an attempt to find the father. The three football players first and then, just before involving half the school, some teachers and neighbors, my father was tested. His DNA was a match. I had my father's child. Neither mom nor I knew how to respond to that. I was 15 and the mother of a baby born out of incest. We both began counseling and a couple from my mom's church adopted the baby.

"For the first time in my life I was being told that what I had been doing was wrong. When people from the church heard about the baby being my own father's child, gossip flew. Mom couldn't walk in without every head turning and shaking. So we finally quit going.

"Mom fell into a deep depression and her counselor began to prescribe pills for the depression and insomnia. Nothing seemed to pull her out. She was fired from her job and she laid in her bed, sleep alluding her as her thoughts overwhelmed her. She'd cry and pray for hours at night when she didn't think I heard her. Guilt plagued her mind constantly.

"The couple that adopted my daughter couldn't take the gossip either and decided that they wanted better for her. 'It would be best for her future,' they explained 'not to have to know the whole story.' I agreed and cried because I hadn't considered never seeing her again. They moved to Oregon when she was almost a year old.

"I was doing much better and I'd met a nice guy who didn't judge me since he didn't know about my past. I was 16 and he was 24. He never even tried anything with me. He was a church-goer and didn't want trouble.

"One morning I left for school after peaking in to say goodbye to mom. She never woke up to say goodbye and I was so glad she was finally sleeping I just went on to school. When I returned home, I realized she had not gotten out of bed all day. I went in to wake her up only to find that she was dead. The coroner ruled it suicide. He said that she must've taken all her sleeping pills the night before. Her time of death had been set approximately 15 hours earlier. When I left for school, she had already been dead.

"I was scared and sad so I went to my boyfriend. I told him about my mom and broke down completely. I cried for days. Depression began to rule my every thought. So Jay asked me to marry him. He didn't want me to be in foster care. I lied about my age and we were married by the justice of the peace right away.

"Not more than three months after our wedding, someone decided that it would be important for Jay to know all about my past and why my mother would kill herself. After that he changed. He no longer treated me with respect, instead he saw me as a whore. His demeanor changed. He began emotionally abusing me to the point that I didn't know if I could go on. I tried suicide but failed and was put in the hospital. There I met a nurse. She was kind and gentle. She spoke with true concern, not in a fake condescending tone. She took time daily to explain what it meant to have faith in God's Son, Jesus.

"She told me that Jesus gave his life as the ultimate sacrifice so that my life didn't have to be sacrificed. She explained that everything I did that didn't meet God's standard of perfection was a reason for my death. That as I released all the confusion, anger, hate, hurt, fear and brokenness into His hands, He would forgive me and wipe out all I'd ever done. That was an internal spiritual cleansing that lasted forever. Once confessed, all my sin and shame would be cast away from me and forgotten by God forever.

"She was also the one who explained forgiveness to me. I thought if I forgave my father, it meant I okayed what he'd done. Like when I'd say I'm sorry for sneaking the cookie before dinner and mom would say, 'It's ok. Just don't do it again.'

"My father destroyed me. He took my innocence and my childhood. He created a sex toy for any and all to use and abuse. My body was never mine. I wanted him to pay forever. I asked God for forgiveness, but didn't want the same grace for my father so I held that hate tight.

"This incredible woman became like a mother to me. She took the time I needed to help me see that I was only hurting ME. By being the victim, I let him continue to victimize me. I lived in fear of him and his prison release. I even prayed for his death. Tawny was God's, and still is God's wisdom in human form. She gently talked with me for months until early morning hours about what forgiveness actually is. It is, in her words, releasing that person to God's vengeance instead of my own. He said in His Word that vengeance is His. I ultimately understood that my hate, fear, and focus on my dad bound me by unseen chains. I didn't sleep well, I ate very little; I couldn't even go to the bathroom. Every part of my life continued to be a victim to my past. Once I said 'God, I forgive him' things began to change. Still have not seen my father and may never see him here on earth but, I am no longer his victim, I am God's victor.

"Every day I know that whatever God deems reasonable will be done to him. He may die in his sin and be tortured forever in Hell, but I hope he finds forgiveness as I have. Either way, leaving it all up to God was the turning point in my life.

"I was about to turn 20 and I had never known love in my life. Don't get me wrong, my mom loved me but she was busy with work and church things. She loved and trusted my father completely. She loved her church family and everyone turned on her. She was lost and it never got better for her. She loved only God at the end, because she hated herself and couldn't give love to anyone else anymore. She prayed constantly. My heart says that God just took His precious broken child home.

"As for me, I couldn't comprehend love; not giving it and especially not accepting it. That beautiful woman came to my room daily, willing to talk to me about the reason for her joy and her peace. She led me in a prayer that gave my life to Christ but I still had no concept of what it meant to be a Christian. I'd seen so much hurt from "Christians" toward my mother. It was unimaginable how another human being could love me. I went from church to church. I'd visit each for maybe a month and if I didn't feel joy or peace, I'd move along. I visited about 18 churches before finding this one.

"The very first day I was welcomed by two women, Constance and Fancy. They are why I stayed. The two of you are the first women to ever, ever treat me with respect at all."

I had contained myself until now, but I can't anymore. It's like a dam broke and the floods came. I am bawling. *No one can understand. No one must ever know. I'm so jealous of her; her beauty. How horrible I am! How did I reach her when I'm so wicked at heart? Me? I showed her respect? God, how? How can I be so wicked? How can You still love me? I'm so unworthy of her friendship. She truly knows You. She should be teaching this class. I can't. I can't do this, God! I'm wicked!*

Everyone is crying.

"Let's use this time," I begin through uncontrolled sobbing. "To repent and to praise." I gather my composure somewhat so I can lead, but Maraschino speaks again. She's solid and controlled. She's weeping but not becoming a blubbering idiot like me.

"Ladies, God has healed me of a great deal of past hurts and has to deal with me daily on today's hurts. My husband is still very cruel and hurtful to me with his words. It is only by God's unending grace that I can go on daily. The understanding of what forgiveness truly is and pursuing that, is what has changed me. I first had to ask God to forgive me and know beyond a shadow of a doubt that He did and does. Then I had to forgive many, many, many people; to remember not to condone their actions but truly let go of all my hurt and just throw it into God's lap and let Him take care of it. I had to let Him choose how to deal with them. I needed to understand that being the victim only held me in bondage. All those boys moved on. My father was living a life of imprisonment, but would someday be released. I couldn't continue being imprisoned by my own unforgiveness. I was released from my emotional imprisonment. I now live as a victor not a victim. I live only because Christ lives in me.

"Statistics are that 1 in 3 women have been abused sexually, physically, or emotionally in their lives. That number is astronomical! Have any of you been abused in some way by anyone?"

Hands go up all over the room. Everyone has their hand raised. Every woman here has been abused somehow. I am amazed at the enormity of the situation. Our group rate is higher than the national stats. Everyone looks at the hands raised. Is it shock? Relief? Sorrow? Guilt? I don't know the range of emotions everyone else feels but I think we're all the same. The reality that I'm not the only one with a dark past eases my mind and at the same time pulls me into despair at the magnitude of hurting women out there... in here. If this number is this high, what about the rest of our church? What about other churches? Is this why we don't get too close to others?

*Is this why, God?*

**Yes, Constance.**

"Ladies, I would be honored to lead us tonight in prayer." Maraschino offers calmly. Everyone else nods, unable to respond any better. "Oh, precious Heavenly Daddy, You see the open wounds on our souls tonight. You've been beside us during the darkest moments of our lives. Your Son took 39 stripes for our healing, for the seeping ulcers on our spirits. You alone are capable of healing those deep wounds, Daddy. You are the only one we can release our hurts to. You originally forgave us and want to teach us about the peace that comes from our forgiveness of others. I lift each of these, your beautiful daughters, to your throne tonight. I pray that You will heal their pasts and their hurts. Remove from them hurt, anger, sorrow, bitterness, unforgiveness, and guilt. The feelings of insignificance, the dirty feelings that have been heaped on us and that we have put upon ourselves. The shame. Those feelings like we need to hide our true selves. God, help each of us to understand that we can't hide who we are from You. That above all, You understand and love us. That You don't blame us and You're not angry. Give us instead a 'peace that passes all understanding and joy that is unspeakable and full of Your glory'. Teach us, Daddy to rest in You. Teach us how to love ourselves so that we can in turn love others the way that You do. God, teach us to not only forgive others releasing them into Your hands, but teach us to completely forgive ourselves. You, Daddy have hand-picked each of us to be the bride for Your only son. Thank you.

"Jesus, You are our betrothed. You know the depths of our wounds. You've seen all we've done and all that was done to us. You know our thoughts and how we continue to cut our souls deeper with our own words. But for the joy that was set before You on the day of Your death; You died rather than to have to spend eternity without any of us. For that we are overwhelmingly grateful. Help us, Jesus, to trust You and to accept Your love. Give us the ability to physically feel Your arms around us as the true lover of our souls.

"Holy Spirit, You are the great and mighty comforter. Jesus sent you here when He left the earth to comfort us and to guide us. I pray that You would teach us to rest in that comfort like crawling into a soft feather bed and sinking deep; able to sleep a sleep of security like children. Love on us, and help us to allow ourselves the luxury of the peace that You offer.

"Daddy, counsel each of us this week so that we can stop ripping open wounds You're trying to heal. We love you and are thankful for what You've done, what You're doing and what You will do in our lives. Heal us completely. I love You, Daddy, good night."

## Inside My Head

Silence. Eyes begin to open and look around. "Amen." I say to let everyone know she's done. The tears are mixed with smiles. Hugs are exchanged between everyone.

*I have to hug everyone and I have to talk to Maraschino.* "Maraschino, thank you." I shake my head and my mouth is open in awe at her beauty, now more abundant as I've just been given this rare opportunity; to look inside her soul. "Thank you." I say again. She smiles brilliantly. *A saint for sure. I hate myself for how cruel I've been.*

"Constance, thank you, for letting me speak; for loving on me; for being Christ to me." She'll never know how unbelievable those words are. *Me? Christ? I can't begin to think of how completely insane that is. Not me! I don't get it.* "I've wanted to thank you for so long, but I never knew how. Church seemed too open and big and impersonal, but you mean the world to me." I begin to cry again. *I'm such a phony! I'm jealous! I have never loved her, I wanted to replace her. I wanted her face, her body... her husband. Oh, God how? Why? Please, God strike me dead!*

"Maraschino, I am no good! I'm so wicked." I shake my head and lower my tear-filled eyes. "I've been jealous of you. I wanted to switch places with you. I thought you'd never last a day in my shoes. You're stunningly beautiful! You're perfect in every way. I can't compare to you. I'm horrible! I'm sorry!" The dam of tears is now released. Tears are gushing.

*Couldn't I have at least waited for everyone else to leave before confessing? Why did I have to confess everything? Why does everyone else have to know how wicked I am? I'm not worthy of being the leader of this group. I can't stop crying and Maraschino is hugging me! No! I don't deserve it! I wanted her husband. I said mean things about her body. Well, I thought them. Please don't hug on me. I'm wicked!!! NO! Everyone is hugging me! NO! I can't God! Please make them stop. I've been truly hateful to all of them deep inside my mind. They don't know. I'm a fake! I'm a hypocrite! I'm horrible! God please help me.*

**I am Constance, let me love on you.**

God, I can't, I can't. I'm horrible, You know this better than anyone. I'm not at all who they think I am.

**But, you are who I think you are. I know the depths of your soul, and I love you, Constance.**

God, (I close my eyes and shake my head, tears streaming down my face.) I don't deserve your love. I deserve your wrath. You should just kill me... now. You should torture me. I've even been angry with You, I don't tell You, but I am. I think about how You left me and how You weren't there in the beginning for me. I get so angry, God. Now You know. I'm pure evil. My mind is a cesspool of every wicked thing. I'd choose a man over You. God, I'm sorry! I'm sorry!

**Constance, I know... I've always known.**

I start crying again, loudly. Maraschino and Fancy tell the guests goodbye and then tend to me. The two beautiful gentle angels I've always hated. The two I can't begin to compare to; they stay and love me.

**I hear your heart cry out to me.** God speaks compassionately to my mind; my heart physically feels the pain I've tried to suppress, the pain I've felt and even caused myself for years. **Your wounds are deep and your heart far from me, but I know. I continue to love you and wait.**

*Wait for what?*

*For you to stop hurting yourself. You don't hate Maraschino, or Fancy, or Porter, or Tommy or even Me. You only hate you. You've piled on so much hate you can't dig out. Let me help you.*

"Constance," Maraschino's voice is soft and sweet. "I love you for your heart. You have a heart of gold. You were able to treat me so kind when others assumed I was street trash." I looked at her as if for the first time.

*I had never considered her street trash. How could anyone think that? Because she's beautiful?* My look reveals my confusion.

"See you heard all I said tonight and still don't see me as street trash."

"No." I sniff and barely mutter but I can't look at her. *She's everything I want to be.* I glance up and see her and Fancy smiling. I close my eyes. *How do I have any friends? I'm not worthy of their friendship or even their kindness. I'm a slug. Oh, God step on me! Pour salt on me not sugar!*

Fancy hands me a tissue so that I can wipe my eyes and nose.

"Maraschino, I..." *how do I continue?* I shake my head. "I have hated you! You are gorgeous! You are perfect! You are everything I only dream of being! I'm horrible. I'm sorry. I'm a fake. I have been so jealous I can't stand it." *I know that had to hurt but I can't let her believe in me. I have to see her face. I have to know.* I look up and she is smiling. My face hides nothing. Confusion overtakes it.

"Constance," she begins again in her soft loving voice, as she smoothes my hair. "Honey, I love you. You are a true friend. Your honesty is commendable, but you don't hate me, you hate you." My mouth drops and my eyes widen.

*Is she on a direct connection with you, God? Did I say that? No! That was definitely you, God, did you tell her that? What's going on? That's freaky. You just said that.*

"Sweetheart, God really wants to heal you. Did you pray with me earlier?"

"I tried, but I got sidetracked in my head. I began thinking about you thinking that I'm something that I most definitely am not. I suddenly realized what a hypocrite I am, and how cruel that is to others."

"See?"

My head tilts like a dog as I put thought into that. "No." *I can't begin to imagine how or what she means.*

"Even during the prayer you condemned yourself. Do you ever lift yourself up? Do you ever look in a mirror and see the beauty that God sees?"

"No." My voice rises only slightly above a whisper.

"You are beautiful." She smiles.

"I guess I don't see myself that way."

"Have you ever?"

I have to think for a moment before replying. "No, I guess not. It seems that everyone has always been prettier and sexier than me." I pause before clarifying. "Not that I didn't get dates in my youth, but I knew why guys asked me out and so that I got asked out again I always complied. I even got to the point of thinking that I was just better at it than other girls so I prided myself in that. But, I always knew I wasn't one of the pretty girls." The pain of actually saying that out loud was more than I thought and I broke again. "I always hated girls like you and Fancy. Like I'd have to compete with you and I knew deep inside that I couldn't." My sobs are so heavy I don't know how much more they actually heard but both of them are crying with me.

After a lengthy silence, Fancy broke the tension. "Constance, Honey, all I see is beauty; beauty deep inside ya. Bless yer heart. How 'bout I come over one o' these days an' putcha on some make-up and do up yer hair. Maybe then you'll see the woman I see."

"I don't really have any make-up any more. I just go to work and home and church, I gave up a long time ago I guess."

"Not a problem, Honey. I got all kindsa make-up an' every kinda curlin' arn ya can imagine. I jus' love makin' girls over. I jus' got a knack for it I guess." She smiles that simple beauty kind of smile, the kind I wish I had. This time I don't hate her for it.

"Wow!" I gulp back my emotions. "O.K." *Don't talk, you'll just cry again and I can't believe how much I've already done that!*

"O.K." She agrees with a grin and giggle. "Constance, let God jus' love on ya, Sugar. He adores you. He hand-picked ya ta be the bride o' His only Son. Yer heir to th' throne o' Heaven. You're extremely special to our Daddy." She looks me in the eye and smiles with so much eloquence.

*It's hard to believe just a little while ago I was thinking that she was stupid. Since Kendra moved to Oregon, I haven't* had any close friends. It's been so long and this is so cool. We give a group hug.

"Thank you both for staying and listening and for everything." Tears well up again. *Please just go before I start to cry again. My face is already red and puffy and embarrassing. I hate crying, especially in front of people.*

"Good night, Constance." They both call out as they leave the porch and wave.

*They called me Constance. Only you call me Constance, God. How cool! I like the name Constance so much more than Connie.*

**I do, too. Constant and Faithful.**

I continue to watch as they walk down the driveway to their cars. "I'll call in a couple o' days ta see when we can do that makeover." Fancy calls out and waves goodbye again.

"O.K., thanks again to both of you," I say as I close up for the night.

*Constant and Faithful, huh?* I have to smile.

**It suits you.**

*Thanks, God, I'm so glad You love me so much even though I don't deserve Your love.*

## CHAPTER THIRTEEN

*What kind of sick freak would do that, God? Treat his little girl like her dad treated her?*

**One filled with lust, Constance.**

*Yeah, well that's the type of person who should be hung by twine by his big toes and tortured mercilessly till he nears death then drop him on his head causing severe spinal pain for the rest of his life so that they could understand the emotional pain they've caused that will never leave. You must have really bad things waiting for him.*

**What about you?**

*What about me?*

**You lust constantly.**

*Yes, but I lust for men, not children.*

**Lust is lust, Constance.**

*Not really. Lust for children is wrong. Very wrong. I think it borders on unforgiveable.*

**Well, in my Word you'll find that it says the sexually immoral will go to Hell.**

*Yeah, but this is the worst kind.*

**No, it doesn't say that does it?**

*No, but I'm sure you wouldn't want anyone hurting a child. Oh, wait a minute; it does say something about that in the Bible. Something about punishing one who causes your child harm, right?*

*You're my child.*

That can't be what it meant.

*Why not?*

I'm not a child.

*So it's O.K. for you to lust?*

Well, I haven't had sex in about 10 years.

*So that makes it O.K.?*

This isn't supposed to be about me. It's supposed to be about people having sex with children.

*So would it have been better if he would have only kissed her and touched her?*

No! She was only a child!

*What about when she lusted for Jay and he lusted for her?*

What about it?

*She was 16 and he was 24, was that better?*

Not really, I guess. I mean she was still a minor. But they did love each other.

*Did he really love her or was he just lusting after her?*

I don't know.

*What is the cut-off age? Would it have been better for Jay to have been 17? Or for her to have been 18? Is the day of her birth plus 18 years a magic day when lusting and being lusted after becomes O.K.?*

*Whew! I don't know.*

**Lust is lust. Sexual immorality is the same whether it's adult/child girl/girl, boy/boy, human/animal, incest of any kind, even adultery, and fornication fall into the same category. It is all sexual immorality.**

*You're saying I am no different than Maraschino's dad?*

**I'm saying because of your sins, you both deserve Hell. And BOTH can accept my Son, and BOTH can come to Heaven. BOTH get my mercy, when you ask. My grace is sufficient for EACH of you. Constance, my Son did not have to be begged or even told to go to the cross. It was His joy and my pleasure. Look up Hebrews 12:2 and Isaiah 53:10 when you get home. You are His crown. Remember, you are His Bride. You were the joy I set before Him; you and all the others that I have given to Him. He prayed for you, remember?**

*Not really. Not sure exactly what you mean.*

**Look up John 17 also.**

Silence, (even in my thoughts) for what seemed to be an hour or so.

*God? I was His joy?* Even in my mind I can barely get the words out. *Me? I'm no good. I'm a sinful, lustful hypocrite. I'm mean to others and to me, in my head, of course. I'm nice on the outside; but inside, where nobody hears, I'm horrible. How can it be? Ooh! That song! Amazing love, I know it's true and it's my joy to honor You; with all I do let me honor You,* I sing. *I'm forgiven because You were forsaken. I'm accepted, You were condemned. I'm alive and well, Your Spirit is within me, because You died and rose again. Amazing love, how can it be that you my king should die for me? Amazing love, I know that it's true and it's my joy to honor You; in all I do let me honor You. The Newsboys sing that on the radio... I never got it this way before. I sing it at church but, wow! I never really got it.*

*God, I do want that. I'm sorry for all the bad thoughts, so sorry. I'm so bad. All the good on the outside is such a lie. I'm such a sinner. I'm rude and condemning. I'm hateful and hurtful, even to my friends. Only on the inside; but, God, that's so bad! Why do You even talk to me? I want to change but I don't know how. I'm so sorry.*

"Ron, I'm going to the bathroom if anyone needs to find me."

"Sure… you O.K.?"

"Yes," I say as I shake my head no. I can't hold back the tears anymore, so I hurry to the solitude of the bathroom. I can't imagine having to explain these tears.

*God, will you help me? What do I do? I don't want to be like this anymore, but I don't know how to change. I've always been this way.*

**Constance, my dear, nothing brings me greater pleasure than to hear 'I'm sorry and I want to change' from one of my children. I love you, my darling. Present your body as a living sacrifice, holy and acceptable to Me which is your reasonable service. And do not be conformed any longer to this world, but be transformed by the renewing of your mind, that you may prove what is My good pleasing and perfect will. (Romans 12:2) That's how you change. Focus your mind and your attention on me. Breathe me. Eat my Word which is the Bread of Life and drink from my well of living water. Let me be everything you need. Delight yourself in me and I will give you the desires of your heart. I will put them there and be sure that they line up with my will so that when they come to pass you will be pleased as well. (Psalm 37:4) I am able to do**

*exceedingly, abundantly above all that you could ever ask or even imagine. (Ephesians 3:20)*

My tears are uncontrollable. *I'm a mess. I don't know what to do. I can't go back to work like this and I can't stay off the line much longer. I can't stop. I haven't cried in years and now, all of a sudden, I can't hold it back. I'm sitting in a toilet stall crying. What in the world? Deep breath, Constance, get it together.*

Connie? Are you alright? Ron said you practically ran in here and you have tears in your eyes."

*Oh, Sheila, I wish you could understand, but then I'd have to explain how horrible my thoughts have been about you too. See, God, I don't have anyone I'm nice to.*

"Connie, what's wrong?"

*I can't believe she is so concerned. I don't deserve her friendship either. I can't stop crying. I can't answer. God help me.*

"Do you need to go home? I'll make an excuse for you."

"O.K." I barely get out. *I am jealous of you. It's not fair! I'm jealous of everyone. I'm mean to her too. Is there anyone I'm not mean to inside my head?...Kevin, I love him...well, at least I want him. I wish he were in here. I wish he would hold me and tell me everything is going to be alright. I wish he'd kiss away all my tears...* "Oh, my gosh!" I say out loud. *You were just telling me that I need to not lust and here I go again! Do I ever stop? I'm sick!*

"You go punch out and I'll get your things. I'll call tonight." I leave the stall and check the mirror to see my red swollen face. I'm so embarrassed. I look worse than usual and this is two days in a row. Man, I hate this! I'm so stupid! She gives me a hug like I'm her best friend.

"Thanks," I sniff.

"No problem. You'd do the same for me... In fact you have." She smiles and wipes my tears. "You gonna be O.K.?"

"Yeah." *I wish she wouldn't make me talk.* I walk to my van slowly. *I can't think. I can't think. I'll cry. I don't want to cry anymore. Radio! I'll listen to the radio.*

I was made to love and be loved by you. "I love this song. Mmm hmmm mmm hmmm. I wish I knew all the words. I look like the bobble head thingy on my dashboard. Toby Mac is great."

**I want you to meet Ron's wife.**

*Just a second God,* "Is this breakfast or lunch?" I question the faceless voice.

"Lunch," Comes the dull reply.

"Oh, good, I'll have a double cheeseburger, fries and large coke with no ice, please."

"Is that all?"

*Well, I really want a fillet mignon, baked potato, and a glass of wine with something chocolate for dessert but...* "Yes, thank you." I hand the heavy-set white woman with corn rolls the four dollars. *Wow, Honey that is not the look for you. She looks too young to be out of school. I wonder if she just looks young or is maybe a drop out. Maybe she got pregnant and now she has to support her baby any way she can. I wonder if the father stuck around or, like the typical man today, he left.*

## Inside My Head

*Oh, Constance! Get a grip. She could be fresh out of high school and working her way through college. You never know, she could be happily married and just wanted to make extra money. Whatever! It doesn't matter! After 5000 of these burgers they kind of loose their taste; same with fries. I gotta do something different. I'll never be thin again on this diet; the ever-popular fast-food-in-the-car-diet. I can never wonder where all my money goes. Four bucks here, thirteen there, It all adds up. Between me and the kids and the gas for the car I bet half my check is gone each week on junk. I just don't have time to cook anymore. Well, what would I cook anyway? I got time today. I'll go to the store before I go home.*

**I took care of you.**

*God?*

**Yes.**

*How did you take care for me?*

**I suggested to Ron to tell Sheila you needed to go home because you are having such a rough time right now.** My head tilts like Duke when I call him. If I had longer ears they'd flop over.

*You did that for me?*

**Yes.**

*Not that that's not great, but I could use the money.*

**Trust me.**

*I guess I have to. I mean… I don't know what I mean.*

**You don't even trust ME, do you?**

*Yes! Of course I do.*

## Inside My Head

***Constance, you forget I know your heart and your thoughts.***

Well, I want to, but trust doesn't come easy for me.

***Trust doesn't come at all for you.***

Well, I don't know about that, but it is hard.

*I'll fix lasagna and surprise the kids. I'll need everything. Oohh and special bread sticks. Oh, cool! I used to love to cook. What happened? Oh, yeah, life. I gotta make money and the kids have so much to do. Ground chuck for $1.99 a pound that's good. Let's see... It's been a long time. I guess two pounds will do. Oh, yeah, sausage mixed in makes such a difference. Chili sounds good too. I could go ahead and make a pot while I mix up the lasagna and that way we can have homemade meals for a few days. We need to have cornbread with the chili.*

*God, I'd love to not have to work. I could make dinner every night for my family, but of course I couldn't make the bills then.*

*If I were a rich man, na na na na na if I were a rich man... I don't know any more of the words, but that really says it all anyway. If I were a rich man... I should watch that movie again. I haven't watched that in years. Well, I haven't watched any movies in a long time. I used to do that every weekend with the kids. Maybe this weekend we'll rent a movie, there has to be something good out.*

*Forty-eight dollars and seventy-six cents, whew that was a lot more than I expected to spend. But we now have food at home and don't need to go out so often. Besides, we needed the toilet paper and dish detergent and dog food. Eggs sound good for breakfast. I'll put the groceries away and then start cooking. This'll be fun.*

## Inside My Head

*Constance?*

Yes, God?

*I brought you home so we could spend time together.*

Oh, what do you want me to do?

*Take a hot bath and look up those verses. You'll have plenty of time to cook.*

O.K., that sounds great anyway. A hot bath... I can stay in the water till it gets cold. Oh, (sigh) that does sound good.

*Then cook a fantastic dinner and rest all evening enjoying your children.*

Today is Wednesday, I've got church tonight.

*Don't go.*

Well, that was obviously me and not God. He'd never say that.

*Why not?*

Well, church... church is where I go and what I do since I am a Christian. What would it say to my kids if I didn't go?

*What does it say to them when you spend no time with them? What few minutes you do have, you're tired or rushed. How is that good? You love me and today you're learning what I want you to do by staying in my presence. Do my will. I have what's best for you and Jade and Porter in mind. And this is best.*

O.K. I can't believe it. Not go to church? Oh, this water does feel good, God. Good suggestion. I breathe deep and let the warmth envelop me.

## Inside My Head

*I alone can fill you the way you need to be filled. I alone can meet your deepest desires, I put them there. I alone can provide for you. Listen to me and your life will begin to change, my love.*

*O.K. Let's see what verses did you tell me to look up?*

*Hebrews 12:2*

*Right.* " Looking unto Jesus, the author and finisher of our faith, who for the joy that was set before Him endured the cross, despising the shame, and has sat down at the right hand of the throne of God."

*Isaiah 53:10*

"O.K...here it is...'Yet it pleased the Lord to bruise Him; He has put Him to grief. When you make His soul an offering for sin, He shall see His seed, He shall prolong His days, and pleasure of the Lord shall prosper in His hand.'"

*And John 17:20-26*

"O.K. 'I do not pray for these alone but also for those who will believe in Me through their word; that they all may be one, as You, Father, are in Me, and I in You; that they also may be one in Us, that the world may believe that You sent Me. And the glory which You gave Me I have given them, that they may be one just as We are one: I in them, and You in Me; that they may be made perfect in one, and that the world may know that You have sent Me, and have loved them as You have loved me.'

"'Father, I desire that they also whom You gave Me may be with Me where I am, that they may behold My glory which You have given Me; for You loved Me before the foundation of the world. O righteous Father! The world has not known You, but I have known You; and these have known that you sent Me. And I have declared to them Your name, and will declare it, that the love with which You loved Me may be in them, and I in them.'" (New King James Version used)

Wow, I thought that meant His disciples.

*You are one of those that I gave to Him. One that would not see with human eyes but with the eyes of faith. You are even more blessed. Look up Mark 3:33-35.*

"O.K." The pages flip quickly as I search for yet another verse to make sense of what He is trying to get inside me. "But He answered them saying, 'Who is My mother, or My brothers?' And He looked around in a circle at those who sat about Him and said 'Here are My mother and brothers! For whoever does the will of God is My brother and my sister and my mother.' Hmm..."

*Now Look up John 20:29*

"Let's see... 20...29, O.K. Jesus said to him, 'Thomas because you have seen Me, you have believed. Blessed are those who have not seen and yet have believed.'(New International Version used)\* I do remember reading that before. It just seems to have more meaning today. Thank you, God, It's so cool when You're showing me what to read and what it means and all. Church is nice but sometimes I don't get much out of it, You know?"

*Well, what if this Sunday you try something new?*

*Sure, God, what?*

*Try praying before you go. Pray over your mind, that it would stay clear and able to focus on the message. You will get more from it if you're not looking at every other woman there as your competition. You look at their clothes, their shoes, their hair, their makeup their hands, their weight. You look at every man wondering if he's "the one". I Am The One. You need to focus on Me. Treat Me as though I am your betrothed; your beloved. Remember the first week of Bible study?*

Yes.

*Jesus is your bridegroom; I hand-picked you to be His bride. The bride of My only Son. I didn't choose everyone. But, I chose you. Blessed is the one I have chosen, and cause to approach Me, that he will dwell in My courts, you will be satisfied with the goodness of My house, of My temple.*

I don't know how to treat You as anything more than who I pray to or read about. How can I teach this class? I should quit.

***No, you should learn. How would you treat Kevin, given the opportunity?***

God, You've got to be joking! I can see, smell, touch and even taste Kevin. And Oh, my gosh, would I like to do all those things to him. Problem is I wouldn't want to stop... ever.

***O.K., put Jesus there. Put Me there. Long to see Me, experience Me. Long to touch me. Find full delight in being near me.***

My forehead wrinkles and I'm looking older by the second. *God, seriously what is that supposed to mean? You're invisible – I can't smell, taste, touch or even see You.*

***Draw near to Me and I will draw near to you. Meditate on me—who I am, who you want me to be to you. Possess Me. Let Me possess you. You certainly can focus on being with Kevin and you've not even talked to him. I talk to you all the time.***

# Inside My Head

*Well, you do have a point there, God... O.K. Let me think.* I sink down until I'm almost completely submersed in the warmth of the water. *Hmm, God, You're strong... incredibly strong, intensely strong; and powerful. Wow, You are sooo powerful. You're power is sooo incredible! All You did was speak and the entire universe was created. You stopped the sun for hours and hours. Your power is beyond all imagination. Hmm...what a magnificent man, there is no one stronger or more powerful than you; a strong powerful man who can definitely take care of me.*

*You know me, God. You know all of me. You know everything about me. You hold me in the darkest hour. You touch me in ways no one else could ever do. Parts of me that no one else knows or ever will know. You're there. You know all my thoughts, all my parts. You're there in my bed at night. You walk with me into the factory every morning. You reach me when I'm unreachable. You touch my deepest, most sensitive places. You know how to touch me like no one does.*

*Ooh! God, this is not enough. If you were a man I'd have sex with you right now. Look at me, God, my breathing is ...Oh, my gosh! I want You. Your creativity...the beauty of flowers and trees and mountains and all of nature! And water, water...* I sink even further in and turn the hot water on with my toes. *Oceans,* (deep longing breaths) *the depth of the oceans; the powerful movement of the waves, and the beauty of the creatures there. You're creativity made it all so beautiful. Your powerful words spoke your thoughts into existence. God, I'm really turned on!* "This is insane! Oh, my gosh, I'm a freak!"

**That may not be exactly what I meant, but at the same time it is exactly what I meant. I long to be intimate with you, but the only intimacy you understand is sex. The intimacy we will have will satisfy even more so. I can satisfy your soul. Your deepest most intimate and sensitive parts, I'm there. I'll never leave. You can trust me fully. Don't let go because I won't. The longings you have**

*are actually more on a soul level than a flesh level. You've always used men to try to fill that longing you have for Me. I gave sex to you as a gift, but that isn't the ultimate gift and it doesn't actually take the place of the desire I gave you for love. It is merely a substitute for you. Intimacy is more than sex. Intimacy is deeper. It can satisfy all of you. Find Me. Focus on Me. You'll begin to understand as you grow with Me.*

*Does that mean I'll never have sex with a man again?*

*I won't answer that for now. But I will say with the intimacy we can share, all intimacy with another can be felt more powerfully. When you experience My love and you begin to love you, you'll be able to love on a whole new level. Therefore intimacy will be at a whole new level.*

*God, this is what I want. You do want me to be loved and love others or at least one other fully. You do understand! And You want that too! ...You do right? You want me to share this love with someone, not just You, Right?*

**Yes.** I can hear the smile come across His face. ***But it has to begin here with you and Me, for you to understand it fully.***

*Thank you, God. I'm starting to.*

***Now Constance, you need to start cooking so that you don't run late picking up the kids for your night together.***

"Mmm hmm hmm la la la ti da. I love you, God. Thank You, thank You, thank You." I hum and sing while I dry off. "What a feeling! Wow, it's so good. Good isn't good enough, It's awesome! It's stupendous! It's superwonderifical! Yeah, yeah, yeah." I laugh not for any reason, just because. *This feeling is beyond my explanation. I love it. I'ts almost like I did have sex. I mean, not exactly, but* kind of. I don't know this feeling. I don't get it but, I love it. I love You, God!

*Hmm mmm, la la la la, I love lasagna. The kids will be so surprised. This is going to be a beautiful night. I am so glad God's O.K. with me staying home with the kids tonight. I never expected that. Hmm, God, You're full of surprises, aren't you?*

**You have no idea. No eyes have seen, no ears have heard, no one has even imagined the things I have prepared for you, my child.**

It's like I can see my daddy smile at me. How cool. Hmm hmm hmm La, la la.

……..

God, the kids are asleep, the house is straight and dishes are done. I'm not as exhausted as usual. This has been a wonderful day. The lasagna was terrific, Jade and Porter were both surprised about not going to church, but all of us enjoyed spending the time together. We don't get to do that very often. Thank You for letting us do that.

**Constance, you have freedom in me. You are not required to go to church. I want families to celebrate their time together. Besides, you are my true temple, church, as you know it, is just a place where my body meets. If everyone comes only out of obligation no one benefits, least of all Me. Jesus said that the greatest commands are what?**

*Love the Lord your God with all your heart, mind, strength and soul, and love your neighbor as yourself.*

**Right! Notice it doesn't say work yourself into an early grave. It doesn't say go to church a certain number of times a week or read your Bible an hour a day. When you truly love Me with all your heart, soul, mind and strength**

*you will want to read My Word. You will long to be with Me at home, at work, at school, and at church, even when you're doing things like driving and exercising. You will enjoy taking the time to experience Me. Our intimacy will fulfill desires in you. Focusing on me won't be a chore. It won't even be something you have to think about. It will happen naturally.*

*When you understand My love for you and My desire and acceptance of who you are, you will be able to love yourself and then others. It all begins by loving Me fully. Sleep well, Constance. Rest in the knowledge that I love you.*

*Goodnight, God. I love You too.*

## CHAPTER FOURTEEN

I explained to Sheila the necessity of spending time with the kids, and learning to love God and myself more. It seemed adequate to satisfy her curiosity about my not attending church.

*After picking up the kids, Jade and I will make dinner together. Making that chili was a great idea. I'm already getting hungry. I still have salad stuff and it won't take much to make the corn bread.*

*This is so wonderful, God. I'm not stressed over what to have and we will be able to eat right away. I am so relaxed today and work has flown by. I didn't pay attention to music and the noise was pretty much in the background. I feel like I'm in love. I want to go home and read my Bible with Jade. She'll love that. What should I read?... Maybe Psalms or John. You know, I think Ruth would be fun, since it's a love story. Maybe I should wait till you tell me.*

Buzz, buzz, buzz

"Last break!" Ron says as he catches up to me. "I've been watching you today and you look so different somehow. It seems like a good thing. Yesterday you were so… well, you were having such a rough day and today…Hmph! It seems like you're a totally different person." He sits down across from me at the table and we both open our pop cans.

I smile as I begin the explanation he will understand. "I spent yesterday afternoon with God and yesterday evening with my kids. It was amazing." I take a long drink and look at him again. He's smiling back at me.

Mark joins us. "Hey you two," he starts, "everything O.K.?" He looks at me as he continues, "You missed Thursday and Friday last week and went home early yesterday. I was just, ya know, concerned." He nods. I looked at Ron and then Mark and smile.

"Mark, everything is wonderful." I pause for a long drink.

"Oh." He looks at Ron and back at me. "Oh… you two an item now?" He asks as he points at each of us and the smile leaves his face.

Ron laughs, "No, man, I'm married to an amazing and beautiful woman whom I love with all that is in me."

"Oh, sorry I…" his voice trails off and he shrugs as embarrassment covers his face. I smile.

"Mark, I spent Thursday and Friday with Jade because she was sick; in fact, I had taken her to the H.R. Thursday evening. We didn't even go to church on Sunday, but she's better now." *How do I explain spending time alone with God to him? I don't think he'll get it.*

"Oh, I'm glad she's better. So, yesterday?"

Buzz, buzz, buzz; *saved by the bell.*

"I had a rough morning and went home to spend time alone…" I look at him and continue, "with God." I look away.

"Oh, O.K., so all is well now then?"

"Yes, thanks." *He didn't seem too distracted by that, maybe he does get it. Hmm, interesting.*

I happen to notice Mark peeking around his machine to look at me periodically the rest of the day and I ignore it like I don't notice.

Buzz, buzz, buzz

"Hey, Connie!" Mark rushes through the crowd of workers leaving and coming in for the next shift.

"Yes." I barely look at him as I put on my gloves and hat.

"Maybe we could get some dinner tonight."

Now I look at him. *Could he be the one?* "Umm, well, I don't know, Uhh, I was just going to hang out with Jade and Porter." *Should I invite him? What if he's the one? Maybe God knows something I don't. Maybe the Brady bunch isn't so bad. They got along well on TV*

"Well, if you're busy it's O.K." His eyes search the floor.

"No, I mean I don't know. Maybe you could come over and have dinner with the kids and me."

"Oh, O.K., cool! What time and where?"

"Well, we will probably have dinner around six, so I guess sometime around then would be fine and my address is 711 Burkdale. Do you know how to get there?"

"I have a map! Boyscout, remember?" He smiles showing his teeth and his eyes light up.

"I do." I nod, "O.K. then, see you around six."

"What can I bring?" He stops at my van.

"How about a dessert? Would that be O.K.?"

## Inside My Head

"Sure. And what kind of meat are we having? Is wine O.K.?"

"Well, I don't really drink and we are just having chili, corn bread and salad." *That's not really all that impressive, that's for sure.*

"I love chili! No wine then. I'll just have to impress you with my dessert. See you after while." He smiles and waves as he continues on to his van. *He just might start to skip.*

*Well, God, he's not really what I wanted, but if he's the one then I guess that would be fine. At least I wouldn't be alone anymore.*

Jade and I work together to fix the best chili bar ever. We sing every song K-Love plays and by 5:45 our house looks like a restaurant. The 'bar' is set up with everything we could think of to top the chili all in their own little dishes and plates; silverware and napkins at the end. Placemats at the table with ice filled glasses and water and pop in the fridge getting cold. I run upstairs to change after finally looking at the clock and being pleasantly surprised that he was not there early.

Jade straightens up the living room a little and then answers the door. I check the mirror one last time wishing I were as impressive as the dinner. A nice sweater and tan cords, a classic, like me, my hair is down and I put a bit of makeup on before going downstairs. *Not too bad, I guess. There's only so much I can do with what I have. I look forward to that makeover. I hope she hasn't forgotten.* I fix a smile on my face and descend the stairs to see Mark waiting for me with a death-by-chocolate cake, sugar cookies, and pudding cups.

"Wow," *seriously? Do I look like I need that much dessert? Maybe he's just thinking that if dinner isn't very good he'll have plenty of dessert.* "So many choices." I nod and smile as I take the cake and lead him to the kitchen.

"Well, I don't really know yet what you like so I figured this way there would be something for every taste."

"Thank you, it all looks so good." *Smart idea.*

"Wow! Dinner looks terrific! I never realized chili could look so amazing!" He looks around wide-eyed and nodding. "Perfect tunes. Not as annoying as the ones at work. I mean soft and kinda peppy at the same time."

"Do you listen to K-Love too?"

"Nope, never heard of it, but it sounds nice."

We all enjoy the conversation and music as we eat. Porter joins us about half way in.

"Mom sings really good. Sometimes I pull out my keyboard and we play karaoke." Porter begins with no forewarning. "One of her favorites is La Bamba. She even dances while she sings sometimes." He smiles at me. *I just want to wring his neck.*

"Really?" Mark glances over at me then back to Porter. "How do we get her to perform for us?" he asks as though he is relishing the idea of me making a fool of myself.

"Oh, no you don't!" I protest, but Porter and Jade laugh and Porter rushes off to get his keyboard with La Bamba prerecorded on it. "I haven't done that in ages and I don't think I can remember the words anyway." *I hope this will allow for grace as I back out.*

## Inside My Head

"Mom, you were just singing it the other day." Jade adds her two cents teasingly. I glare at her and Mark witnesses the lack of intensity in the gaze and realizes that I am a pushover.

He smiles at Jade and then winks before turning to me. The three begin to clap and whistle as Porter plugs in the keyboard. Mark takes the initiative to be the announcer on the wooden spoon Jade had retrieved from the stovetop utensil holder. "Now performing for the first time in front of a live audience, Connie Stone and La Bamba!"

He said it with great enthusiasm. "O.K., you three! Remember this when I start and you realize what a mistake it was." Mark looks at me with a grin and states matter-of-factly that he has the entire evening set aside for us. I hope that doesn't mean what it sounds like. I haven't heard a come on like that in years and it takes me by surprise; so much so that the first of the song was nearly missed. Everyone claps and eagerly encourages me as I sing a very funny rendition. I couldn't think of some of the words, so I just filled in with whatever I could come up with at the moment. Every one of us laughed for a long time at the finish. I suggested that everyone take their turn. While the kids run off to get music to accompany them Mark leans in and whispers that the kids are gone for the weekend and he's free as late as I want. His grin is still across his face when Jade walks in.

The song I am going to sing has been my favorite since I was a little girl. She pops in a c.d. of Locomotion and begins to sing with the wooden spoon microphone and dance the same way we have always done, silly and in a single file parade of sorts so Porter falls in and Mark and I follow. *I only went out with him once and we haven't even talked on the phone. What makes him think he can stay the night? Does he really think that or is he just thinking that he can stay till like 11 or something? We are having a good time, and the kids are laughing more than they have in ages. I do wonder what it would be like to have sex with him now that I am beginning to understand intimacy a little better. But that is wrong. I don't even know if I like him that much. Plus I haven't been with anyone in so long...*

Porter sings and dances to some new song I've never heard and Mark sings an old Journey song. *He sounds pretty good. I can't get caught up in all of that. He is nice and all, but I need more time to make a better decision, and the kids are here and there is no way they are waking up and finding him here. This is crazy! It's our second date and we have never gone out alone. How stupid! I bet he didn't even mean it like that anyway. I always take things wrong. He probably doesn't think of me like that yet anyway, I'm just so desperate for someone to think of me like that, that I am taking things out of context. Connie you're so stupid it is unbelievable.*

"Dessert is the perfect end to a very fun evening." I start into the kitchen to begin opening all the desserts Mark brought, hoping that he would get the hint. Jade and I had already claimed the cake and Porter followed me in to see the choices. He and Mark decided on cookies, several cookies apiece.

"I have lots of homework." Jade says as she finishes her cake.

"Me too," Porter adds. "Maybe I can go to the E.R. this weekend and we can all stay home next week again." He states with a full mouth.

"Porter, that's awful! I don't want you sick and I can't miss any more work." I smile and muss his hair. It just lets me know how much this time together has meant to all of us.

"It's been so cool the last few days and I don't want Jade to be sick anymore so I can take a turn at it," he offers with a half-smile.

"I don't think so, Son, but I have also enjoyed our time together lately; I want to make it happen more often. We have the holidays coming up soon. We'll think of something special to do then, O.K.?"

"I hope so." He picks up his plate and cup and goes up to his room to get started on his homework.

Jade begins to clean up the kitchen before going upstairs but Mark stops her and smiles and with a wink tells her that he will take care of it for her. "You don't need to worry, and besides you don't want to be up too late with homework since you've been sick and all, you should probably still rest more," he added as he put the plates in the sink. Jade looks to me for approval and I nod so she thanks him and goes upstairs with her backpack and cup.

"What a nice night," I start without looking at Mark. I search for small dishes to put leftovers into. I feel Mark's gaze. It's a kind smile, but I still feel nervous. He combs his hair over with a side part reminding me of a little boy. I hadn't noticed that before, but then again it usually seems a bit disheveled. Mine is usually in a ponytail. *I guess he was trying to look nice. I don't know if he's the one but I do know I want Mr. Right and not just Mr. For Right Now.*

"Can I kiss you?" He leans in close and whispers. *I can't believe he actually asked that. Maybe he is a gentleman. Does he think he has to ask that but feels free to offer to stay the night. Oh, my gosh! What if I took that all wrong. I knew it! I'm so stupid! Who really wants me like that? No one! Oh, how embarrassing.* My eyes close at the thought of such a terrible misjudgment and he takes that as a yes. His lips are a delight to mine. After years of nothing this is a very welcome change. *Oh, my gosh! This feels so good.* His hand softly touches my neck as I feel his tongue softly on my lower lip. *As good as my imagination is it fails in how amazing it is to feel a man's lips touch mine again.* As my tongue meets his I taste the sweetness of the sugar cookies. *Oh, my gosh, this feels so good, I don't want it to stop. I feel like a kid again. Kid! What if the kids come down? What if we get caught? What if he stayed?*

I set the dish down and put my hand around his waist. My pinky slides along his belt line touching bare skin. He gently pulls me closer till our bodies are touching. I allow my hand to explore his lower back, feeling him tense up. His hand mimics mine and my body heats up. More than anything I want to go upstairs.

*It's like I'm a kid again. Tommy and I are hoping no one would catch us. We would make out till we couldn't take it anymore then we'd "go for a drive." I want that again. I want this. I really want this. I don't want to stop.*

**Do you really?**

*Oh, crap!*

**Is this really what you want?**

*Oh, yes.*

**Is he who you want?**

*At the moment? Yes!*

*His back is hairy like an animal. I wonder if he'd be like an animal in bed. Like a caveman. Strong and in control, powerful, all man. Yes, right now this is what I want. It's what I have wanted for a long time.*

"I brought protection." He whispers and his tongue slides along my ear.

"My kids," I barely get out. I feel his tongue down the side of my neck. I lift my chin and he continues to tease me. I swallow hard, realizing that I don't want to explain this to the kids.

"We can go for a ride." His voice cracks a little and my eyes spring open almost expecting to see Tommy. I swallow hard as I am reminded who I am with. *I am not even attracted to him. I don't want it to be this way.* I take a deep breath, relishing the last few seconds of this embrace, realizing that it may be the last for a long time.

"I can't do this." I say softly but firmly as I pulled away and turn toward the counter once again. He's stunned.

"What? Why? I don't understand. You seemed like you really wanted it. What happened?"

*God help me!* I close my eyes and take a deep breath. "I'm so sorry, Mark. I haven't been on a date in years. Your kiss felt so incredible, I almost gave up everything I believe for a night with you."

"It doesn't have to be just one night. I really like you. I've thought about this for a long time. I watch you at work when you don't know. I imagined how I could approach you. How it would be to be with you." His hands continue to caress my sides. "I have wanted you for so long. Kissing you just makes me hungry for more."

*Oh my gosh! God, I don't want to say no. He wants me. He fantasizes about me. Me! Oh, I want this so bad. Help me.* I swallow hard again and move his hands so that I can concentrate better. "I am a Christian."

## Inside My Head

"Me too."

"O.K., but my relationship with God means too much to me to lose. It is very clear that sex without marriage is wrong, and even though you feel incredible right now, I can't lose my relationship with Him for anything... or anyone. I am teaching a Bible study to women right now about the Proverbs 31 woman and verse 12 says 'she will do him good and not evil all the days of her life.' It's talking about her husband even before they meet. Having sex with you would not be doing good to my future husband."

"He would never have to know."

*In other words it won't be you. That cinches it. I don't want Mr. For Right Now, thanks, God.*

"I would and I have to say no. Goodnight, Mark."

"This wasn't at all how I imagined it. I'm sorry if I moved too fast. We can go slower." His last ditch effort was over and he turned to leave. I didn't try to stop him. I didn't even follow him to the door. As it closed I returned to putting dirty dishes in the dishwasher and started it before checking on both of the kids and telling them goodnight.

*God, I can't even pray out loud. I don't want the kids to hear me. I do love You but I didn't want to stop. It felt so good to be wanted. It didn't matter who it was. I suddenly remembered our whole conversation about all the guys I was with before and how they didn't love me and how I didn't love them and didn't, and still don't, know what love is. I remembered You telling me that You love me and that I can trust You.*

*I don't want to be alone tonight. But, I don't want to be with someone I don't love either. I can't believe he said we could go for a ride. That's when it all clicked. How did he... I mean... I*

## Inside My Head

*don't know what I mean. God! I want to be married. I love You so much, I don't want to mess this up. I'm sorry, God. I almost gave in. I wanted to. I'm glad I stopped though. Help me, God. I can't help but cry and wrap my arms around myself as I fall asleep.*

Jade woke me at 4:30. We rushed to get ready and ran out the door with lunch money instead of bagged lunches by 4:45. I don't know how I got to work on time, but here I am.

Mark avoids me all day and I stay busy away from him.

## CHAPTER FIFTEEN

"Hello?...Really?... Oh, my gosh!" My eyes close and I sigh. "Are you coming today?... Oh good, I'm glad you're both coming. What about Chuck?... O.K., good. Will Patty come?" I bite my lip as I do so often when waiting for something. "O.K., well, maybe she'll talk to Jade. They seem to get along. I know they're not best friends or anything but you never know. I'll see you in a little while. In fact, meet me up front by the water fountain, O.K?... O.K. then, goodbye, Sheila." As I hang up Jade just appears by my side. I look at her. *I'm so proud of her. She'd never get pregnant before being married*. As I touch and then kiss her cheek she asks what that was all about.

"Well, Sheila called to tell me that Patty told her last night that she is pregnant. I guess she's about 10 weeks or so. I don't know what to say to her. I guess it's not the most horrible thing but it's not a good thing either. She's only about 15 or 16." I close my eyes and shake my head.

"Mom, it'll be O.K. Is she coming this morning?"

"Yes."

"I'll talk to her but not about that, she doesn't need to know her business is all out there like that, ya know? I'll just make myself available." She smiles and the whole world eases. She's magical like that. I return the smile with my best effort.

*I've never been beautiful. I can't imagine how she turns everybody down 'cause I know guys are all over her all the time. They'd be crazy not to try. God, You've done a great job with her. I'd've never been able to raise her up to be so good... thank You.*

## Inside My Head

"Thank you, Honey. O.K. you two, everyone ready? We'll get donuts on the way today, but we have to leave right away so that we're not late."

"Yay, donuts!" Porter yells out of his room and runs down the hall in my general direction. Jade just smiles and begins to stroll down the stairs.

*Her beauty blows me away. I wish I were half as beautiful as she is. Maybe then Kevin would say hello. I really should understand that I can't keep thinking about him, but he is everything I want in a man. Those shoulders and those arms, oh, my gosh! Those arms! He is fantastic! How can I not think of him? What I wouldn't give to be with him; touching every part of him. I'd be willing to do anything for him. One look in my direction and I'd melt. He could mold me any way he wanted. One time with him and every memory would be replaced. Touching that fantastic body would be a one way ticket to Heaven. I'd never want to come back.*

*His hands touching me...* (I take a deep breath and my pulse races).

"Mom, the donuts!" Porter yells and points at the little locally owned Donut Hut. I remember stopping here when I was a kid. Their donuts are the freshest. Sometimes if we get here at the right time we can request ones that have just come out of the deep fryer. One won't do, they are all so good we get a dozen. 'I never met a donut I didn't like,' I told the man a long time ago and it is still apparent today as we name off practically one of every kind. I have to go around the block since I was in my other world and swept right past it the first time.

"A dozen," I say to the new face behind the counter, "assorted." The kids are each solely focused on the layered shelves of donuts. I am transported into my own private paradise as I inhale the blended aroma of fresh donuts and assorted frostings and fillings. My paradise does not exemplify youth, nor does it worship tall thin women exposing midriffs and lanky legs protruding from mini-skirts. This paradise allows for the simple luxurious pleasure of surrounding oneself with the most delectable goodies and delighting in the sumptuous soft aroma and almost sensual flavor of anything sweet.

The imagery of me licking melted chocolate from Kevin's chest was interrupted by "Ma'am, four more."

"Oh, sorry, I have so much on my mind lately. Umm... one each of these, chocolate frosted raised, Bavarian cream filled straight *(what I can do with that imagery)*, strawberry filled and apple fritter."

"Nine forty-eight, out of twenty, ten fifty-two is your change. Have a great day." All with a 'yay-for-my-first-job' smile. I return my best 'just-give-it-some-time' smile and we all practically run to the van with our treasure in hand. She'd given us each our own bag, thus eliminating the fingering of each donut in order to find the right one and giving us each a feeling of importance as we singularly held our very own treasure.

At church the kids hurried to their classrooms as I hunted for Sheila. Fancy, Maraschino and she were chatting by the women's restroom. We all enter the foyer part of the restroom together. Scented with fresh flowers, the large mirrors and chairs become even more inviting. Resting in here is a welcoming experience all on its own. When the church was remodeled a few years ago the women were excited about this new addition along with the extended length providing for a total of six stalls and three sinks in the main part of the restroom. I don't believe any woman enters the sanctuary before checking herself in the ceiling-to-floor mirrors. We all sit down and continue to chat about Sheila's news of her pending grandmotherhood. Maraschino had plenty to say and it was all so comforting. I sat quietly and listened and nodded, it seemed like the best idea.

Once in the sanctuary, Sheila sits wide-eyed, as always, listening to every word of every song and announcement as though it were of utmost importance. It all runs together for me.

*I wonder how she is going to help Patty when she doesn't want help. She is so rebellious. It just seems so pointless. Should she even keep the baby? Now, how can I even think that? Look at Maraschino, she had her baby and that was a worst case scenario. And someone is happy about that. And look at Kendra, she was so happy to adopt Celeste. I miss her so much. It's been so long since she moved. I need to call her soon.*

*This song is a good one.* I close my eyes and listen intently to the comforting words. Holy, holy, holy are you Lord. *You are holy, Lord. You are truly amazing. I have never understood that before. I am learning so much about You lately. I don't understand holy very well, I think it means special or unique or not like anything or anyone else... You are those things.* Holy, holy, holy are you Lord. My eyes open to see Sheila with her eyes closed and swaying gently to the music as well.

Prayer, announcements, a special song and Pastor Roberts begins.

"I know that it is not Christmas, but I feel that today is supposed to be about the importance of babies and children. God could have chosen to send Jesus in any form. He could have been a man that just appeared one day. He could have been born into the royal family or even the family of the high priest, but instead he chose to place His only Son in the home of a humble carpenter and a young girl. And, He was born to them in a stable during a long unexpected trip. They were not a significant couple; no, quite the opposite, they were very average. Yet wise men from the east traveled nearly two years to find them. They bowed and offered extravagant gifts to this tiny child and His parents. Herod became so jealous that he had all boys born within the past two years murdered.

That one child was the foundation of an entirely new way of thinking, praying, and expressing dedication and love to a once-distant God. As well as a new way of showing love to others. That one baby, who by the way was completely unplanned and nearly caused a breakup of his earthly parents before they were even married, grew to be the perfect sacrificial lamb—He was the Messiah.

We need to remember that every life is a gift from God and that every insignificant seeming child could be the one that could be the next leader of our people, the one that brings new life to our nation. We need to thank God daily for our children and speak blessings over them. Jesus Himself held the children and proclaimed blessings over each of them. He had a lot to say about children. Matthew 11:25 says that the Father reveals hidden secrets to children. Matthew 18:3-6 states that unless we become like children we cannot enter the kingdom of Heaven. And whoever humbles himself like a child is the greatest in the kingdom. And whoever welcomes a little child welcomes Him. It goes on to say that if anyone causes a child that believes in God to sin it would be better for him to have a large millstone around his neck and drowned. Matthew 19:14 says that the kingdom of Heaven belongs to children.

Children—all children—are extremely important to God. We have had such an uprising in this country about abortion and so many of us sit still and let these important lives be taken without a fight. So often we not only let some of them be given up to death, but the ones that are born are sent into a cruel world unaware of the blessing they bring to our homes.

Speaking blessings over others has been found to be a game changer. Children that have very little monetarily thrive with parents that encourage and bless them. Prayer for protection is not just a nice thing to do anymore, it is imperative! We send them to schools that could be the next one on the news in which some hopeless person enters with a weapon, and our child may be the one not coming home ever again. In fact, the child that has no concept of a loving God and loving family may be the next hopeless person with a weapon.

We NEED to teach our children of their value as human beings and the delight that God finds in them. We NEED to speak these blessings over our children and over ourselves. So many adults have missed the importance of this because they themselves were never blessed as children. Mentors and godly friends are important for us to learn of His desires for us. Jesus said that we should have life and life abundant. We cannot have abundant life when we don't recognize that it is for us and reach out and accept it. We need to have hope and a love for ourselves. Not a prideful love, but a godly love and appreciation for who He created us to be. Our worth is priceless when we look at ourselves with His eyes. Let us begin today to praise our children for their lives. Read over them the promises God's Word says about them... The Kingdom of God is meant for them; they are blessed and loved by Him. His delight is toward them. They are each fearfully and wonderfully made. Read all of Psalm 139 to them before a meal or at least before bed. Let them know how important and thought out their lives are to God. He creates each new life for a purpose.

I hope that today will be the beginning of an entirely new life for all of you and your families.

God, today I speak blessings over these your important children. We are all your children, no matter our age. Thank you, dear Father for the significance you place on us. Thank you, that You created each of us in Your likeness and Your image. Thank You that we are special, not just some random thing that formed after thousands of years of nature's guess work. Thank You for sending Your Son to a common household so that we could find ourselves in this picture. I declare this day to be the first day of pure blessings on this body. I humbly ask that You reveal hidden things to us. Give us ideas, thoughts, goals, dreams, and desires that would bring glory to You and Your kingdom. Help us to realize the changes being made in our homes as we begin to speak out and declare blessing over our children. I pray a hedge of protection around each person as we leave here today. Thank you, God. Amen."

I realize that some people went forward to be prayed for, but I just want to get out of here. I am stopped by a strong hand on my upper arm. It is Sheila.

"Did you tell him about Patty?" She asked with a look of unbelief.

"No, I hadn't told anyone except Jade and that was because she overheard me on the phone with you."

"How did he just come up with that kind of speech today without having been told?"

"I do have to admit it is strange, but I have recently begun to see how God is involved in our lives in so many ways that we don't even comprehend. It is almost freaky sometimes how He answers my prayers quickly and precisely." My voice trails off a bit as I look out the sanctuary door and catch a glimpse of Jade and Patty walking together slowly toward the restroom. "Look." I point toward them.

Sheila catches a glimpse of them as well and shakes her head and smiles. "I don't know how or why He is doing all this but Oh, my God, I am so glad He is." She says, pointing upward.

Chuck and Porter approach and we sit down, giving the girls plenty of time to discuss anything that may come up. Discussing lunch is plenty to keep the boys mentally occupied until the girls join us. "We decided to go out to eat together." I smile at Jade and continue, "And we determined that a buffet would best suit this crowd so we will have time to talk there, O.K.?" They both nod and we are on the way.

..........

*What a weekend. It was so different than the average weekend, a date and an announcement of teen pregnancy from my new best friend. I don't know how to respond. Work is going to seem like forever today. I used to love this music; well when I first started, and now I just don't even want to listen to anything. It's most frustrating to listen to the same songs at the same time every single day.*

*I did enjoy the karaoke the other night. I always have so much fun singing; even though I know I don't do it well. Mark was a lot of fun up until that point in which he wouldn't stop. What the heck? I didn't think I'd ever stop a man. I have wanted that for so long and then what? I don't get it. I mean I do get it, kind of. If it had been just a few weeks ago I'd have been thrilled and now...*

## Inside My Head

*God, I don't even know how you're doing it, it just seems like I'm the same but I am totally different at the same time. It's not like you did some miraculous lightening-striking something. But I am thinking differently and still somewhat the same. I have heard people talk about how they were changed completely and thought they were making it all up. Look at Maraschino, she was changed and I guess it may have been slow as well. Talking to her now I would've never known her past or even her life now was, well, is so tough. She is someone I should get to know better. Maybe I could learn a lot from her about You.*

**It is almost always a slow change, but it is a lasting one like that. So many times when people change quickly they revert back to their old ways. It has to be something that will last. You will never be the same. You are learning daily how to look like me. I am so proud of my daughter.**

I smile, realizing that I am having a conversation with my Heavenly Daddy. It is so different than I ever expected. I always thought him to be an angry god like in some Greek myth. I don't know how I feel now except that He is definitely not that way.

## CHAPTER SIXTEEN

*I need to cram for this week's Bible study. JoAnne volunteered this week to share her testimony. Let's see... we will start the review at verse 13. She seeks wool and flax and works willingly with her hands. The NIV says 'eager hands'. Verse 14: She is like the merchant ships; she brings her food from afar.*

*O.K., to start, she works hard. She looks all over for the best material to use, and at a good price. She then sews; well, we will get to that in a few minutes. She brings food from afar and gets up while it is still dark to cook for everyone in the family and her servant girls. She buys a field and plants crops that would be beneficial to her household and financially beneficial as well. She works in the fields and at home till late at night. She sees that her trading is profitable. This is why in the beginning it says that her husband trusts her explicitly and knows there will be no lack.*

*Verse 19 says in her right hand she holds the distaff and grasps the spindle with her fingers. This is indicative of the sewing that she does with the wool and flax.*

*Verse 20 says that she opens her arms to the poor and extends her hands to the needy. She doesn't keep everything to herself; she understands that when God blesses us with gifts and talents as well as financial freedom we are to share that with others instead of hoarding it all for ourselves. She is obedient and willing to do exactly as He wants.*

*Verse 21 says, when it snows, she has no fear for her household; for all of them are clothed in scarlet. This indicated wealth and authority. She had the money to get the finest thread and materials for everyone under her roof. No one went without. Again she sewed this warm clothing for everyone. I can't even mend clothes, so to me this is important.*

*Verse 22 says she makes coverings for her bed; she is clothed in fine linen and purple. Purple is a statement as was the red. It showed wealth and royalty. It was one of the most expensive materials one could buy. She also quilted. This woman was truly amazing! I have seen quilts at craft shows and admired the work and I can't begin to imagine the time someone would have to put into just one. She made quilts for every member of her household.*

*I want to add here that in the beginning I read a commentary which states that this is actually a composite of many women and not just one. It would be nearly impossible to accomplish all this woman did. She would definitely not sleep.*

*Everything mentioned in her repertoire of abilities says that she is willing to do all this. Therefore, no complaining and whining that she stays up late and wakes early, or that she helps in the fields as well in the kitchen. She has servants and still she does all the sewing, shopping, cooking, planting and harvesting and, and, and...*

*What this also reveals is her gratitude for her abundance. She has the means to purchase the top-of-the-line everything and goes out to the "store" far away and buys it. She takes pride in the way she and her family dress. Today it would be like going to the mall and buying all the hottest names and not on sale either. Women were taught as young girls how to sew and take care of a household, but the wealthy women hired it done. She had servants according to verse 15, and yet she still did her own stuff because she took pride in making sure it was done to certain specifications.*

*Verse 14 tells us that she cooked gourmet foods. She brought her food from afar. She had a farm, as seen in verse 16, well, a vineyard anyway; she sold her harvest and purchased the finest foods and seasonings from others that had brought it on ships to that region. She could have gotten spices from India, and meat from hunters nearby. She didn't go without and had items that not all of her neighbors were able to afford.*

*Let's go back again to verse 15. She gets up while it is still dark; she provides food for her family and portions for her servant girls. The King James Version says that she gives meat to her household and a portion to her maidens. I have been reading from the NIV for the most part so if I have a different version I will let you know. Anyway, she gave them meat; that means she had to get up early to begin cooking so that no one went out to work or school or wherever without a hot breakfast. That would've taken hours of preparation, to get the wood hot enough in the stove to cook meat, also the meat would've taken a while all on its own. She could've afforded to sleep in yet, she got up and cooked for everyone.*

*Kinda like me getting up at 3:30 so I can work my butt off, well, go to work at the factory to make sure we have food, clothes, heat, lights and water. Not that we have top-of-the-line anything, and by all means I look for sales, not garage sales or thrift stores like some people do, but I do try to get good deals.*

*When I was growing up I had it a lot better since both of my parents worked, but that stupid man I married... lame excuse of a man, I should say. Sometimes I can't believe I fell for him. Well, to be honest, I didn't fall for him; I got stuck with him when I got pregnant. Man! I love Jade and Porter but I so wish I would've used the pill or something. I am so tired and I hate my life. I want something different, whew.*

*I'd love to travel. I want to meet some strong tall gorgeous tropical tan body and have a wild and crazy vacation. I don't have to ever see him again but just enjoy the moment.*

*I want to... oh, I don't know... I want to be rich. If I got hungry for Chinese food I'd love to go to China. Or I would just hop on my own private jet and fly off to Italy for some fresh lasagna. Oh, my gosh! I can't even imagine that lifestyle as being real. Well... I can, I am. Right now if I want something special I have to plan around my paychecks and bills. School, gas, lunches, clothes, repairs, and everything else that just pops up, I'm lucky if I have enough left for McDonalds. Well, actually we do get fast food way too often. In fact I almost never cook anymore. Man, I'd love to be able to cook again. In fact, I'd love to bring my food from a far away grocery store and cook it up gourmet style, or even plain dinners like meatloaf or pork chops or spaghetti. Oh, I am way too hungry. This studying is making me hungry. What doesn't make me hungry? What a cow! I hate that I want to eat all the time. If I keep going I'll look like JoAnne.*

*Man, how does anyone let themselves get so huge? She's enormous! Everybody says her husband cheats on her all the time. Who can blame him? I do feel sorry for her. He's no prize himself. Geez! I don't get it, why would anyone want to sleep with him. He's so-so, not gross or anything, but certainly not worth cheating with. Maybe the sleezeballs he's sleeping with don't know he's married. Maybe he pays them. Maybe he gets them wasted first then anybody will sleep with anybody. What a loser! What a creep. I mean, hmm, I know she's huge and all but why not just leave her? Why hurt her?*

*She has to know. I wonder if they ever have sex anymore. I mean that would make it a dead give-away. I wonder if she cries herself to sleep.*

*Oh, my gosh, I feel so sorry for her. She's so nice. I don't really know her all that well but she seems nice. Of course, so do I, Man she'd probably hate me if she knew what I really think about her.*

*I hope her testimony isn't like Maraschino's. I thought hateful thoughts about her too. Well, I really was jealous of her. I'm anything but jealous of JoAnne. I'd kill myself if I looked like that. She must go 400-450. How does anybody eat that much food? I mean, I eat, obviously! But, geez! She's more than two of* me and I'm huge. Where does she find clothes? Nope, I'd rather be dead.

Her testimony is this week. I'm going to quit studying for now and come back to it later. I'll have some supper since the kids will be home soon. It was so nice of Martina to take them for the afternoon. It gave me all this study time and I can go get some food and not spend a whole lot. What do I want? Well, I really want a pepperoni lover's stuffed crust pizza.

Hmm, hmm... I could have leftovers for a couple of days. The ultimate pizza for days... wish it was the ultimate man but I will take the pizza. Of course I'd give it all up if I could have Kevin. Oh, my gosh, I'd give up anything if I could have him.

His arms, his chest close to mine, touching mine; skin on skin, strong hard body. Huge hands touching me everywhere... I really have to stop! I really want God more and I can't walk the fence anymore.

God, help me. I don't want to sin against you. I don't want to be alone anymore. I'll take anybody, ANYBODY! Please God! Deep breath in and out... slow in through the mouth out through the nose... "O.K. dinner, pizza it is."

..........

One-forty-five, come on come on, I want out of here! Some days I hate my job. I have so many things I don't want to do and never enough time. I don't feel like I'm ever going to accomplish anything of worth. My life goes from one nothing on to the next without a breath in between. I'm always rushing and never getting anywhere. I have tons to do and it seems like nothing is ever done completely. Deep breath... in through the nose out through the mouth. This yoga breathing thing is a good thing. In slow... out slow... calm...get out of here, get gas, pick up kids, drop off kids at dance and ball, call Bonnie, home to feed the dog, eat the leftovers I hid in the oven, shower and don't

## Inside My Head

*forget to grab notes before getting over to the church for tonight's study. Chris! Gotta call Chris about the church keys.*

"Connie?" *snap back to reality.*

"Yeah?"

"Hey, Mia said she really wants to be there tonight and I was wondering where it is exactly."

"Oh, sure. It's at the Believer's Church on West Cherry Street. Did I tell her it's at 7:00?" I tilt my head like Duke. *I hate it when I do that.* I straighten up right away.

"Excellent, I'll be right by there anyway. How long does it last?"

"About an hour and a half."

"If I'm done early with my appointment can I sit in the back or something till you're done?"

"O.K. I guess that's cool."

"Great! See you there then."

Buzz, buzz, buzz *None too soon.*

"See ya there." *Cool, now I have a friend I invited; it's growing like wild fire. Last week we were packed like sardines at my house. Like 15, I am so glad we could use the church tonight. I am so glad Chris was available. I hope he didn't forget...*

"Connie!" My head spins like the 'exorcist girl' to find Sheila.

"Hey! You will be there, right?"

"Yep, and I have a few friends comin' with. Oh! And I need to talk to you." Her face is overtaken with a sly grin.

"What? I have to know." I demand jokingly.

"Nope! Later. Alone."

"What about?" I urge.

"Pepperoni lovers stuffed crust pizza," she says while walking the opposite way. My forehead wrinkles and I age by the second. *What? Does my breath smell pepperoni lovers stuffed crust pizza? What the…Oh, my gosh! NO WAY! Kevin?! Could she mean Kevin? Oh man, oh, man! This could be good by the look on her face. Or maybe not I couldn't tell she walked away too fast. Does she understand the whole don't date a non-Christian thing? The no sex before marriage thing? What if he is a Christian? Yeah, in my dreams, but then again, if so, what if he wants… oh, I don't know… someone pretty, or skinny, sexy…someone…not me? Oh! Do I really want to know?*

*Yes*

*NO! I don't know.*

*Why now? Why did she say that now? I got so much to do. So much to think about, and now all I can think about is him. I can't think about him right now. I will be a mess if I start to think about him. I am really trying hard not to lust, but he is so delicious! His hair, and oh, my gosh, that face. Those lips, what I wouldn't do to feel them touch mine softly or any other part of me for that matter. Oh, crap! Music… I need music.*

"What a beautiful mess I'm in… I can't get enough of your love…" I flip through the stations

"Oh, yeah that helps. What else is on?"

"Lying beside you here in the dark feeling your heart beat with mine. Softly you whisper love so sincere, how can our hearts be so blind. We sail on together; we drifted apart, now here you are by my side. Now I come to you with open arms hoping you'll see what you love means to me..."

"Journey, Oh I love all their stuff. Crap! Something else..." I change the stations frantically looking for something to get my mind in the right place.

"Come on baby do that conga, I know you can't control yourself any longer..." *Songs always take me somewhere else.*

*Oh, I want to see that! Kevin unable to control himself any longer. Oh, my gosh! One touch, one kiss, just being near him and I can hardly control myself. Oh, shoot! This is not working. It doesn't matter which station or what kind of music I turn on, it all turns me on. I guess I really wanna go there. I know I shouldn't, but Oh, man! Oh, man! What do I do, God? How do I not lust? I want sex. I know You really are trying to teach me, but I guess my head's thick as steel. I'm sorry, God. Will I ever be able to change? How do You put up with me? I am such a loser! I should not be heading up a Bible study, I need one. I need someone to tell me what to do.*

"Hey, Mom! How was your day?" Jade's attitude always knocks me out. She's always so happy. I hope she never gets like me.

"Hi, Sweetheart. My day was good, I guess; same as always. How 'bout yours?"

"Mine was spectacular! Right at the end of the day I was in biology and we were talking about trees and vines that produce fruit and Ms. Baurshcmidt brought up the obvious. Each particular tree or vine produces a specific fruit, and that tree is called its fruit. Like an apple tree, blueberry bush or strawberry plant, which of course is a vine."

"Of course."

"Then you can get even more specific, like gala apple or Clementine or mandarin oranges, etc." She looks at me with an excitement I can't figure out.

"Hmm," I nod like I'm interested.

"Mom! It was so cool! Right then and there God spoke to me!"

"Yeah?"

"Yeah! Even a child is known by his doings and they will be known by their fruit. I need to look up those verses, but even better Galatians 5. Look, I had to pull out my Bible and read it while I waited for you. Listen…"

"O.K." She has my curiosity now.

"Verse 16 till… I don't know, but anyway listen… Let the Spirit direct your lives, and you will not satisfy the desires of your flesh. For what our human nature wants is opposed to what the Spirit wants, and what the Spirit wants is opposed to what our human nature wants. These two are enemies, and this means that you cannot do what you want to do. This is early. Sorry, hold on. I like this Good News Translation, it says it so plain.

Well, I guess verse 19 is more what I wanted, what human nature does is quite plain. It shows itself in immoral, filthy, and indecent actions; in worship of idols and witchcraft. People become enemies and they fight; they become jealous, angry, and ambitious. They separate into parties and groups; they are envious, get drunk, have orgies, and do other things like these. I warn you…da, da, da, da, O.K., verse 22: But the Spirit produces… this is it! Produces love, joy, peace, patience, kindness, goodness, faithfulness, humility and self-control. There is no law against such things as these. O.K., anyway, these are the **fruit of the Spirit,** and before that, the fruit of human nature. Hey, Porter!" She acknowledges him as he climbs in the van then returns to our conversation without skipping a beat. "Mom, we are just like the fruit of the trees and vines in nature. Whether we're producing flesh fruit or Spirit fruit, we are producing some kind of fruit, AND…we are known by that fruit!

I know girls that are easy or mean and jealous, they fight and gossip. They are known by that fruit. We should be known for our fruit, loving, joyful, kind, peacemakers, gentle etc…"

My smile hasn't left my face, but as usual she doesn't know the real reason. Only God and I know that.

"But, producing the fruit is up to us. We have to allow the Holy Spirit of God to do His work in us. We are the soil; He is the food and fertilizer. Jesus said to the woman at the well that the water He offers would make it to where we'd never be thirsty again. This is an everlasting flow of water. This water is inside us. So with this endless supply of water and food and fertilizer supplied by the Spirit! How cool is that?!!! Oh, my gosh, Mom, I never got it like I did today!" She beams.

"My young preacher. God speaks through you. You are going to change the lives of millions. The next Billy Graham, I'm so proud of you. You have no idea how often God uses you to teach me. Don't lose that excitement and willingness."

## Inside My Head

*Thank you, God. What was the first of that? Let the Spirit lead and you won't fulfill the lusts of your flesh. So, You had my own daughter tell me what to do... again. Let the Spirit lead me. Let You and the Holy Spirit do the work of producing self-control. O.K., God, thanks; I'll work on that. Actually, I'll let YOU work on that.*

"Jade, Porter, I got that Bible study tonight. I know you know that, but as a reminder we're doing it at the church tonight so Aunt Bonnie will pick you both up and take you home. She will feed you and I will be home like 8:30 or 9:00."

"O.K., Mom, bye." Jade smiles and waves as she bounces out of the van. I wave back.

"Mom?" Porter starts.

"Mm-hmm."

"I'm proud of you. This Bible study is going really good and everyone tells you at church how much they love it and appreciate it and you don't let it go to your head or anything. You act the same. You are amazing and I love you so much."

I can hardly believe my ears. I look at Porter with sheer delight. "Really?" is all I have to offer. He's never said anything even remotely like that before. "Thank you, Son. You have no idea how important that is to me. I truly appreciate that. I love you so much and sometimes I get so caught up in my own world." His smile says it all. "Have a good practice, Sweetheart, I love you."

"Bye, Mom."

"Bye, Honey." I watch as he runs up the path to the field. Everyone says that he is built like a football player. Coach Carter says he could get a college scholarship if he sticks with it all through high school. I'm sure he will; he loves the sport.

*Her children will arise and call her blessed.*

*Thanks, God.* I shake my head. *Wow!*

..........

*Amazing! There are so many here!*

"It's seven, so we're going to go ahead and get started. I'm Constance and we have been growing with leaps and bounds. This is only week four of our study of the Proverbs 31 woman.

"Maraschino gave her testimony last week for anyone who wasn't here you missed an incredible word about God's healing power. I know God has begun a work in me because of her life. So, again Maraschino, thank you for sharing.

"Tonight is JoAnne's turn to testify. I'd like to explain to everyone why we're giving personal testimonies. Revelation 12:11 says 'And they overcame him (meaning the devil) by the blood of the Lamb (Jesus is called our perfect sacrificial lamb) and the word of their testimony. Each time you give your testimony, which is telling others about what God has done in your life, each time you do that you strike another blow to our common enemy—the devil. So, tonight we'll rejoice as JoAnne attacks him and strengthens us. JoAnne…"

Everyone claps as I take a deep breath and sit down. She closes her eyes and then looks out at about 45 people or so. Then she smiles nervously.

"Yeah," she says with a sigh. "When I agreed to do this I expected six or seven. I'm not good at talking in front of people, so I just want to apologize ahead of time for how this may come out.

"I was always the big girl. The one no one picked in gym to be on their team. My mom always told me I needed to lose weight so she could buy me pretty clothes, but my dad loved me just like I was. His acceptance was the only thing that kept me going in junior high and high school.

"I contemplated suicide many times but each time my daddy would come through for me. He never knew. He was my inspiration to live. He'd put his arms around me and sing Jesus Loves Me and then he'd tell me that I must be extraordinary in God's eyes because he put so much more into me.

"He told me every day how beautiful I was and how proud he was to be my daddy." Her tears are mirrored in every woman here. She shakes her head and gulps back more tears before starting again.

"When I was twenty three my daddy died in a plane crash coming home from a business meeting." She sighs hard. "I thought my world had just come to an end as well. I knew no one that loved me or accepted me like he did. At that time I was a size 18. Not terribly large but my mom was a 3. She saw me as an embarrassment and I couldn't face the comments so I hid in a college dorm studying like a maniac and eating my way to a comfort zone I didn't want to leave.

"Another girl in our dorm noticed that I went nowhere. Even at Christmas I didn't go home. Mom called to tell me I could come home if I wanted but when I declined she just said 'O.K.' and we hung up. After the first year she didn't even make the call.

That girl from college was Jessica. She came to my room and brought her books and we'd study together. She also brought Christian tapes and her Bible. After studying to her music we'd break out some munchies and her Bible and we'd look into what God says about us. She had a thyroid problem and couldn't gain any weight. Everyone assumed she was anorexic, but she could out-eat me." She smiled and gave a slight giggle for the first time tonight.

"For the next three years we would declare God's Word over each other. We'd use verses like Genesis 1:27: God made them male and female in His image, and Psalm 45:11: The king is enthralled with your beauty; honor Him for He is your Lord. Psalm 17:8: ...keep me as the apple of Your eye (a paraphrase we used). And Psalm 17: 15: I will be satisfied when I awake with thy likeness. There were lots more but I just picked a few for tonight to give you an idea.

"Because of these amazing verses of acceptance and love that God has for each of us I got to know Him personally. I could accept His love for me. He doesn't judge our physical beauty or activity, He simply judges our hearts.

"Eventually a doctor diagnosed me with diabetes and hypothyroidism. I felt such relief to know there was a medical reason for my size; however, I was finally at the point where I didn't care. I knew my Heavenly Daddy, The King of the universe, finds me beautiful. He loves me. He accepts me. And He delights in me.

"Jessica lost a battle to cancer one year out of college. I knew that God had placed her there for me because He loves me that much.

"Please understand one thing, no matter what the world tries to say, we as women should be or do or look like, God has already given His stamp of approval. Rest in Him. Allow Him to show you how magnificent you are to Him. You will be pleasantly surprised. Thank you."

Claps ring through the room as she turns to go to her chair.

"JoAnne, will you pray for all of us?" I ask, hoping she will. *I know I need it. How can I pray when I can't get where she is yet?* She looks up from the floor and around at all the teary smiles and rolls her eyes as if to say O.K. and fixes herself right back in the same spot.

"Daddy, here we are, all of us, Your beautiful chosen daughters. Some of us get it. Some of us crawl up into Your lap and let You love on us. We understand your pure love. We feel accepted. But the majority here do not. Daddy, God, I pray from the very deepest part of who I am that You will shine Your light into each one of those who are hiding in the darkness of their minds. Those who haven't felt Your perfect delight in who they are. Let them catch a glimpse of You dancing over them.

"I pray tonight would be a new beginning for each girl here. That Your enemy would feel the desperation that we have felt. That we would overcome him this night, halleluiah! Amen."

"JoAnne, thank you so much. I know personally I will gain ground in this battle, thanks to you. Thank you." I hug her with a sigh and a smile.

"I was thinking as I studied about this woman of Proverbs 31. She was truly grateful for all she had. She has the means to go and purchase the best of everything and she is still not haughty or cold hearted. She loves selflessly all those around her. She takes pride in the way she and her family dress and in the foods they eat. She is confident in her own abilities. She knows her family is warm and healthy; which brings us back to her husband's confidence in her. Verse 11, from the first night, says that ...her husband has full confidence in her and lacks nothing of value.

"This is truly striking. How many women today are really confident? In their own strengths, abilities and just who they are in general? My perception of women is that the majority of us are insecure; uncertain of the way others feel toward us, especially when it comes to our husbands. Many women are suspicious and in turn become vicious. This is a cycle of folly. JoAnne put it so beautifully by saying that some women accept who God says they are; His love and admiration is plenty, and yet so many are unable to do this. The ones who are unable to do this tend to play mind games causing fear, hurt, anger, anxiety and jealousy. These are walls we build around ourselves, glass walls which allow people to see into our world only what we allow them to see. The fakeness of most women is difficult to get through. I want to thank each of the women here who have given their testimonies so far. The openness you've allowed us to experience is extraordinarily refreshing. I know personally I have grown tremendously from you allowing us to enter your glass walls. Thank you all so much.

"Now, going back to the Bible study...last week I passed out a questionnaire, a test of sorts. Would anyone like to share a couple of their answers?"

Hands go up all over the room.

"O.K., to stay within the time frame we have I'll ask the questions and call on two people for each answer." All hands go down as I begin. "What do you enjoy doing? Hobbies or whatever." Women I don't know answer these so that we can get to know each other. The answers were short but with ten of the questions and so many women the time flew.

"I really enjoyed getting to know so many more women tonight. I'm not too good with names but, I am trying. Please don't get mad if I forget your names by next week. I will possibly remember your faces and even your answers. It's already 8:00 and I would like to get a little bit of the study in tonight. I have been reviewing each week but tonight I will need to be quick. I'm sorry.

"For those that are new tonight we have gone through Proverbs 31: 10-18 so far. We got through the first part of verse 18 anyway. So the second half of that says 'and her lamp does not go out at night.' Verse 19: 'in her hand she holds the distaff and grasps the spindle with her fingers.'

"This means that she stays up super late and makes her own thread to weave her own material to make her own clothes and blankets that it talks about in verses 21 and 22. Just peeking here it says that she sews clothes, warm beautiful clothes, for her whole household. That includes her servants.

"She also makes blankets or quilts for everyone. Her clothes are top-of-the-line and represent their social status. In today's terms that would be like being dressed in Dior or Vanderbilt or some other designer, as would everyone in her household including her servants.

"Anyway, verse 24 shows that others admire and want her clothes because it says she makes linen garments and sells them, and supplies merchants with sashes. She has her own clothing line! There is nothing she can't do! Please keep in mind this woman is a composite woman.

## Inside My Head

She is able to do everything; but, I don't see it as a possibility that one woman can do everything.

"However, she definitely has a handle on her time-management skills. She works now looking ahead to the future. This assures healthy eating and warm clothes and bedding for the winter. Purple and scarlet as noted in the verses indicate wealth. The poorer people could not afford the products necessary to create these dyes.

"In these few verses alone I feel inadequate. I tend to get up at the last minute in our fast-paced world where breakfast tends to be a cereal bar on the way to drop off kids and get to work barely on time. I run kids here and there, study very little for this class and pray that God would work through me anyway to touch someone. I am not sure why I agreed to do this study except that God has been doing some major work in me these last few weeks. I can't honestly tell you that I'm going to be up earlier or fixing healthier meals, but I know God is teaching me what my priorities should be. Does anyone feel me here?"

It seems every woman's head is nodding. I'm so glad that I am not looking too lazy. "You know if anyone has any ideas we could use it looks like we could be open to those."

JoAnne raises her hand, so I nod at her and she begins, "I could put together a few recipes that are easily made ahead of time and frozen so that you could eat healthy quick meals if you'd like." One woman begins to clap and then the whole place breaks out in clapping.

"It's a unanimous, yes. I know I would appreciate it. Would you be able to get them to me early so that I could have the church make copies for everyone?" She nods with a wide smile.

## Inside My Head

Martina stands up sheepishly. "Martina?" I question. *That's strange, she's so cold and does nothing. She's exactly the opposite of what we're looking for.*

"Well, my maid is here with me tonight and she does a fantastic job of cooking and cleaning for our family. I bet she would have lots of ideas to make housework quicker. Maybe she would be willing to give everyone ideas on how she does things. My house is always spotless and I'm always so proud to have people over. She's also an extraordinary cook. She specializes in vegetarian meals, but makes a mouth-watering steak as well." Martina turns and looks at the beautiful yet plain woman to her left. She smiles from ear to ear and reaches up to brush a long dark stray hair from her eyes. Her cheeks are flushed; it's easy to see she's not comfortable with the attention.

"What's your name?" I hope the easy question will break the awkwardness of the moment for her, but her face shows the opposite reaction.

"Rochelle." She answers weakly.

"Would you be willing to write out some time saving tips for us, Rochelle, since you come with such a high recommendation?" *Maybe the realization that we're not expecting her to get up and speak will help.*

"O.K." *quick and to the point.*

"Thank you, Rochelle; I look forward to getting help from these two ladies as I know we all do." I pause for only a moment before finishing.

"We'll stop here, but, during this week think of the Proverbs 31 woman. She is strong, wise, admirable, respected, talented, and trusted by many people. This week please take the time to write down your talents if you were not here for the survey and test we took last week. And for everyone, if you could do or be anything you wanted, what would that be? Then write down what it is that is stopping you from doing or being what you really long to do or be. That may take some thought for some of us. Be honest with yourselves.

"It would be easy to say 'because I got married young and started a family,' but, we're reading about a woman who probably got married at about 14 or 15 and has children and servants. So think hard and be honest about what is really stopping you. I will do this too. Let's see what can change. God says in Philippians 4:13 we can do ALL things through Christ who gives us strength.

"Any questions before we pray? ...No? O.K. then, I'll close in prayer. Dear God, thank You for opening our eyes to your love tonight and your acceptance through JoAnne's testimony. Thank you for helping us to catch a glimpse of understanding of who we are in You. Bring that home to each of us this week. Give us insight into who we are purposed to be. Go with us as we leave tonight and keep us safe. Thank you, Lord, Amen.

"Goodnight ladies and I will see you all next week, if not before. We do have services here on Wednesday nights at seven and Sunday mornings at ten. There are caregivers for infants and teachers for toddlers through teens. If you don't already have a church home you are welcome here."

Before I can get off the platform women are already approaching me and thanking me for this class and my insight and willingness to do this. I love the attention far more than I expected. I really didn't think I would be able to do this a month ago. It's amazing what God can do when we let Him. The socializing lasted for about an hour.

## Inside My Head

Ron came in and Chris followed shortly thereafter sitting together and chatting in the back. Slowly but surely several men, assumedly husbands or boyfriends, fill the back row. I completely enjoyed conversing with many women. I was introduced to at least fifteen women. Each had stories of who invited them and why they came. Chris was able to close up about ten.

# Inside My Head

# CHAPTER SEVENTEEN

*Another day another dollar, hi ho, hi ho, it's off to work I go. I'll take the kids and drop them off thank God there is no snow.* I laugh at my silliness. *The good thing about singing to myself is no one can hear me butchering Disney songs. Well, any song.* "Jade, time to start getting ready for school, since you're up and all. Porter, time to get up." *Hi ho, hi ho it's off to school they go, with bags in tow and lunches too, hi ho, hi ho, hi ho. Hi ho, hi ho, we dance and sing into the clothes we have to wear each day… that's funny. I never thought of that before. The clothes we have to wear each day. It could be a bad thing like we have to wear those particular ones, or it could be a good thing like the clothes that we have. How many people wish they had more than one or two pieces of clothing in this world? I have a lot of clothes, comparatively; and a job too. Man, how many people don't even have a job to go to?*

*How many women wish they had children to get ready for school? I have two. How many people want their kids to be good and not make them go to jail just to see them? Mine are wonderful! I have a house; not an apartment and some people are without either.*

*Oh, my gosh, Lord, I am so thankful for so many blessings! Sometimes I get lost in stupid things and can only focus on not having as much money as I want, or a dirty house or an older van. I am materialistic! I hadn't thought of it like that before, but I am. I consider things more important than people. I have very few friends because I just don't like women and I couldn't get a man to give me attention even if I paid for his time. But! I have clothes and a house and a job and the best kids in the world. What do I ever have to complain about? Oh, God, I'm sorry.*

## Inside My Head

Jade, Porter, I will be taking some time this weekend to hang out with you guys; let me know what you want to do.

"Will you go to my game Saturday? It's pretty much the last one," Porter immediately asks.

"Yes, I will. Jade you wanna get some hot dogs at his game? No! Let's go to lunch together afterward. Maybe we can get some popcorn or something. Is that what you do at a football game?" I throw that out to whoever wants to answer, as we climb in the van.

"I guess, but only because it's you, Porter, I'm not into football at all. But lunch does sound good. Do you think you'll start Saturday?" Jade whips from one subject to the next like me.

"I never know, but coach says I'm getting better. Maybe if he knows you two are coming he will start me." His rare but beautiful smile strikes me as another blessing.

"Think about lunch. Where should we go?"

"Sit down or take out?" Porter asks.

"I don't care, whatever you guys want. I don't have a lot of money but we can definitely do something. I have a job." Both kids look confused, but I understand the significance of that finally.

"Have a great day, you too." They wave goodbye as they continue their conversation about lunch all the way into Aunt Bonnie's house.

..........

"Hi, Ron." I wave as I pass and get to the machine I will be positioned in front of for the next eight hours.

"Hey, Connie, how long has this Bible study been going on? Chris and I were impressed with the number of women there and Mia was so excited again this week."

"Well, last night was week four of the six weeks."

"Are you serious? Only four weeks in? How many did you start with? And what do you mean four of the six weeks? Is that suggesting it's about to end?" He and I get ready for a long loud day turning on machines and putting plugs in our ears.

"Yes, it is a six week study on the Proverbs 31 woman." He gets a little closer so he can hear. "There were six of us to start. I remember thinking how ironic it was to have six people for a six week study. In fact, that's how we started doing testimonies, one girl each week. We could get to know each other better and I wouldn't have to fill the whole time. It was at my house until this week as well. Six people, six weeks and 21 verses; it seemed simple enough." I mused.

"That's impressive! In just four weeks it has grown like a wildfire!"

"Yes, I had eight people sign up and I could fit up to 10 in my house. We'd be tight but it was possible, so I told the ladies the first night to feel free to invite others in hopes that we could get at least the original eight. The second week there were nine and by the third week we crammed 15 into my house. They were all over the place." I smiled as I remembered them in the living room, dining room and on the steps just to find places to sit.

"That's when I asked if we could use a room at the church. Chris kindly opened the sanctuary since there was the possibility of over 20 last night and I was still surprised at the number of women there. Many of which I had never seen at church before. All invited by someone. It keeps growing, like you said, like wildfire."

"See! You can't let it end. Just think about everybody coming and inviting others. And think about the changes being made in their lives, like Mia, she's excited to come and to invite family; and what about Sheila? My gosh, Connie! This wildfire is what we all need, and you started it! Don't put it out, I beg you." His baby face and puppy eyes somehow define the seriousness his words expressed.

*Wow. I hadn't thought of any of that. I definitely hadn't thought of continuing the study.* "I'll definitely pray about it, thank you for the idea." *You heard that, God, you tell me what to do.*

"Oh, my gosh, there's Kevin." I whisper to myself while taking in a deep breath.

"Yeah, he's a great guy." My eyes shoot next to me where I thought no one was, until Ron spoke. My eyes must have said it all.

"Oh, sorry, I thought you were still talking to me."

*I guess technically I was.* My eyes close as I realize just how embarrassing this is. *Oh, my gosh!*

"He goes to my church. In fact he got me this job. He's cool." Ron says matter-of-factly while nodding, as if he wasn't talking about the most incredible man ever.

*Cool? He goes to Ron's church? Does that mean he's a Christian? What does it mean? Is that a good thing or a bad thing? Well, obviously it is a good thing. When I get to Heaven I'll have a beautiful body and maybe we can hang out. I know here it's out of the question…* "He's far too perfect for me here…" I sigh.

"I'm not sure that he's that cool." Ron is looking at me again.

*Don't tell me I just said all that out loud. Oh, my gosh! How completely stupid! When will I learn? Why do I have to embarrass myself all the time? What an idiot!*

"Hmm?" Ron asks.

"What?" I ask as though I don't know what the heck he's talking about since I was lost in self-destructive thinking.

"Do you want to talk to him?" He repeats

"NO!" I shake my head and act as though that would be the most disgusting thing ever.

"No way!" Ron looks excited.

"What?" I ask cautiously. *I wasn't thinking anything out loud since I wasn't thinking at all. Which could be worse, I don't even remember what I did say. Oh, no.*

He laughs. "You act like a junior higher. You like him that much, and you don't even know him?" He laughs again, "Kevin!" he yells out before I could even consider that he would do that.

*No way! No he isn't! Oh, no! Oh, my gosh!* I close my eyes and pretend it's all a dream. *I am such a child. Breathe, breathe.*

"Kevin, I would like you to meet Connie."

I look up to see those entrancing green eyes. The ones I've only seen from afar. *They are so beautiful. I wish I could touch him, he's so close. Am I at least smiling? Oh, I hope I don't look as stupid as I feel. Oh, my gosh! I hope I don't say*

## Inside My Head

*something out loud.* I roll my eyes as I concentrate, *No, I don't think I have.*

"Hi, Connie, I've seen you here for a long time."

*His voice is deep and strong. He is all man! Don't touch. Don't act stupid.*

"Mm hmm. I've worked here for like five years." *Stop messing with your hands! Don't roll your eyes. You look like a ditz.* "You've been here a long time too, haven't you?" *Duh! Can't you even talk like a grown up? Oh, my gosh! You are so dumb.*

"Yeah, about seven years, but I don't get to meet anybody really, since I'm always being called for some kind of repair or clean-up. You know what they say... a man's work is never done."

I laugh... and laugh... and laugh *I can't quit laughing! I am such a moron. If there had been any chance in the universe that we could have ever gone out you are blowing it right now.* "Sorry." *That's all you can say is sorry? I wish I could crawl into a machine, but then he'd have to save me and it'd be even worse, if that's possible.*

He laughs a little and we hear his name over the loud speaker to get to line two for a repair. He points up, "See? Gotta go, nice to finally be introduced to you, Connie."

"Bye, you too." *You too? You too? Are you serious? You too? What an idiot!*

"I haven't seen anybody act like that since grade school. You got it bad, girl." Ron shakes his head and smiles. "He's really not that perfect, don't worry." He goes back to his machine and leaves me to my thoughts.

## Inside My Head

*It's about time. ...A Christian, huh? I wonder if that's what Sheila was going to tell me last night. I had forgotten she had started to say something. Strange, I would have never remembered that before, or I mean forgotten that. Man! I am a child. I wish I had the body of a child. Well, not a child-child more like an 18 year old child; that would be sick. But, if I looked like I did then I would've already come on to him. He would've definitely come onto me, well, into me. Yeah, life would be so good. I was so much more beautiful and so sexy, everyone told me so. Not like now, (sigh), God, I think I just blew it big time. You're inside me, why didn't you stop me from making such a huge fool of myself? Doesn't that embarrass you?*

Buzz, buzz, buzz

"Oh, Connie!" Sheila sings.

"Oh, Sheila," I groan.

"Hey, last night was great! So many women! Like they came out of the woodwork. I think the tip ideas are cool. I look forward to them. I'm bringing more people next week. In fact Betsy from Bonno's is coming. She finally got that day off. And my sister said she would come. Do you think Patty could come, or is she not old enough?"

"Well, she could come and see if she likes it. I'll have Jade come; her class is taking a break for now. Sheila, you were going to talk to me last night about...?"

"Oh, yeah, Kevin."

"Shh! Geez!" I look around like a criminal. She laughs and shakes her head.

"Connie, you are so funny! Kevin is a Christian, he goes to that really big church on Oak. He's 41 and single. He was married once before but she died. He has no children. He's been here for seven years and three months. No felonies. Hmm, anything else?" She thinks; "No, I guess that's it. Is that good enough?" She's beaming.

"Where in the world did you get all that info?" I smile curiously.

"Oh, I got my ways." Her voice reminds me of when I would tease my friends about the boys in high school. *I wonder if she slept with him. I know she's cool with Joe now and God is changing her.*

"Did you go out with him before?" *I hope not.*

"No," she still teases, "I talked to Joe, they're friends." She tilts her head and smiles. *She's really very pretty. I bet she wouldn't have acted like an idiot in from of him.* Deep sigh.

"Well...?"

"Well, Ron introduced us a little while ago. He and Ron are also friends from church and he got Ron the job here and..." *Do I tell her? Well, I told her the pizza thing, so I guess...* "I made a fool of myself. He said, 'You know what they say; a man's work is never done.' And I started laughing and I couldn't stop. I looked like an idiot. Oh my gosh, Sheila." I shake my head, "I can't believe it, I finally get to see him so close I could touch him and he was actually talking to me with that voice that would melt a glacier, and I just laugh... at nothing!" My eyes roll back and my body sinks.

"I'm sure it wasn't that bad."

"Oh no, don't stick up for me. It was definitely that bad. I can't imagine it much worse. Unless I just up and peed my pants." I shake my head and roll my eyes.

## Inside My Head

Buzz, buzz, buzz

"Connie, I'll talk to you later. Don't worry." We both go back to work.

*God, what do you think? Should I keep the Bible study going? Is that just an ego thing? Would I do it just because I like hearing everyone praise me because of what's going on? I don't even feel adequate enough to do the first six weeks. I'm way behind if we're going to finish in two more weeks, but I have to say I am enjoying it. I know I'm changing. I am thankful.*

"Oh, crap!" I push the stop start buttons but my machine won't work. "What in the world?"

"Gene, my machine just up and quit."

"I'll call maintenance; we don't have time for this." He rushes past in frustration.

*I can't believe it just quit! What in the heck?! I've had it miss-press, start and stop or need some sort of adjustment but, just stop?*

"Connie, is this your way of talking to me again?"

My eyes close before looking up into his face. That sweet smile is incredible. I'd do anything for him. "No, I don't know what happened, it just quit. I pushed the stop and then the start. I checked for stray pieces that might've gotten stuck but I can't figure it out. It's never done this before."

"No? It didn't really do it this time either, look here." He bends down and points at the cord lying on the floor, not plugged in at all.

## Inside My Head

My eyes widen as I begin to realize how this looks. "Oh, my gosh! Who would've unplugged it? I never thought of checking that."

"I don't know but, at least this was easy. Have a good afternoon, Connie." He walks away casually.

'Connie.' He said my name. I wish it was more passionate, breathy, like…'Connie, I've wanted this for so long,' or 'I love you, Connie. I want this to last forever. You feel so good.'

Anything, just to hear him say my name. Actually it would be even better if he called me Constance. Oh, yeah it couldn't get better than feeling him inside me and telling me how much he wants me and loves me.

Deep breath out and eyes closed. *My world is so much better than this one. And Kevin is everything I could ever imagine as the perfect man.*

"God, I'm sorry, I'm lusting again. I want to change. I still don't know exactly how. Especially when I see him. He's incredible, God! You really outdid yourself there. I think he's the closest thing to perfection I've ever seen. And he's a Christian! Wow! Would you set it up that we could get together? Two single Christians; of course, he'd have to like pleasantly plump and fluffy, beached whales. But, God, maybe you could just put me to sleep and do an overnight miracle to make me beautiful enough for him. What do I do, God? I know I've never tried hard enough or I'd be thin. It just takes not eating junk, eating less and exercising. But, I never find time to exercise and I eat whatever is there. I don't want to. What I really want is to get serious about it and lose weight. It's like a fight constantly inside my head, a tug-of-war. Eat right, work out… eat something quick and rest before running after kids and work.

I hate being fat and ugly but I feel like I'm stuck; like I have no choice now. God, I hate it! I hate me! I hate my body! I'll *never be with someone again if I don't lose weight and yet here I sit. I hate my job and here I stand. I hate my life, work, kids, activities, dirty house, dirty dishes and clothes, a hungry needy dog, church. No social life, nothing for me!!! I have no life and no fun. All I can do is fantasize and that is wrong! That's not fair, God!!!*

**Constance, I love you.**

*Yeah, I know and that is important, but I want a man to love me; a human that touches me and kisses me, I'm sorry, God. I guess just coming face to face with reality. The reality that I'm unwanted is too hard sometimes.*

**Constance, read Romans 7:14 through all of Roman's 8 when you get home.**

*Why?*

*You'll see.*

*O.K.... Is that all you're going to say?... God?...O.K.*

The remainder of the day I just listen to the music replicated each day. My mind closes off to the world around me.

## ChAPTER EIGhTEEN

Duke barely has time to go out before work and after picking up kids, going to church eating fast food and unloading the car. He's getting fat like me. Time just gets away from me all the time. I don't even make plans because I can't do anything. I sigh as I lay down. I check the alarm out of habit and notice that it is already 10:30. I'm so tired."

**Constance.**

*Oh yeah, good night, God.*

**What about Romans?**

*Romans?*

**Yes, Romans 7:14 through all of chapter 8.**

*Oh yeah, Can I do that tomorrow?"*

*I never force you to do anything. So when you are ready...*

Yeah, when will I have time? Really, I'll just put it off till I forget altogether. Do I really want to change? I guess I just need to start. Oh, I'm so tired. "O.K.," I say as I take a deep breath and begin to read out loud.

"Sold as a slave to sin, hmm, I understand that.

"I do not understand what I do. For what I want to do I do not do. Yeah, that's me. But, what I hate I do. Yep! That's exactly what I do. My work! I eat when I'm not even hungry. I want to be like you, God. But I don't do anything to get me there. I should pray, not just talk at you. But, I don't.

I lust. I hate me, and life and I'm jealous. I'm lazy. I'm fat; I'm not very sociable anymore. I just go through the motions every day. I really don't want any of it. I want to like me. I wish I was nice. I wish I was skinny. I wish I was pretty. I wish I wasn't jealous of every woman. I wish I had friends. I want to be like you. I am what I don't want to be. I can't change. I'm stupid. You keep talking to me. You keep trying and I don't get it. I don't change for long. From one day to the next I'm nice for a minute and then I'm the same as I was a minute ago.

God, I'm no good! I'm terrible! I do love you. I want to love you more. I want to be like Maraschino. She's so good. She's so beautiful, she's gentle and kind and she forgives. She loves you. I wish I was like her.

God! Why am I like this? I've been a Christian for years. I am worthless as a Christian; as a woman, as a person! I can't change, I'm so tired." I want to cry but I can't even do that. I fall to sleep realizing that maybe I'm not really sorry enough.

## CHAPTER NINETEEN

Kendra moved to Oregon about eight years ago after her and Geoff adopted Celeste. I wonder if she knows about Celeste's parents. It would be very strange if Kendra adopted Maraschino's daughter. I wonder if that would be possible. It is a small world. I'm pretty sure that's where Maraschino said they moved. I'm going to call tonight after work. Wow!

I remember Kendra moving. It was so hard for me. She was my last close friend. She and Geoff just said that things were getting complicated with the birth mom. That would make sense now, if Maraschino is the birth mom. I even left that church after that. Since Kendra couldn't trust the people there I wouldn't either. I like my church now. Besides, none of it was the same after Kendra left.

I wonder if it would be O.K. for Maraschino to meet Celeste. I don't know how that would be possible but, God You said that what is impossible with man is possible with you. So, I'm, at least going to try.

They may be glad to know about Maraschino's walk with God. They could be praying for her. That's the kind of people Kendra and Geoff are. Maybe they would at least O.K. me to tell Maraschino about her daughter if Celeste is in fact her daughter. Oh my gosh, that would be so great! Oh my gosh, that could be why I'm doing this Bible study in the first place, so that I could help Maraschino get in touch with her daughter, or at least let her know that she is doing well.

"God, could that be possible?"

"Connie?" I jump back into the real world of the factory and see Ron looking at me like he's been there for a while.

"Yeah?"

"How do you work like that? I'm afraid you'll cut a finger off one of these days." I quickly look down thinking I'm in trouble but everything is fine. I look back at him quizzically.

"What?" I ask, confused by his statement.

"Well, the bell for last break went off two minutes ago." I look around and Ron and I are the only ones here.

"Oh, thanks for letting me know." I wipe my hands on my jeans then in my hair, as we walk toward the break room.

"In your own world again?"

"Yeah, I tend to like it better there. Besides I was thinking about an old friend that moved away years ago."

"Oh. Well, I know you go to church all the time and all but Mia wanted me to ask if you'd consider joining us Sunday. She wants to introduce you to some women at our church. She's been talking non-stop about the Bible study and people want to meet you before they go."

"Wow, really?" I ponder the incredibleness of anyone wanting to meet me.

"Yes, so what do you think?" He continues to stare at me.

"Uhh, O.K., I guess. Porter wanted to visit there with some friends from school anyway. He will be so excited. O.K. we'll come this week. What time does it start?" I listen but only half-heartedly. *Why would someone want to meet me? I am not doing hardly anything. It's everybody else's testimonies that make it so cool. I am learning from them. The Bible study has gone slower than it was supposed to also. I hope they aren't too disappointed when they meet me. I'm just really nothing.*

"...about 1:00, O.K.?"

"Your church doesn't start till one?"

He tilts his head like Duke and squishes his eyebrows as if to determine if I really just said that. "No, we go to the second service and it starts at about 11:30 but we get there at about 11:15. It lasts till about 1:00... You need to stay in this world for a while."

"Yeah, sorry, we will be there. Thanks," I say, nodding the whole time.

"Awesome! Mia will be so excited! I'm going to call her right now." He walks away pulling out his cell phone.

*Hmm, introduce me to friends? I'm no one. I don't even do much. Maybe it should keep going. God, I haven't even prayed about it at all. Is this Your way of telling me to continue? There are only so many verses in Proverbs 31. I know I've been reviewing and haven't gotten through them all but we are at verse 22 and we do have 2 more weeks. What would I talk about after that? Would we keep hearing testimonies? Would I still lead it? Should I have someone different volunteer each week? I don't know. I was scared to do this one. True, it's going good, but how long would that last?*

**Constance?**

Yes.

**Yes. Keep going. I'll show you what to study and share. I have a plan.**

O.K., like what?

## Inside My Head

***I'll show you when it's time.***

*O.K., so I will announce it next week. We will continue to meet on Tuesdays. Oh! I need to talk to Pastor John and get permission to continue using the church. I haven't talked to him since it all started. I just asked Chris if he'd let me use the room and he got it okayed... I'm sure it won't be a problem.*

I realize that I am in the cafeteria and don't even remember getting here. Its final break and I didn't even hear the bell ring. *Ron is right. How do I work like this? It's crazy! I need to focus on work when I'm here; although it's rather apparent that I can be on the line doing my job and not have to think. Well, not about work anyway. I pretty much hate my job. The monotony, the same stupid songs repeated every day, the most boring work, loud, white noise from all the machines. I'd rather think about anything else... Jade and Porter, church, Sheila and Joe, whatever... Kevin!!! He's my favorite subject no matter where I am. He is so exciting. Oh, crap! He goes to Ron's church! What the heck was I thinking? What am I going to wear? I don't have anything. Maybe Jade will do my hair.*

*Yeah, there goes the little black dress, wind blowing, sexy look thing. Why'd I say I would go there? I didn't think at all. I can't go there. Maybe I could tell him I changed my mind. Ugh, I don't think I have a choice now. He called Mia and everything.*

*Man! I was having such a good day. I have got to get my mind off of Superman. Superman, those gorgeous green eyes, those huge arms of steel, so strong, so sexy. I sure would like to fly away with him. Like Lois Lane when he flew her away to his secret place in the ice castle or whatever. We'd melt the bed.*

*Oh, God! What am I doing? Didn't I just say I want to be like you? Just last night! I was right, I can't change!* I shake my head and let out a deep breath. *I'm such a stupid loser!*

## Inside My Head

God doesn't speak to me all day. *He's probably mad because I'm so stupid and stubborn. I say I want to change but obviously I don't really or I would. Loser!!! Loser!!! Loser!!! Just tattoo the L on my forehead. God! Why don't you just change me?*

God is silent.

..........

Just before I fall asleep I pull my Bible back out, "verse 16: ...and if I do what I do not want to do I agree that the law is good. As it is, it is no longer I myself who do it, but it is sin living in me. I know that nothing good lives in me. *Whew! I know THAT for sure. Who wrote this?* I flip back to the beginning of Romans and find it was Paul. He wrote this after his conversion. *Paul? Wasn't he like a super-Christian? Why did he write this?*

Anyway, nothing good lives in me, that is, in my sin nature. For I have the desire to do what is good, but I cannot carry it out. For what I do is not the good I want to do; *Paul, you and I have a lot in common. He understood this years ago, centuries ago.* No, the evil I do not want to do- this I keep on doing.

God! That is exactly what I said earlier today. This is describing me perfectly! Verse 20: Now if I do what I do not want to do, it is no longer I who does it but it is sin living in me that does it.

O.K., God, I don't really get it. If You're living in me, how can sin be living in me?

*Still silent, I must've really made Him mad this time. Great! He finally starts talking to me and now I made Him so mad He already quit. Loser! Loser! Loser!*

## Inside My Head

Verse 21: So, I find this law at work: when I want to do good, evil is right there with me. For in my inner being I delight in God's law; but I see another law at work in the members of my body, waging war against the law of my mind and making me a prisoner of the law of sin at work in my members. What a wretched man I am. Me and you both Paul! Me and you both.

Who will rescue me from this body of death?...And fat, and stupidity, and hate, and anger, and loneliness, and fear... Verse 25 Thanks be to God –through Jesus Christ, our Lord! So then, I myself in my mind a slave to God's law, but in the sinful nature a slave to the law of sin.

*God, I'm sorry. I didn't mean to make You mad. I do get this. I feel like a prisoner in my mind. I'm trapped with no way out. I don't like me and know others don't really like me either. How could they? I don't like them. I know you don't really like me either. How can You? I am not good at all. I know some people think I am but I know I am not. And You know my thoughts. You must hate me.*

Tears in my eyes, I can't think I close my eyes and begin to drift into sleep.

# Chapter Twenty

Beep, beep, beep...smack!

Beep, beep, beep...smack! "Oh, I hate that thing! No condemnation, hmm. Jade time to get up." I knock on her door on my way to the bathroom. *No condemnation, none, nada, zilch, none. How is that possible, Lord? Sin calls for death. Jesus died because of sin. If sin lives in me how is there 'no condemnation'? I don't get it.*

"Porter! Porter! Get up! Get ready for school." I head back to my room and hear Jade getting ready.

Jeans, t-shirt, pony tail, work boots, my uniform. Dog out, pop tarts down, lunches made, this day starts like every other. At work I slip out of reality and the music takes over my thoughts. First break comes and goes as I hide out in the bathroom. My mood does not improve.

Lunch and the promise of a warmed up frozen pizza from the food truck doesn't offer much pleasure. Seeing Calvin in his tight jeans doesn't either. Pleasure is hard to come by when one realizes how truly loathsome they are. Everyone else must know to stay back since I find myself sitting alone. It's been a long time since I sat alone at lunch. Now, I made God mad. I realize I am a slave to sin and everyone stays away. The day can't get worse. Last break brings a glimpse of sun. "Whatcha doin this weekend?" Sheila asks as if today is the same as every other.

"Well, I know she will be at church with Mia and I on Sunday." Ron pipes up and looks over as if he's reminding me.

"O.K." Sheila says as she looks at him and then back at me. "What about the rest of the weekend?"

"I don't know." I gloomily offer.

"Joe and I and Chuck and Patty are going to a corn maze, you wanna come and bring Porter and Jade? It should be a lot of fun."

"When?"

"Tonight, we're going to get something quick to eat on the way right after work. It's about 15 miles south of here but it's supposed to be funner as the sun sets."

"Well..." I can't think of a good excuse quick enough so I agree. We make arrangements as the break ends.

On the way home even my mind is quieted. Jade is excited about the maze but I had forgotten that Porter had practice and can't go. *What kind of a mom forgets about practice? I know the kids schedules they are routine! I needed an excuse and that would've been perfect. Of course, I never go to practice, or games for that matter, but still... What a sorry excuse for a mother.*

We meet at the maze. I've barely spoken but Jade hadn't paid attention since she loves to listen to music and do homework while we drive. I can't shake this depressed feeling.

*Slave to sin. Slaves are bound they are owned by their master; mine being sinful thoughts. How can I claim to be a Christian and be owned by sin?* My attention remains fixed on my dilemma as we enter the maze. Then my eye caught a sign.

# Inside My Head

<u>Anyone breaking stalks or making their own "doors" through the maze will be prosecuted for destruction of private property. The fine is up to $500 per "door".</u>

The beginning seems harmless enough but the narrow path becomes crowded as we near the next group. They are lost. The sun is going down and the moon is not yet offering its light. Children are crying and teens are laughing and making obscene comments. Part way through I trip and tear a "door" in the maze.

"Oh, no! Mom, are you O.K.?" Jade asks as she helps me up.

"Yes," I murmur as I look around at the teens behind us laughing, "just embarrassed."

*What am I going to do? I can't afford a fine. I can't deny it or not tell the farmer because that would not look good to Sheila and her family. Here I am a Christian and contemplating lying. This is no good. I am so clumsy. I always have been. It's like I was born that way. I hate that about me, I always have.*

A small boy runs up behind me with parents close behind threatening him if he doesn't stop. I turn just in time for him to slam into my knees. Down I go again, my back crushing several more stalks. We're close enough now that the worker at the end hears the commotion and heads our direction.

*Great! Now I can't lie even if I wanted to, there's no way out. I seem to attract trouble. I was born clumsy and I'll die the same way. I thought one day I'd grow out of it...but NO!*

"Who broke the corn stalks?" The voice is obviously closing in us and I'm not even up yet. *The day did get worse! Oh my gosh!*

"Bobby!" Sheila shouts.

"She-dog!" He responds with a hug. Joe watches silently. Chuck and patty walk away openly embarrassed by the entire situation.

"Oh, my gosh, Bobby it's been forever!"

"Please tell me it wasn't you that broke the stalks," he pleaded.

"No, not me personally, but my friend here was tackled by a wild toddler and went down. It was an accident." She defended. While those two catch up Joe and Jade help me limp back to the van.

"You sure you can drive?" Joe asks kindly.

"Yeah it's my back and my pride more than anything. And my lifelong clumsy curse has afforded me much more pain in the past, but thanks." He waves as we take off.

"Are you sure you're O.K., Mom?"

"Yes, Jade, I'll be fine. Thanks."

"I guess it's all in who you know, huh?" Jade states like I have any idea what she is referring to.

"Hmm?"

"Well, you are clumsy, and have been forever. It's like it's your nature to fall. Sorry, but you know it's true. Anyway, those falls would've made you a criminal and according to the sign I read on the way in, if condemned in court you could've gotten a fine for up to $1000. But, because you know Sheila and she knows Bobby you are cleared! No condemnation at all."

## Inside My Head

*No condemnation for my nature. I don't want to be clumsy but I am. That clumsiness could've cost a high price but Sheila got me out with one look.*

Before bed I reread Romans 8 "Therefore, there is now no condemnation for those who are in Christ Jesus, because the law of the Spirit of life set me free from the law of sin and death. For what the law was powerless to do in that it was weakened by the sinful nature, God did by sending His own Son in the likeness of sinful man to be a sin offering. And so He condemned sin in sinful man in order that the righteous requirements of the law might be fully met in us, who do not live according to the sinful nature but according to the Spirit.

O.K., that is a bit much, I need to break it down. No condemnation for me, because I am in Christ or He is in me, and His Spirit set me free." I reiterate slowly.

For what the law was powerless to do in that it was weakened by the sinful nature... The law meaning, everything in Deuteronomy and Leviticus, the law of perfection God demanded, and we as humans are incapable of because of our sinful nature.

So, like the impossibility of me not tripping over my own two feet, since my very nature is to be clumsy. Even if the fine was high for holes in the maze I couldn't stop myself... that makes sense! So, God did by sending His own Son in the likeness of sinful man to be a sin offering...

O.K., so, God met the law to the 'T' through the only one who could...His own Son. He condemned the law not the man and therefore set up the new order of things. Righteousness can be obtained through His Son. If, we are in Him and He is in us, then we technically meet the requirements. So... it's not the letter of the law but the

Spirit of the law. Jesus sees us fall through the maze in our clumsiness so-to-speak and says 'yeah, I knew that would happen, so if you depend on me I'll take care of it.

He offers His hand, I get up and apologize for the gaping hole and then put one foot in front of the other, doing my best not to trip and fall again. He steadies me for a second and then I'm off. He fixes the hole and catches up. If I stumble but reach out He stops me from falling and I keep going. Eventually I'll make it to the end and He will be right there.

I get it!!! Thanks, God. Not that clumsy is a sin by any means, it's just that that's part of who I am and I try not to be that way but at times I am anyway. You steady me; You put me in the right direction again, Oh, God!!! There is so much I understand when it's simplified. Thank you, You are not mad at me, You're "fixing holes" and steadying me. You're setting things right and teaching me how to be more careful. I get it! Thank you, thank you, thank you. I love you!"

*I can sleep now. It's 11:30, I get to sleep in.*

## CHAPTER TWENTY-ONE

This entire day went by so fast and I got nothing done. Porter had his game so I spent the morning cleaning house while Jade studied. Here it is 10:30 and I don't even know what I did. Some laundry… I vacuumed…I did cook a good dinner, and the kitchen is clean. Jade walked Duke; I don't know it's not that much. I hate days when I feel like it was just wasted. I can't justify anything I did. I get one day off and I become so lazy. This house should be spotless. I didn't go to Porter's game again, I keep saying I will get to one. What if he doesn't even play? What if he sits on the bench…well, I was told that he's doing pretty good but I still hate football. I got up late and I'm still tired. I did nothing.

"Mom?" Porter calls in from my door.

"Yes, Porter."

"Can I come in?"

"Sure, Honey, sit here on my bed."

He climbs up and we snuggle for a beautiful moment. "It's been so long since we did this. Remember when you and Jade were little and we'd have movie night in Mom's room?"

"Yeah. We'd get popcorn and pop and we'd take turns picking the movie." I catch a smile in the mirror on my dresser.

"I miss those days," I lament.

'Me too." We sit together for a few more minutes.

"Mom?"

## Inside My Head

"Mm Hmm.' I sit with my arms around him and my eyes closed, soaking in the moment.

"You promised you'd be at this game but you weren't. I looked for you and Jade to come, even late but you didn't. I really want you to watch me play. We won again and you didn't even ask how we did. Will you go to my game next week?"

"I'm so sorry. I never liked football and it doesn't dawn on me that it would be important to you to have me there when I don't get the game. I am sorry. I am so, so sorry. Yes, I will come for sure. I look forward to it. I'm so sorry that I still have never seen you play a game."

"I want you there. I don't have anyone there. All the other boys have someone. I feel very alone there. I like the game a lot and have done very good this year. I hoped that if I got better you would go. Is that why you don't go?"

"I don't know." I don't want to lie. "I was thinking about that a little bit ago. I'm sorry, Honey. I never wanted you to feel alone. I will go next week. Oh! Talk about going next week, I almost forgot, I promised Ron at work we'd go to his church tomorrow."

"Which church is that?"

"Zion Temple."

"Really?" Porter sits up and turns toward me wide-eyed.

"Yes, and it doesn't start till 11:30 but we need to get there a little early. His wife wants to introduce me to some friends that might start coming to the Bible study."

"Cool! Remember I wanted to go there?"

"Yes, I told Ron that too. I don't know how I forgot to tell you."

"Oh, my gosh! This is so cool. I'm so happy. Thanks, Mom." Porter, obviously satisfied with the finality of the tender moment races out of my room.

"Porter!" I call after him, "tell Jade please, and I love you, good night." I take the last word.

*What am I going to wear? I almost forgot all together. That's what I should've done today. Well, after going to my only son's game. I should've figured out what to wear, and how to do my hair. Oh, crap! Kevin will be there. Now I'm really nervous. I need sleep. That blue flowered dress... I hate that one. I wonder if I could wear pants... probably not a good idea since I'm being introduced to people and I don't know how they feel about pants at church. That brown skirt? Maybe a skirt is best. I have several skirts. Oh, I need to shave! Longer shower, it doesn't start till 11:30. I want my hair nice. Leave by 11:00, so up by 8:00 at the latest. I need sleep.*

..........

*Good thing I asked Jade to do my hair. I wanted to look nice and looking at this place I know there are far too many women who know how to look nice, and I am going to be meeting some. And Kevin, it will be a whole different look from the usual pony tail. Hopefully...*

*Oh, my gosh this place is huge! I'm glad the kids know people here, it could seem overwhelming. The designer did such a good job on the alcoves and stained glass with the sun shining through perfectly; the effect is magnificent. I wonder where Ron and Mia are. Eleven twenty, the place is packed. I don't know anyone and only the designated greeter at the door has said hello. I like my church – small and very friendly.*

*Maybe I'll get some coffee or something.*

# Inside My Head

"Hi, how much is a cappuccino?" I ask as I look over the menu above the young woman's head. *I guess if you have to ask you can't afford it but I would still like to know ahead of time.*

"Everything is done by donation. There is a donation box by the door so that no one knows how much or if you give at all. We just want you to enjoy your experience here." She replies in a kind voice with a smile that would light up any room.

"Oh, very nice. Umm I guess I will have a double mocha cappuccino then." She smiles again and gets right to the order. *She must be all of 22, no ring. I wonder if she goes to college I'm surprised she goes to church the way the world is today. She does seem extraordinarily kind though. I wonder if she is like that outside of these doors.*

"Have you been coming here long?" I make small talk.

"Well, I'm attending college here so I took the summer off to return home, but this is my second year here. I love it."

*College, I knew it!*

"Do you attend church back home?"

"Yes, I was raised in a much smaller church in Mount Prospect, Illinois." She explains as she hands me a cup.

"Thank you, it looks wonderful."

"No problem, enjoy; I hope I'll see you again."

*There were probably 25 to 30 people behind me, yet she took her time and was very pleasant. Come to think of it, so were all the people in line. That's a change of pace. Starbucks and Biggby are a nightmare. Get that many in line and there are bound to be angry voices heard.*

"There you are." Ron says as I enter the foyer again. "I see you found the coffee shop."

"As long as it's mocha I love it. Hi, Mia," I offer my hand but she hugs me.

"Oh, I'm so glad you're here! Can I introduce you to friends now?"

"Sure." I take another cautious sip.

"Tammy, Sierra, Franny, and Juls this is Connie, the Bible study woman I was telling you about."

"Hi." They say simultaneously and offer free hands and smiles.

"Hi." *Tammy, tall, dark hair fair skin. Sierra, young, black, pretty. Franny, maybe Francis, younger than her name, brown hair, crooked teeth. Juls, short for? Beautiful blonde hair and blue eyes. I'm not too good with names but this always helps. Picture the name.*

Church begins with loud music and everybody quickly finds seats. The lights and the band are reminiscent of a concert I'd normally have to pay for. Everyone seems to get into to the music. Then the pastor comes up to the stage.

*He's wearing jeans and a sweater. Even if you're just doing announcements you should dress appropriately to be on the platform on Sunday morning. Come to think of it, the worship team wasn't dressed well either. I guess that's part of the laid-back atmosphere.*

# Inside My Head

"I'm Kane for any of you visiting for the first time today; I am the pastor of this great place to worship. My wife Nichole and I will be in the foyer after church and we would like to meet each of you. Please stop by and say hello. There are pamphlets that tell about the church, what we believe and teach here, along with flyers from all the small groups around the city. We encourage you to check one of those out so that you can get to know each other and spend time getting to know God on a personal level.

O.K., it's time to give an offering of thanksgiving. Then we'll have a short drama before I return.

God, thank you. Thank You for the freedom to speak Your Name. Thank You for the joy You give that strengthens us. Thank You for peace in every situation. Thank You for jobs to pay bills. Thank You for wisdom in every area of life, and thank You for the opportunity to live forever with You. Amen."

The band starts up again and people stand and walk up front leaving orderly and dropping money and envelopes into larger wicker baskets before returning to their seats in the same single file manner.

*I definitely prefer this way of taking an offering. No begging or badgering and everyone acts eager to give. Hmm. Oh! There's Kevin! He looks amazing in real clothes. I didn't even pay attention earlier. Very Fall-like in that gold shirt and brown slacks. I'd love for him to be my treasure, all that gold. And a Christian, wow! I wonder how good a Christian he could be if he goes here, I've heard a lot about this church and how it's only to get attention and not really about God. It's one of those seeker churches. I wonder what all that really means. I mean, everything seems legit, but there are no pews and no Bibles, they have a full coffee bar and a huge band. Pastor Kane did say to get to know God or something like that at a small group. I wonder if Kevin goes to a small group.*

## Inside My Head

The actors enter and are dressed in filthy rags. They are bruised and their hair is knotted, they just lay there talking. Two of them direct the conversation, telling the others about God. Even though they are miked I can tell their voices are hushed.

The other four begin to sit up a bit and pay attention. Before long the jailor comes in screaming and proceeds to beat those two. He orders two other men to drag their bodies across the room and the three verbally humiliate them as they go. They are forced to watch the others eat large bowls of gruel while they get only water.

There is pity on the faces of the four other men. All dishes are taken with the jailor and his minions. They talk again in hushed voices, the four refusing to believe that life with God is better.

"We are healthy," one of the two states; "We are filthy and beaten as are you. We have gotten only water for three weeks yet we remain healthy. Our God is protecting us so that He can reach you four. He loves you that much. Each of you has sickness. Vomiting, diarrhea, fever and chills, you can't' sleep. Tell me what is better."

Pastor Kane reenters as they leave the stage. "If it became illegal tomorrow to speak God's name in public would there be any reason to believe that you would be arrested? Let's pray. God, you are magnificent. You are worthy of praise. Speak to our hearts today. Teach us, God, how vital our actions are in keeping our freedoms."

"In this scene from the Bible, Paul and Silas were thrown in jail for preaching the new philosophy of Jesus. They were beaten repeatedly. They were freed and re-arrested multiple times. Once in the book of Acts it talks about how at midnight the jail was quiet except for the worship of Paul and Silas. They sang praises to God for all to hear. They didn't hide their faith in Jesus; they put it all out there.

"They praised Him even in chains. That prison was not like the ones here in the States today where you get three squares and medical attention. They were beaten with whips and chained to a wall.

"The story goes on to explain that the praise made God so happy that He decided to set them free, not just them, but everyone around them. All chains broke and all prisoners listened. They stayed to hear about this God that could give anyone a reason to sing in prison. The chains were broken and the doors opened and everyone stayed and listened and learned.

"Now, letting prisoners escape was a death sentence for the jailor. He felt the quake and ran to the prison which was more like a dungeon, and pulled out his sword and prepared to kill himself. Paul yelled out 'Wait! We are all here!' The jailor listened. He put down his sword and listened to these men about their God who would allow them to go free and yet compel them to stay just for him. He brought the two of them to his home and he and his family along with everyone in the prison were saved that night. You can read this in Acts 16.

"Does your life show others that there is always reason for praise? Is anyone listening or are they mocking? We need to live lives that make people sit up and take notice; ask questions and really listen for the answers we have.

"If there were a warrant issued to search your home would there be enough evidence to convict you? Would there even be a reason to issue a warrant?

"God, speak to us this week. Show us areas that need change. Give insight to small group leaders as people come and ask the tough questions. Help us to sit up and listen to You this week. Now, God, go with us as we leave. Protect us and keep us safe, amen."

The music starts again and people everywhere get up and rush out.

*No altar call? No 'let's pray for you?' I don't get that.*

Ron and Mia hold on to each other and to me so that we don't get separated.

"Good service." I yell in Mia's direction above the music, she nods. "Do you go to a small group?" I yell out over the noise again. She nods again while pulling me to the corner of the foyer where we stop briefly and she begins the introductions with her sister-in-law, Connie.

*Ronnie and Connie, twins hmm.*

"Yeah, that's why I think we have such a connection at work." Ron says, "She's my twin."

"Good to meet you," I say with a smile.

"You too," she quickly states before rushing off.

"She doesn't usually come," Mia starts, "She doesn't believe."

"In church?"

"In God." She replies matter-of-factly.

"Oh, of course." *You idiot, that would make more sense.*

"Nichole! This is Connie, the woman I've been telling you about. Connie this is Nichole, Kane's wife."

"Hello," I nod as she takes my hand.

"I am so grateful for your small group; several ladies have come to me raving about the meetings. Although it's quickly becoming more than just a small group I hear. There would obviously be plenty of reason to put out a warrant for your arrest, huh?"

"I hope so," I stammer. *Several from here? I didn't know that.*

"I'd issue it myself!" she laughs. "Kane, Honey, this is Connie." She turns to her husband and back to me.

"Hello," I nod, "please call me Constance." *What the heck? Why did I say that?*

"Constance, constant and faithful, great name and describes you perfectly from my understanding. Thank you for taking the time to do the small group, and for allowing our ladies to join you. We as a body need to unite. United we stand, divided we fall, huh?"

"Right."

"Good to meet you, finally, Constance. I hope to see a lot more of you. Not trying to take you from your home church, just if there is anything we can do to help your efforts to allow women to sit up and listen to the Word you let us know, O.K.?"

"O.K."

"She may need our sanctuary soon if it keeps growing." Mia smiles, as we shake and search for my kids.

Jade is in the far corner holding on to Porter like a teddy bear and searching the room for me. I wave as we get closer.

"We are going to dinner if you want to come." Ron offers.

"Oh, sorry we have to get home, but maybe another time. I'd really love to get together with the two of you." We all hug and part ways.

*The pastor and his wife talk about me? She would put out the warrant herself? Wow! I can't believe it. They have the biggest church in the county and I think maybe even the state, I don't know the whole state. He knew the meaning of my name. And why did I tell him anyway? He said it exactly like God did. They want to see more of me? Oh, my gosh, I had no idea. I'm not even very good at what I do. I don't even know how it's gotten so big.*

**Constance, My faithful one, I spoke these words to Isaiah, '...your righteousness will go before you and My glory will be your rear guard.' You are experiencing that now. Read all of Isaiah 58 when you get home. You are finding your joy in me and I will cause you to ride on the heights of the land and feast on the inheritance of your father Jacob. I am so pleased with you.**

God, a tear runs down my cheek, *I am not worthy of Your love. I'd be like the men eating food and not wanting to be happy with water. I don't get Your love for me at all.*

**Constance, my dear, I desire obedience above sacrifice. You were obedient to start this Bible study and you see how many have been touched by Me. By your obedience you have even begun to change. You have opened yourself up to Me so that you can learn from Me. Grace is my unmerited favor and My grace is plenteous for you daily, not only on the days you feel like you've earned it. It is more about Me than you. It has never been about keeping the rules, it's always been about being willing to. It was impossible to keep all the rules, even though they are there**

to keep you from getting hurt, they are also there to show my mercy.

*If you are obedient I will make the changes in you that are necessary for you to continue to obey and therefore be blessed with peace, joy with abundant life. I sent my Son, the ONLY one worthy to be THE sacrifice so that by accepting that sacrifice you could live abundantly. No one can truly live an abundant life without the peace that comes from resting in my Son's sacrifice on the cross. He was obedient unto death.*

*All I asked for you to do was to start this Bible study. You were obedient. Through that one simple act I have reached many people that you do not even know about. I am pleased with you. See, it's not up to you or anyone else to clean the person up spiritually, that's my job and I am good at my job. I love my job. It is actually for you to bring them to me and let me do the rest. You need just to love them right where they are; like I do.*

*When I sent Jesus to Earth I didn't tell Him to condemn anyone, just save them. He watched Me and saw that My desire is to completely heal people from the inside out and to transform their lives. That brings Me overwhelming joy. Laying down your life, dreams, goals etcetera as a sacrifice allows Me to use you and transform you into the absolute best you, you can be. Then as you reach those goals, and achieve those longtime dreams you enjoy them all the more. I have put desires in your heart and I long for them to be fulfilled, however, without Me there will always still be something missing. That little something that people can't quite understand. That is why people strive for more; they are looking to fill that place I reserved in every person for Me. Once you are obedient to My call I replace brokenness with wholeness and insecurity with security, fear with rest. I love unconditionally and long to be one with each of My children and so many don't even know I am their father.*

*Constance, pray that others will turn their hearts back to me, their Father. I will prove Myself to them as The Father; the One that will never leave them alone or turn My back on them. I will provide for them and be gracious to them, forgiving them and casting all of their sins as far as the east is from the west, never allowing them to be counted against them. I love all of My creation and it is my desire that none should ever have to die without me.*

*I watched as My Son was beaten and right up until I couldn't take the pain anymore and I turned My head in great sadness. He is the only one that has or will ever experience My turned head. I cried that day. People there said it rained, but it was My tears. The pain was excruciating. I do understand the pain people go through. When Lucifer rose up out of his arrogance I was so hurt. I had allowed him into My inner circle. He was the head of the music that surrounds me constantly. He was close to My heart and he betrayed Me. He continues to attack My creation and hurt them. I don't want anyone to be trapped in eternity with him. I made a way for everyone to be with Me. It's so simple and yet people fight against its simplicity.*

*Accept that I Am God and that My Son has already paid every price necessary through His sacrifice on the cross. As a reward for His sacrifice I gave Him the throne at My right hand and He intercedes for you all day and night.*

*When He was on the cross I allowed Him to look out across time and see all those who would live and choose to believe; that was His joy. That is why He didn't call angels to rescue Him that terrible day. That moment of anguish was worth the reward.*

# Inside My Head

*He loves you, Constance, as do I.*

# CHAPTER TWENTY-TWO

"This is the night that Martina will be sharing her testimony with us. I do want to let everyone know that next week is the scheduled end of this six week study." Mouths open and there is a hushed murmur throughout the room.

"It has been suggested that it continue and I am open to that idea as long as that is what God wants. I wanted to see how all of you felt about the idea since you basically signed on to do a study of the Proverbs 31 woman and we are going to complete that next week. So, if you would like to continue would you mind raising your hand?" Immediately every hand in the room shoots up. "O.K., I guess the entirety rules and we will continue as long as it is O.K. and Pastor Roberts agrees to let us use the sanctuary.

"I am not sure exactly what we will be teaching on, however, we will continue to give the opportunity for women to give testimonies each week. We will continue to defeat the devil like it says in Revelation 12:11.

"O.K. then, Martina if you are ready we will hear from you after prayer." She nods. "Would anyone like to open with prayer?" Mia raises her hand cautiously. "Great, Mia, thank you."

"Dear Jesus, thank you for keeping us safe this week and bringing us all together. Please help Martina and Connie as they bring forth your Word tonight, amen."

Martina walks up to the podium and takes the microphone.

## Inside My Head

"I was born and raised in California. I went to private schools and took tennis lessons from the finest trainers. I practically lived at the beach. My friends and I partied all the time. I was only 13 when Vietnam began. The draft took my brother and my boyfriend, who was obviously a great deal older than me.

"It was 1973 and I found myself with child, an embarrassment for my wealthy family. My parents sent me to live in New Mexico with my mother's sister. I had never gone to church before, but my Aunt Martina, my namesake, took me in and showed me an entirely different life.

"I went to church Sunday morning and evening as well as Wednesday evening. Everyone noticed the weight gain, of course and I became the talk of the town. It got so bad that Aunt Martina left the church. We stayed home and read her Bible and prayed. She was a saint. Her love for God did not diminish. She taught me well.

"The baby was put up for adoption and my story was well rehearsed before returning home so that I would not embarrass my family. I told everyone that I had spent the year in Spain with my father's cousin. My parents had even travelled to Spain in my absence to make it all more believable. Gifts were brought back for my friends and postcards were put in a box and sent to me to mail to my friends, they had gotten Spanish postmarks and everything. It was an elaborate scheme which worked very well.

"I never forgot the kindness of my aunt. Each year on the anniversary of my baby's birth I wondered about her wellbeing.

"Once home again, I picked up where I had left off. My boyfriend never made it home. I was very much a part of the free-love movement, until I turned 22." A smile softened her face.

"My Aunt Martina called and asked if I were willing to visit for a month. I wasn't sure that the boredom would be welcome; however, due to my feelings of obligation, I went. She was in her mid-forties and had very little. I pitied her. She had not returned to the same church. In fact, she now volunteered on a Native-American reservation.

"Her kindness and generosity to those very impoverished people was heartwarming. I stayed only a short while. I was longing to return to my life of parties on the beach and the latest drug along with a never ending supply of alcohol.

"I saw many of my friends losing jobs and social standing due to their addictions. I became an expert at hiding mine. I lived a double life, the princess and the pauper in the same body. My father overlooked the obvious signs, however my mother would not.

"Once again she contacted my Aunt Martina. It had been five blurry years. Aunt Martina welcomed me back, anticipating assistance on the reservation. I made contact with a dealer there. I was only given a small amount of money to provide my keep so as not to burden my poor aunt. That was gone within the first month and I turned to the beds of those willing to keep me high."

Everyone in the room is blown away, by her nearly impossible to believe past and her transparency. Mouths haven't closed since she revealed her pregnancy at 13.

"My aunt was very naïve and was clueless to my lifestyle. It was only six months after arriving that I found out that I was again pregnant. I expected it would be easy to abort this one as easily as I had the three or four since my daughter's birth. But, I had been so drugged that by the time I realized what was going on I was already 20 weeks and I couldn't find anyone who would do it. I didn't know what to do.

"Aunt Martina took me to her pastor and the three of us talked. I knew I needed to be free of my addictions but I was so trapped. I didn't have the slightest idea who the father was. I had embarrassed and hurt my aunt so deeply. When she found out that she had taken me daily to the reservoir of wickedness she was crushed. She believed she was introducing me to the fountain of life.

"Seeing her broken spirit crushed me. I had believed I was past feeling anything. We contacted my parents and they paid for a private rehab. Careful attention was taken for the sake of the baby. I got clean slowly as to not harm either of us. And while in rehab my son was born early. He was addicted to cocaine. He had several birth defects and died after only two weeks. I was at the point of suicide as I was now clean and realizing all that I had done."

Eyes are filled with tears and jaws are still wide open. Never in a million years would any of us have seen this potential in Martina.

*Ms. Prim and Proper a druggie? Oh my gosh!*

She begins again, "One night, while lying in the room my aunt had so lovingly set aside for me fourteen years earlier, I was contemplating the best way to end my life. I decided on the how and the note of explanation. The where had been narrowed to only three possibilities, and the when was my final concern. It was late but sleep eluded me. Death was so final, but life had become impossible in my mind. I had put to death three or four babies and caused the death of yet another child. A boy; a boy that I had held and named. His little face and painful cries haunted my every waking moment. The pain and embarrassment I had caused my aunt and the embarrassment to my parents, who had now decided that it was too much to bear and disowned me, it was more than I could take.

"I heard voices coming from the front room and rose to spy on my aunt and her guest.

"I am afraid for her." My aunt spoke with a sadness to her voice.

"I understand, but God has a plan for her life. He has protected her up until now. He won't ever leave her or forsake her," came the deep male voice.

"She had me so fooled! I believed that God had begun a work in her. She was so willing to go and help every day. I took her directly into the snare of the fowler daily." At this, Aunt Martina began sobbing. I wondered how many conversations like this had preceded this one while I was gone. I headed back to bed determining that as soon as I could get the place set I would stop hurting everyone forever.

Suddenly the man spoke with such confidence I stood still and listened.

"Martina, you know I have loved her for so long. I know that God is working in her. Remember His promise. He alone is the author and finisher of our faith. What we cannot force, He will woo to perfection.

"His proclamation of love for me was beyond my comprehension. I didn't even know who was speaking, yet he said he'd loved me for a long time. I snuck back into the space I'd been hiding in order to see my admirer. I was shocked to see her volunteer assistant, Michael. He was attractive and kind; far kinder than I had ever personally experienced. In the light he looked soft and gentle. I would not normally have been attracted to his sun-leathered features, but that night everything inside me melted as I peeked into that tiny room and for the first time saw what true love looked like.

"Since I was twelve the only 'I love yous' I heard were precursors to sex. This man had never even alluded to sex. I will never forget how those words changed me. I returned to my room and lay awake all night, now contemplating my future. Everything had changed in that moment.

"I volunteered beside my Aunt Martina for the next three months. Both she and Michael expressed their pleasure in my new attitude. I listened with delight at the Bible lessons and watched as they helped everyone who requested it.

"Finally, I returned home, begging for my parents' forgiveness. I explained to them in the best way I could about the new way I saw life. I explained to them about the volunteer program and Michael. I asked my mother to retrain me on being a lady. I worked hard. I wanted to be the trophy wife that he deserved. I had no understanding of any other way to be a wife. I became proper and well-mannered. I was once again an upper-class lady. I walk, talk, eat, and act like a lady should.

"When I returned to New Mexico, Michael had moved to Ohio. I volunteered next to my aunt for a year. When Michael came for a visit I was so excited. He stayed for a month rather than the original week he had planned. Before he left we married on the reservation. I had accepted Christ into my heart only a few weeks before his return.

"My parents accepted Christ after our wedding as Michael explained his faith and my new self to them. They returned home as a new couple. Our wedding gift was the purchase of our home. Michael had moved here and accepted a position at the medical college. He is a doctor for those that don't know.

"God blessed us with Gabriel a year after our marriage. The greatest miracle I could have ever hoped for. I love him so much.

"Anyway, I have lived for the past seven years as a trophy wife on my doctor/professor's arm. I have planned elaborate parties and benefits. We have provided help to the reservation that Aunt Martina still volunteers at as well. I have lived the life, but it wasn't truly fulfilling.

"Five weeks ago I came to this Bible study at the urging of my husband. Previously I had only mingled with wealthy empty women. Women who had also mastered the fineries expected of a well-bred lady. I learned that night for the first time that I am not his trophy, but his crown! I am as valuable as rubies, which are very rare and expensive! Me, Martina Guadalupe Eaglefeather, am the symbol of my husband's royalty. When others see me I represent his authority and power. I am not just a pretty thing on his arm. I am a physical representation of his position in society. I am a point of pride for him. A glorious semblance of his spiritual inheritance!

"That completely blows my mind! I know who I am and what I've done! That was not always how I saw myself. I never could get past my unworthiness to be anything other than a beautiful trophy. Michael deserves so much better. I have tried for seven years to be what he deserves knowing deep inside I can never be that. I held my breath waiting for the day when he would come to me and say that I am growing old and unattractive and he deserves better, or that my past would blow up in my face and cause him great embarrassment. But, I now see that God says, 'Martina, you are a virtuous woman. Your past is forgiven and you are no longer a trophy to be shown off and set aside. You are THE crown I have placed on Michael's head.'"

Martina finished with soft tears rolling down her cheeks and entering the corners of her smiling lips by saying, "For that, Connie, I am forever grateful for this class and you." She then made her way back to her seat in complete silence.

*God, you never cease to amaze me. Martina, a true fake!*

**Not a true fake; a true lady. One who had never been able to grasp what love really is all about.**

She stops at my seat and hugs me and whispers that she loves me into my ear.

*Wow! I made a difference in her life! I never knew that. That was the night I didn't do much at all. Oh, God, I don't know how I did that. I don't even remember exactly what I said. I barely studied. I just sort of said whatever came out. How in the world did I make that much of a difference?*

**I used the Holy Spirit to speak to Martina through you. I know exactly what needs to be said or done to enlighten my children. I will use whomever I choose to work through.**

"Martina, I am so pleased with your testimony of change, but it was most definitely not me speaking. I opened my mouth and the Holy Spirit spoke."

"I want to be used as you are used. You are so godly. I can't begin to see me as good as you. That you are so filled with the Spirit of God that you just open your mouth and He pours out of you."

"No, no!" I shake my head. She's not getting it. "No, I wasn't saying that I'm good at all. He knew that I wouldn't be able to say anything of importance. I was wicked to the very core of my being. My life was a sham, I was living a lie. I went to church and played by the rules, but I was filthy inside. I am ashamed.

"Like a couple of weeks ago when I told Maraschino about my jealousy and hate, I was filled with those horrible hateful feelings. I was a hypocrite in every way. I didn't see it then. As long as I didn't let the filth escape my mouth I reasoned that it was O.K. to hate, condemn, and think horrible things about people." *I am so embarrassed and I can't stop myself. God, are You making me do this?*

**"I don't force anyone to do anything, I am a gentleman. But you wanted a cleansed heart. This is how it begins."**

*Begins?*

"I was jealous of everyone. I hated myself and couldn't find a way to get past that. I thought death thoughts over myself and everyone around me. "

*God?*

"This study has brought me to a new place in my life as well; the translucence of each woman's heart. God has used each of you to pour into me. I will never be the same. I love you all. I could never have honestly spoken those words before. If I said it I knew I was lying. Every breath held a lie. I was a rotting corpse inside my whitewashed tomb."

*God! Stop me!*

"The testimonies have expressed more love and life-changing power than I had ever believed real before. Yes, I went to church for about eleven years without truly living. I lived according to a set of rules that I hated. I complained, whined, and even yelled at God for making me miserable. I wanted to be thin and beautiful. I wanted to live on the wild side. I didn't like God and His rules but, I was afraid of Hell. I criticized everyone for everything. I couldn't imagine anyone really liking church."

*God!!! Please help me here! I'm embarrassing myself! I can't stop! I don't even know what I'm saying, but I know it's not good.*

"I only started the Bible study so that everyone would say nice things about me. I just knew it would all be just as fake as my nice things I'd say but, I needed to feel like someone liked me."

*What?! I did not just say that out loud! God! Stop me!*

**You want a fresh start and a clean heart. Confession is good for the soul. My Word has plenty to say on that subject.**

"Over the last several weeks God has been really speaking to me. He is using me and I am so thankful. I don't deserve any kindness from Him or any of you." That's it. I am broken, like the stone Moses hit. Suddenly the water flooded out. My stone heart is gushing limitlessly.

## Inside My Head

*I can't believe this! I'm crying again! That's all I do every week! I hate this.*

**These are tears filled with living water. They are cleansing and healing your heart. Transforming the hardened clay into the soft moldable clay I can use.**

*Thanks, God, but couldn't we do this privately?*

**No, others here need to be cleansed as well. Your words and tears are cleansing them also.**

I look around and some are crying just as hard as me, some are smiling with soft tears rolling down their cheeks, and others are stunned. Those are easily read; wide eyes and open mouths give them away. None is left untouched. Between Martina and me, every woman here has been given a great deal to absorb.

"Ladies, I am so glad that God has used this time to work in the hearts of us all. If any of you can identify with either of these ladies raise your hand." Maraschino graciously takes over. I look around at nearly every hand lifted. "There are many things that have been addressed here tonight that really need to be prayed about. Maybe you have never accepted God's most miraculous gift... His personal reconciliation with you. Because of sin we as humans have been separated from Him so He placed our death penalty on His own Son and Jesus willingly and obediently took our death sentence upon Himself. We don't have to live eternally with the consequence of being separated from Him, and His love. Instead, by simply accepting His most gracious gift of love we can live out eternity in His presence.

"Or, maybe you've gone to church your entire life without allowing Him to live through you. Following Jesus doesn't mean that you are now required to be bound by a long list of harsh rules; it is more a new freedom, one we don't fully understand at first. It is the freedom to live fully.

"It's like living your entire life in a city of industry with smoke and poison filling the air. People rush to and fro, too busy to get to know anyone and going home to a lonely efficiency apartment at the end of a tiring day...every day. One secluded day rolling into the next. People all around dying from stress and disease brought on by the chemically-dense air. It's the norm, but it's no good.

"One day you're given the opportunity to move to a ranch in the country, all food grown there organically. The air is fresh. There aren't even highways nearby to fill the air with exhaust. Life expectancy is 103. Everyone knows everyone else.

"Some choose to stay in the city because even though it is a lonely, stress-filled short life, it's what they know and they are comfortable.

"Some move to the ranch. The scarcity of convenience stores and gas stations is shocking at first, but eventually they realize it's not holding them back from life; it's actually more enjoyable. Families are drawn closer. Less sickness and hard work keep them into old age. Friendships are strengthened and it helps to know that neighbors keep an eye out for each other. The immediate response is that they are in your business; however, time reveals that they are helpful and encouraging. Soon it's more freeing than anything you've ever experienced.

"That's what salvation is like: the freedom of a ranch, the hard work and true relaxation, along with the clean fresh air and joy unequaled by the rush of the filthy city. Some express discomfort in not having the big city 'conveniences,' saying that those bring freedom. Others realize that saving money is easier when they aren't tempted by spur-of-the-moment purchases. They learn that discipline allows them more time to sit back on the front porch, swing and enjoy the sunset instead of rushing around all the time.

"It's up to you. Life is filled with choices. But this one choice determines your eternity. It's not a matter of repeating some mantra after me. It is a matter of the heart. I set before you today life or death. It is a choice only you can make.

"As I talk with God tonight, those of you who want to accept His gift just tell Him that. Express your desire to have Him change you like both Constance and Martina expressed tonight. He knows your heart and your thoughts. He knows everything. This isn't something you do for show. It is just between you and God.

"Let's talk to Him now. Daddy, God, You are amazing and I love you so much. Thank you for loving us in our unperfected state. Thank you for choosing to offer us a way out of the filth we've been living in. Thank you for freedom. God, You look at us with delight. Your Word says You dance over us. You hand-picked each of us to be the bride of Your Only Son. I am overwhelmed by Your grace. Just the realization that You would choose me out of billions in the world to experience this freedom I now know is incredible. You love us even in the filth. You offer us purity, something I've never known. You offer new beginnings. Your love is so hard to understand for those of us who never have been loved or have never loved ourselves.

"Some here tonight are hearing about Your love for the first time, I ask that You gently wrap Your arms around us tonight.

"Holy Spirit, You are welcome. Move through this place tonight resting on each one here and loving on them in Your sweet way.

"Jesus, I accept You as my betrothed. Fill me. Change me. Search me. Cleanse me. Create in me a softness that will learn to abide in You. Thank You for teaching me how to forgive myself and how to love myself. Work miraculously in the lives of all those here tonight that each of them can experience You in that way.

"I love You. Thank You, thank You, thank You. I worship You and Adore You. You are my everything. All glory and honor to You, my Lord. Adoration and praise I offer to You. I surrender again all that I am. I trust You and I delight in You. You are my joy." She concludes.

"I worship you, almighty God, there is none like you." I can hold back no longer, I must sing. I must worship. My voice is soft and weak, but my heart intent and bold before Him. Others join and the music is beautiful. "I worship you, oh Prince of Peace, that is what I long to do. I give you praise, for you are my righteousness. I worship you Almighty God, there is none like You." We join together and worship for a long time, repeating this one song over and over.

"Thank you, Martina and thank you Maraschino. Once again tonight God has used my friends in my healing process He is amazing.

"Ladies you're welcome to socialize as long as you'd like. If you made a decision tonight for the first time to walk in the freedom of God's love and acceptance, please tell someone. Exchange phone numbers so that when questions or problems arise you have someone to talk with."

*Socializing is amazing. There must be fifty women here! I don't understand how this is happening. Trula even came tonight; she doesn't attend anything. I know she said it's because if she attends one thing she has to attend everything. I always believed she was just a snob, now I don't know. I'm finally realizing that I don't know anything about anyone.*

**Well, that's a big step, Constance. Why don't you go over and talk to her?**

*There's a lot of people here to talk to, why her?* Silence… *God?* I roll my eyes as I think about the giant step I just took backwards. *Will I ever learn to just obey You, God?*

**Someday.**

The corners of my lips turn up slightly at God's patience as I make my way across the sanctuary to talk with my pastor's wife.

"Trula, I'm so glad you made it out tonight. What did you think?" *I really hope she liked it. She could put a good word in for us to keep going if she did. Smile Connie, at least look nice.*

"Connie, I've heard over and over about this small group study. The lives being changed are impacting our church and our community. I had to see for myself what's going on.

"I'm sorry to say, I didn't expect much. People often exaggerate about God moving. I've heard stories for years about excitement taking hold and it blows away quickly. True movements of God are rare; so rare in fact that I had given up ever seeing one firsthand." She lets out a breath.

"Oh, I know how horrible that sounds coming from the lips of a preacher's wife." She pauses and takes a deep breath again, dropping her eyes to the floor as they fill with tears. I don't respond. I just stand here dumbfounded, curling my lips between my teeth and my eyes wander the room.

"Connie, you spoke tonight straight from the heart. I wish I had the strength… I used to believe." She whispers through tears, and takes another deep breath before continuing so softly I have to lean in to hear. "I hate myself and I'm angry with God. There have been so many times I wished I could go to a bar on a Saturday night with my old college girl-friends. They begged for so long and now we don't even talk. There are days when I don't want to be a preacher's wife or a mother. I long for the 'good ol' days'" She sobs softly, face in hands, and shoulders shaking. I lean in to hug her; something just a few weeks ago I wouldn't have considered.

*God, what do I say? I can't believe she's telling me this.*

**Just listen.**

"You are the only one I've ever told this to. I'm so ashamed. I've never even told John. We've been struggling lately and it's all my fault. I've been torn between what's right and what I want."

*I can't believe no one has come over here. In fact, almost everyone is gone. Wow! I wonder what time it is. I peak down at her watch to see 10:27. Oh, my gosh! It's so late. I wander how long this will take. Oh my gosh, Connie, will you ever change? She is pouring out her heart to you and you're thinking about you.*

"Connie, will you pray for me? I don't want to be this way anymore." She is barely whispering.

"Of course, umm..." *What in the heck! I hate to pray out loud! I know I will sound so stupid. I just stammer and can't think of what to say quick enough to make it sound good. I know she wants me to do that now. God, don't' let me say something stupid in front of her, please!"*

"God, You said in Your Word that when two or three are gathered together in Your name You're there in their midst. So, first, I want to say thank You for being here. Now, God, You alone know the thickness of the muck and mire I have been living in for so long. You have been so patient as I have finally begun to change. I didn't even know how gross I was till You pointed it out.

"You have used the testimonies of several women to break me and soften the clay making me into something willing to change. I hated everyone around me. I even hated You for making me live by so many rules. I felt so trapped by church and religion. God my heart is so wild, as You well know. And I was jealous of the party girls, the pretty girls, and even the nice girls. God, I have been so wicked! I am so sorry! I love You. I don't hate You. I just want to feel love. The love of a man, or the love of a friend. I looked to the world to find the missing pieces in the puzzle of my life. Nothing ever filled it before and I still looked there.

"God, the pieces I need are shaped like You. Fill them in. Make me whole. Please, God, fill me up. Change me. Shine through me. I don't want to be like this anymore. Fix me God." I open my eyes and they burn with tears as I realize this was supposed to be a prayer for Trula. I quickly close them again and continue.

"And God, Trula longs to be whole as well. You said a thousand foul things will flee from me and together Trula and I will see ten thousand flee from our lives. Thank you, thank you. I pray that You will free us from the bondage of our minds. I pray God, that You will open our spiritual eyes to the reality of the freedom You want for us. Help us to view the world as You do. Lord, give us a new sense of what fun is and teach us how to accept and reciprocate love.

I pray that You will strengthen their marriage. Fill her up with desire for her husband. Awaken her to the crown that she is for her husband.

Give us the gift of not wanting the world, but wanting You instead. Help us not to see Christianity as being forced to live by a long list of difficult rules. I don't know what else to say, but bring us back to life inside. In Jesus' name, amen." I look up again and she is smiling.

*I did sound stupid. I knew it. She's laughing at me. Well, trying not to anyway. Nothing I do is right. I can't even pray right. Man! I hate praying out loud. Why did she ask me? Why didn't she just ask someone else?* I close my eyes and tears fill them again. *How embarrassing.* I let out a breath and turn to leave before embarrassing myself further.

"Connie," Trula catches my arm and I turn to her tear-coated smiling face. She seems softer somehow. "I can't begin to thank you. I can't believe how perfect that prayer was. You really do understand." Her eyes close and she sighs while more tears spill out from between her lashes causing more black to run down her face. "I thought I was the only one to feel this way. I haven't felt free in ages. I have felt trapped and angry. I had to hide it since I am supposed to be a certain symbol of sorts. I hated my position. I can't confide in anyone because then I'd be the talk of the church and embarrass my husband. He truly lives what he preaches and I couldn't do that to him. But, I feel like I'm dying inside.

You nailed it on the head over and over; like you could read my mind. Oh, my gosh, and I trust you. I know somehow that you won't tell anyone. I think this was a divine appointment. Can I call and talk with you from time to time? I could really use a good friend. Of course, you can vent to me as well. We can be accountability partners or something like that. O.K.?" Her eyebrows rise with a look of hope. Confusion must have completely overtaken my face and given me away.

"If not, it's O.K." She quickly apologizes.

"No, no, of course you can call. In fact I would be honored, completely. Wow! I just can hardly believe all that's happening. Hours ago I thought you thought you were better than everyone else and that is why you would never attend anything. My whole idea about everybody is wrong. I judged everyone so harshly with no concept of what their reality was. God has opened my eyes lately so much. I...I don't know what to say. My speechlessness is rare. But, umm, yeah. My number is, well here let me write it down real quick." I rummage through my purse and can only find a highlighter and a gas receipt.

*I need to start carrying pen and paper.*

I scribble my number quickly and glance back at her wrist for the time. *10:43 Oh my gosh. I need to be in bed. God help me. I want to be there for people but, I have to work early; I don't want to be mean, but I also don't want to be tired either.* I slide it into her hand and she leans in to hug me again.

"Thank you, again." We exchange simultaneously and pick up our purses and Bibles, which we didn't use and walk out together. I lock up and start toward my van.

"Connie!" She calls ort from a few car spaces over. I turn to face her hoping she doesn't want to confess any more tonight. "Thanks for staying late with me, I know it must be tough to get up for work when this kind of thing happens. But, I kind of have a feeling that since God is using you in such a big way that He'll make a way so that you won't need to work for anyone but Him. I mean I don't like know for sure, but, uhh, it's just a feeling. Yeah, but, anyway thanks again, good night."

"Good night." *Hmm, I wonder… I mean, that would be so cool. I don't know how that would be possible.*

**With Me all things are possible.**

*Hmm, what would I do? I can't really see me as a preacher. I mean this Bible study is turning out to be incredible, but it can't keep going like this… can it? What if it did? Would I want to do this full time? Besides, it doesn't pay. I could never start taking up an offering so that I don't have to work.*

"That's ridiculous!"

"What's ridiculous, Mom?" Jade asks as she opens the door. Confusion again takes over my face.

"Did I say that out loud?"

"Yes. What were you thinking was ridiculous?" Jade can be relentless.

"Well, Mrs. Roberts stayed late talking to me. Then as I was getting into the van she called over to me that she had a feeling that since God is choosing to use me in such a big way that He will make a way for me to not have to work for anyone besides Him."

"That's not ridiculous," Jade says matter-of-factly.

"No, but I was trying to figure out how that could be possible. I can't take up an offering so that a Bible study group can pay my way in life, ya know. That's ridiculous."

"Well, God will make a way if that's what He wants you to do."

"You're up late, Jade. Go on to bed, Honey." I kiss her forehead and hug her with my free arm.

"Yep, I just wanted to make sure you were home first. I love you, Mom." She bops up the stairs as I drop everything and follow slowly behind.

# CHAPTER TWENTY-THREE

"Hi, Kendra, how are you doing?"

"Connie! Hi, I'm doing great! How are you?" Her voice warms me like it always did.

"I am wonderful. How are Celeste and Ben?" *What do I say? Do I just come out with it? Do I make small talk till we get around to it? How do you get around to it?*

"...and Porter?" Kendra finishes.

"Oh, everyone's great! Jade is the most wonderful teen ever. I wish I'd've been like her, but then I probably wouldn't have had her. And Porter is doing good in school and football."

"So...what's going on? You don't sound like everything is great." She always did know how to see right through me.

"No, all is well..." *O.K. do I just ask? How?*

"Out with it, Connie." Kendra demands like a parent.

"Is Celeste Maraschino's daughter?" I blurt out. *Oh my gosh! I did it. I didn't pause or do it gently. And she's not answering. I hope I didn't hurt her feelings. It's not really any of my business.*

"Yes."

*I was right!*

"Why...How did you put that together? How do you know Maraschino?" Kendra doesn't pause between questions. She is shocked.

*How could I do that? No, she's not Maraschino's daughter, she is Kendra's daughter. Oh, man! I hope I didn't hurt her feelings.*

"Well, it's kind of a long story. But Maraschino attends my Bible study and gave her testimony a couple of weeks back and the timing was right. I don't know. I think God put it together for me," I stammer. "Are you mad?"

A long pause weighs heavy before she answers. "No," she speaks quietly and contemplatively. "Tell me more. Tell me everything."

I start with the real me; the one inside my head, and let it roll off my tongue with such pure emotion I surprise myself. I cry and smile simultaneously. She has a split second here and there to insert an 'uh-huh' or an 'Oh, wow!' There's not a pause as I explain the connection between the Bible study, the testimonies and my original question.

"Maraschino gave her extremely personal testimony a couple of weeks ago expressing God's ultimate love and forgiveness. Her life story made me do some deep soul searching. I have finally let God work in me. I've spent so long going through the motions and living the rules..." I finally pause to think; to soak it all in.

"You tried telling me over the years that God wants a relationship with me, but I didn't get it." Tears well up in my eyes, as I begin to contemplate the changes in my life over the last couple of weeks.

Taking this opportunity to put in an entire sentence, Kendra asks about the Bible study. "When is the last one, again?"

"Well, that's tough," I start, "this coming Tuesday is the sixth week and the scheduled end. However, because the attendance has soared from six to about sixty or so and lives are being transformed, many want to continue. I have talked with other ladies and we are going to end the Proverbs 31 study and expand it to actually put into context what we've learned and how to use it in today's busy lifestyle.

"JoAnne is going to teach about budgeting and investing, along with cooking and baking.

"Fancy is going to teach a few weeks about home decorating since, as it turns out, she owns an interior design company.

"Maraschino is going to teach about the importance of taking good care of your body and skin. She'll explain about nutrition and self-confidence. Well, actually confidence in who we are in Christ.

"All of these areas will be under verses and passages from the Bible and how God is still talking to us today. Testimonies will also be an integral part of the entire thing. And who knows what will pop up after they're done. I guess I will still be the leader and coordinator of the Bible study part."

"O.K.," she starts slowly, "well, I want to be there for your last week. Let me talk to Ben and make some arrangements and I will get back with you, O.K.?"

I am speechless. "Why?"

"You don't want me to come?" Confusion envelopes her consistently warm and tender voice.

"What?" *Did I really say that? Shoot!* "No! I mean yes. Yes I want you to come, I love you, I just didn't expect you to come. I thought maybe I would ask for a picture or a note or something that I could give to Maraschino to maybe let her know that Celeste is good and healthy and taken care of. I wasn't thinking about you coming." I apologize.

"Well, I think it's time for Celeste to meet her birth mom."

The silence is freaky. I don't know what to say.

"Really?" is all I can get out.

"Yeah, lately God's been letting me know the time was close, but I wasn't sure how that could ever happen. I never knew Maraschino. I knew her mother and watched her go deeper and deeper into the maddening darkness of depression. I heard stories of Maraschino and how terrible she was. I understood that she continued her wild lifestyle. I heard about her father going to jail and eventually her mother's suicide. After Celeste's adoption we moved so that people wouldn't look down on her. They had already been talking. Gossip is a terrible thing. I believed Maraschino hated Celeste as she did her mother and father and especially God.

"My family hasn't heard anything for quite a while. I figured she never would want to meet the child her own father had forced on her. Now, I guess… it's time." I can hear the tears.

"Are you sure?"

## Inside My Head

"Yes. I am happy for Celeste and Maraschino. God is working things out. It's time," she repeats. "I'll make arrangements and get with you later tonight, O.K.?"

"Of course, and you can plan to stay here."

"Well, my brother is still there and he would probably be upset if I didn't stay there, you know?"

"Oh, I didn't remember you had a brother here. You don't really talk about your family much."

"Well, he's a good guy and he's single too." I catch a sense of teasing there. "We were never very close. He was ten years older than me. Maybe I'll introduce you two. He is a single Christian. And he's cute. Wouldn't that be cool if you two got together? Then you'd be my sister in Christ and in law." She giggles.

*I had forgotten how much I love her. She is wonderful! A Christian brother 10 years older. Hmm that would make him about 45. That's not bad, six years. I wonder if he really is cute.*

"That would be very cool!" *Just being married would be cool. Sex would be cool. O.K., don't go there, Connie.*

"I'll talk to you later, Connie, love ya."

"Love you too, Kendra, goodbye."

"Goodbye."

*Hmm, a cute single Christian brother that I never knew about huh? Yeah, but it's her brother; she would naturally think that he's cute. Cute not hot, well, he is a Christian and how would it be if his sister said he was hot? He's probably a nice guy, short hair, prim and proper. Well, maybe he's got a good sense of humor. Well, at least I might have a date.*

## Inside My Head

*A date... hmm... a date, wow. Well, Mark was a date. Well, a kind of date; me, a man and six kids. But it was the closest thing to a date I've had in years. What if he is cute? What would I wear? And my hair, I need a haircut. A ponytail just isn't a good first impression. Kendra's brother would likely be great like her. I wonder why he's single. Maybe he is dedicated to God and he stayed single. A goody-two-shoes — boring and nearly half a century of set in his ways. Hmm...*

*Maybe he's not really cute. Maybe he's really ugly. Kendra would say he's cute because it's her brother. Maybe I don't want to meet him. What do I do if he's ugly? Or dumb? Oh, my gosh! Maybe he's slow or something. No, not Kendra's brother. Maybe he's super smart; a nerd. Yuck, a nerd. Dress shirt, pocket protector, glasses, dress pants above the shoes. Oh gosh! Which is worse, ugly, stupid, or nerdy? I'm not sure.*

*Well, there is a chance that he's handsome and smart, but not too smart, loves God and kids. Yeah, what if he has kids. Well, Jade and Porter would have to approve. What if he doesn't have kids at all and doesn't know how to be a dad?*

*Hmpf! Porter is clueless, so it wouldn't be any different, I guess. But, maybe he has kids and they're terrible. Mixed families are hard.*

*What if he's single again? What if he's been married two or three times already? What if he's controlling and jealous? Jealous, well he wouldn't have to worry about me, plump and plain. Yeah, does it even make sense? Why would anyone want me anyway? I'm acting like I have a choice. No one wants me and I'm acting like I get to pick and choose. No one wants fat and not so cute. I'm nearly 40 and up to my ears in debt. No shot at job advancement opportunities. A couple thousand saved but if something breaks down that could be gone. I'm never home and my house is a mess. I'm always tired and have just about forgotten how to cook real food from scratch.*

## Inside My Head

*If I were a man I wouldn't want me. I wouldn't take a second look. Heck! I wouldn't take a first look.*

*Geez! Get a grip, what if he doesn't want to meet me? What if he doesn't even have time to see Kendra? She said they were never that close anyway.*

*I get all excited and all she did was mention that she has a single Christian brother. There are single Christian men at church and none of them have asked me out. I am being ridiculous.*

The phone rings and startles me back to reality.

"Hello?"

"Connie, hi again." Kendra's tender smile is coming through the phone.

"That was quick." *I could ask her more about her brother.*

"I talked with Ben and he won't be able to come, but he agrees that it's time for Celeste to meet Maraschino. I booked a flight for Monday evening so that Celeste and I can get in and settle a little before the big day. I'd like to see my brother if he has time. I'll call him in a little while."

"Maybe he could come to my house and have dinner one night." I offer, wondering if that's a good idea.

"Well, that would be nice. I won't be able to stay past Thursday morning, and he works a lot so I don't know, but I'll make the offer. Will you be able to pick us up at the airport?"

"Sure, umm, you have it booked already, right?" I scramble to find a pen or something in one of the junk drawer by the sink.

"Yes, are you ready? I can give you all the information." She offers in her usual got-it-all-together manner.

"Hold on, I'm sorry. One of these days I'll get the time to clean out these drawers. Oh, O.K., here's a crayon and an old envelope. Ready."

"Monday evening at 6:48 on Delta Airlines, gate 12. It will just be Celeste and me, O.K.?"

"O.K., got it, gate 12 at 6:48. What's the flight number so I can check the board and make sure you're on time or whatever."

"Oh, yeah of course, umm… flight 342. Will you bring Jade and Porter with you?"

"Oh, yeah, definitely! Oh, I'm so excited! I can't wait to see you, Kendra. It's been so many years. I can hardly wait!"

"I know! I'm looking forward to spending time with you as well, although this will be a very emotional trip." The weight of the situation comes across fully in her voice.

*I'm so dumb! What a moron! All I can think of is me. Me seeing her and me meeting her brother. What the heck! I'm so insensitive sometimes. She's bringing her only child hundreds of miles to meet her birth mother. How sad.*

"Well, Connie, I need to get a whole lot accomplished before I leave so, I'll have to let you go for now. I'll see you Monday evening, I love you."

"Yeah, Kendra, yeah, and uhh, could you just let me know if it would be better for you to stay here? I want to make sure I have the place ready, O.K.?"

"Of course, Hon. I'll call tomorrow, O.K.?" She answers, still with that familiar joy in her voice.

"Alright, I'll talk to you then, I love you too, goodbye."

"Good night."

*O.K., where will they sleep if they stay here? She could stay in my room and Celeste can stay with Jade. I got that blow-up mattress in the closet. I knew it would come in handy one day. Although I bought it so I could take it camping with the kids. On TV it looked so much better than a sleeping bag. It will be perfect for Celeste.*

*I'll let the kids know when they get home that they'll need to help me get this place cleaned up. Jade's going to love the company. They'll be home soon. We'll have some time Saturday.*

*Oh, my gosh, this place is such a mess. I never did do fall cleaning so... well, I never did spring cleaning either. I used to be so good about all that stuff. It's time.*

*It's time... when she said that I started to cry myself. I don't think I'd tell my kids if they were adopted. I certainly wouldn't introduce them to their birth mother. What if she was prettier than me? Or richer? Or funnier? What if she was able and willing to give them everything they wanted? What if she didn't have to work and could spend more time with them? What if they would have a dad at home? What if her house was clean all the time? What if she had a maid and the kids wouldn't have to help clean? Oh, my gosh, what if the maid cooked real meals every day? What if she was a great cook and they could have whatever they wanted to eat? They could eat healthy.*

*She'd probably have a pool if she had a maid. They'd get to swim all summer. How could I not let my kids get the chance to live with her? She would have insurance too if she had that much money. Probably better insurance than I have.*

*Two parents, a maid and a pool.* I wipe my eyes. *How I could I not let them at least meet her and let them choose? What if she'd been too young and now she has her act together and she's a great mom? What if she has another boy and another girl and Jade and Porter would have siblings to play with and have fun with?* I wipe my eyes and blow my nose. *How could I be so self-centered? I could offer my kids a better life and I would choose to make them stay with me. I wouldn't even give them the option to choose. Oh, my gosh! I'm so mean!*

*What if they both chose to live with her? What if they never wanted to see me again? Or what if they visited me only on holidays and weekends?* I can't stop crying.

*I'd want to see them, but holidays and weekends are not enough. I want them with me all the time. I love them so much. I'd do anything for them. I never want them to leave me! I love them sooo much!"*

I'm now sobbing as I clean the kitchen furiously. *Is my love not enough? I'd do anything for them! I'd give them anything! I want what's best for them. I am best for them. She could never love them as much as I do."* (sniff) *"They'd see that someday. I know they would. I have to believe that, but what if it was years later? What if I died before they realized it? What if they never did?*

*What if they did, but thought I was so mad and hurt that I didn't want to talk to them? What if they thought my choice to let them have the freedom to choose the other mom was because I didn't want them in the first place?* (sniff, wipe, clean franticly). *"What if they went through life thinking that their real mom and their adopted mom both rejected them and even though they had all they wanted they were sad because they didn't even know I loved them? What if they got into drugs and alcohol and one broken relationship after another, self-medicating that pain of rejection and trying to find love? The love only I can give them on holidays and weekends sometimes and eventually not at all. I would've put up barriers of self-protection so that it didn't hurt all the time. Especially if they kept telling me what a good time they were having at their new mom's house. I just couldn't take it. I'd feel like I was rejected even though they'd come see me sometimes.*

*I want their full love. I don't want it divided between me and another woman! I just can't! I can't stand it! I love them so much! If they chose the rich woman with the maid and the pool then they chose! At least I love them enough to let them make that choice. They reject me then they blame me. What the heck?*

*If I never gave them the choice then they'd think I was unfair! They'd think that I didn't trust them enough to make the choice to stay with me. Aagh! I can't win for losing! I hurt! They hurt! I get blamed and all I ever wanted was to let them know there is a choice, but I want them to choose me! I am best for them! My love could keep them safe from some of that hurt. They may not have the maid and the pool, but then again, maybe they will someday. Either way I would never, ever, ever reject them! I would ALWAYS love them! ALWAYS, always, always! No one could ever love them like I do! I love them both so much! I don't know what to do!*

I sit down and cry. I can't stop. It's a horrible feeling.

"God! I can't stand it! I don't get it. This is so stupid! It's not even real, God. Jade and Porter are both mine, they weren't adopted. There is no other mom. There's no one and this pain is so intense. Why? What the heck is my problem? Is this the way Kendra feels right now? Oh my gosh, please help her."

**Constance, my daughter, my dear treasure. You are just starting to understand My dilemma.**

Sniff , Hmm?

*Constance, I am your father. I love you more than you can begin to comprehend, as I do all of My creation. I realized with my first two children that I needed to give them a choice. I didn't want to because I knew they'd choose to walk away from Me. I loved on them all the time. I gave them the most beautiful place in all the Earth to live. I came down every evening and walked with them and talked with them. We played with the animals and smelled the flowers. They'd ask me all kinds of things and I'd answer all of their questions. We shared so much and yet, as I knew they would they chose the 'other mother.' They blamed each other and me. I cried. It hurt in every way. They rejected Me. They rejected My love and the perfect place that I had given them.*

*They cried but the damage was done. I set up times to meet together. It just hurt. When we talked, which was rare, I heard about all their pain and sorrow. I made a way for all of My children to come to Me. To experience real love, to have their needs met and to live with Me for eternity. My first and only real Son gave up his home here in Heaven and went voluntarily to Earth, which He created with me, and He gave up His life for everyone. He was tortured, rejected; He was tormented, and tempted. He was spit on. The others called him names, and lied about Him. Even those who told everyone how close they were to Me hated Him. In fact, they are the ones who eventually ordered His death.*

*My heart broke, I watched my one true Son take all sin upon Himself. It hurt so bad I finally couldn't even look anymore. I turned away. Then the saddest cry came. He called to me...* (I hear tears in His voice) *'Father, Father! Why have You forsaken me?'"* I hear Him sniff, and my sobs become uncontrollable.

*God! No! Please stop! I can't take it!*

## Inside My Head

*Constance, you need to hear this. I cried. I cried and I cried. When He said 'it is finished' I sobbed. The Earth saw it. The skies darkened and rain fell. My tears hit the Earth. The pain My Son felt physically, I felt. The whole Earth trembled as My entire creation feared My response to the death of My Son. I continued to cry.*

Silence. I can't speak. I feel the enormity of the pain of The Almighty. It seems like hours before I hear His deep breath and a sniff.

*I ripped the veil that had always hung between the Holy of Holies in the temple and the Holy room. The way had been made so that anyone who wanted could come straight into My most holy presence.*

*To this day many choose to stay away all the time. I never get to see or hear from the majority of my children. It hurts. At times it's nearly unbearable. They reject me. They lie about me. They assume that because I've given them the choice to know Me or not that I don't care about them. I see their hurt. I feel their pain. They use nearly everything to self-medicate. They try to imitate the love I offer through relationship with others. They don't understand. I want them to but they refuse to even come near.*

*There are those who come only on holidays and sometimes on the weekends. They act like that's enough, but for Me, it's not. I want them to make the choice, not ride the fence. They either need to be hot or cold. When they are warm I just spit them out.*

*Warm is the worst. There are some of my children that say they know Me. They tell others they hear from Me. They lie. They act just as bad as or even worse than those who have just out and out rejected Me.*

*But, Constance, I still love them... all of them. It is My will, My desire that not one of them would spend eternity apart from Me. Reality is that just because that's what I want doesn't make it so. I gave every one of my children a choice. By taking that choice away from them I would become a liar. I AM not able to lie.*

*There are the few that have chosen to remain with Me. They are the ones that I still meet with daily. We walk and talk together. Their earthly surroundings all differ, but their spirits find joy and peace in the surroundings where we meet.*

*I Am so glad, Constance, that you are finally choosing Me. I will never leave you or forsake you. I will never stop loving you.*

I hear the love in His voice.

*Get out your Bible.* He waits, so I get up to get it.

*Read First John 4:16.*

"O.K... God is love. Oh, I understand that better now. You are love is not something I had ever fully understood before." I'm sure He smiled at my childlike words.

*Now, turn to 1 Corinthians 13.*

"The love chapter," I say, as though I can impress Him with my knowledge of His Word. I close my eyes as I realize the ridiculousness of that assumption.

*Yes, the love chapter. You just read that I Am love, so read that chapter replacing the word love with God. Start at verse 4.*

## Inside My Head

"God is patient, God is kind. He does not envy, He does not boast, He is not proud. He is not rude. He is not self-seeking, He is not easily angered, He keeps no record of wrongs. God does not delight in evil, but rejoices with the truth. He always protects, always trusts, always hopes, and always perseveres. God never fails." I read slowly to try to take it all in.

"Wow! I hadn't thought of it like that before. Or, actually, I hadn't thought of You like that before. I always thought of love as an emotion or a feeling, you know like 'I love you'. An action, not a person, but an action directed at a person."

*I want you to read and reread that until you get it deep inside of you. This week at your Bible study tell the women this. Explain to all of them how much I love them. They need to know that. They need to understand it.*

"I will, God, I will." I read it again as the kids come in. I rush over and hug them both so hard they think something's wrong. My eyes are still red from crying.

"Everything is O.K. I was just talking with God about love. I talked to Kendra about Celeste and I just never want you two to choose to not love me." I sniff.

"O.K.," confusion reigns in their voices.

"Is Celeste having problems?" Jade asks while Porter drops his book bag on the couch and heads toward the kitchen.

"No, Honey, but I want you two to sit down so we can talk for a bit." I rehash the last couple of hours in a condensed version while the kids eat a snack.

## Inside My Head

Porter pops in a "So, Celeste is adopted?" And Jade gets in "Maraschino at church?" Other than those questions they are silent till I take a breath.

"So, where are they going to sleep?" Porter asks.

"Well, we have that blow-up mattress we were going to take camping and I thought we'd put that in Jade's room for Celeste, and Kendra can stay in my room and I'll take the couch. It's only three nights."

"Let me have the couch! Please, I'd love to sleep on the couch. It'll be like camping out, sort of," Porter begs.

I smile at my baby. "Porter, you're such a sweetheart. I love you so much."

"So, it's a yes?" I brush the side of his face as I nod, tears starting up again.

"Cool!"

"Now, I'm going to need both of you to help get this place cleaned up."

"O.K., Mom." They say together.

"What's for supper?" Porter asks as he finishes the last of his chips.

"Well, I don't really know. Let's see what we have that is quick and easy."

"Mom, it looks like you've already been busy. Look at this kitchen! You scrubbed it spotless," Jade says with amazement.

"Yeah, I guess I did. I was so upset about the two of you choosing another mother I just scrubbed and scrubbed to release my anger. Here's some bread so we can have sandwiches and some more chips. P.B. and J. or bologna, which sounds better?"

"Peanut butter and jelly," Jade decides, "and I would never choose another mother. There's no one like you, Mom. You are amazing." I smile.

"Yeah, well she had a pool and a maid and could stay at home with you. She had better insurance, and more money and she was far prettier." I sell my reasons.

"Mom, that's ridiculous! No one's prettier than you, and money is no big deal. It's more important that you love us!" Porter states as he reaches for the bologna.

"Yeah," Jade agrees. "But, the pool and maid are tempting," she jeers and we all laugh.

## CHAPTER TWENTY-FOUR

"Connie, brought your Bible today, huh?" Ron observes from over my shoulder.

"Yes, God has been really talking to me lately about love; About Himself. You know the verse, 'God is love'?" I watch as he comes around and sits in front of me. Sheila and Joe join us.

"Yeah," he says.

"First Corinthians 13," I start.

"The love chapter," he finishes for me.

"Yes, but look at it this way. God is patient. God is kind. He does not envy, He does not boast. He is not proud, he is not rude. He is not self-seeking, He is not easily angered, He keeps no record of wrongs. God does not delight in evil but rejoices with the truth. He always protects, always trusts, always hopes, always perseveres. God never fails."

"Wow!" Sheila's voice matches her expression. "I would've never thought of it like that."

"Me neither," Ron says with a wide grin, "that's beautiful."

"It is what I will be presenting this final week of my study." I can barely stop tears from rolling down my cheeks.

"Wait! Final week? No way!" Ron's obviously upset. "I know it's been a couple of weeks but I hoped you'd prayed about it and decided to keep going."

"Well, actually the Proverbs 31 part of the study will end after this week, but the classes will not. Several women will be helping me by teaching different things. Testimonies and the Bible will be the main focus. From there women will learn about physical and spiritual beauty, self-esteem and fitness; purity and strength; keeping a beautiful home, budgeting, investing, parenting and cooking; a bit of everything. So, it's not technically ending, I just won't be the only leader." As I spoke Ron's face went noticeably from concern to peace.

"O.K.," he conceded happily.

Buzz, Buzz, buzz

"So, Connie, you said God's been talking to you a lot lately."

"Mm hmm."

"How do you mean that?" Like, you really hear His voice… out loud… or?" Sheila questions as though she has never heard of this concept. I sometimes don't think about others not understanding this. I hadn't experienced it for years but had heard of it.

"Well, the best way I can put it is that He talks to me inside my head. I do hear Him there. We have conversations there." I had not had to think about it really. If He had talked to me before I hadn't paid attention.

"Can you tell me more later?" she asks as she gets back to work, not waiting for a response.

*You know, God, this is all new to me too. I used to hear people say that they'd heard You speak to them and I couldn't figure it out. Like, how? How did they hear from You? Are You supposed to hear God or are they making that all up? Is it loud or what? Do You look like a lunatic when You "hear" God? I wondered why I never heard Your voice. Now, I don't know exactly how to explain it to someone else. I just KNOW it's You. I don't know how I know, I just do. And I don't know why I hear from You now and never before. What is it, God that makes it possible now?*

*I'm so glad you asked. My Word reveals many times throughout history different people that heard my voice; prophets, judges, David, even when he was still a shepherd and Saul of Tarsus as he set out to kill my followers.*

*Before the temple veil was torn I spoke mainly to prophets and priests; those like Moses, Abraham, and Deborah; men and women of great faith. Their hearts became conditioned to hear Me. The prophets would declare My words to the people.*

*After I tore the veil, anyone was able to enter the most holy place. Anyone could come before My throne. Anyone who so desired could speak directly to Me. Whenever I speak to someone it will line up with the scriptures. I Am not man that I would lie. When a person hears a voice stating anything that does not line up with the scriptures he or she needs to rebuke the liar.*

*While Jesus was on earth He rebuked Peter for speaking a lie. Peter spoke only out of emotion and fear. Perfect love casts out all fear. That's what Jesus did, He cast out that fear.*

*Jesus told His followers that they, and you, are like sheep. John recorded His words in chapter 10. He explained that as sheep they and you would know the shepherd's voice, distinguishing it from all others. You know beyond all things that the shepherd can be trusted. When circumstances don't warrant it the sheep still have an innate faith in their shepherd. The only way they are able to distinguish his voice from all others is that they dwell in his presence.*

*Day in and day out the shepherd sits in the field with his sheep. He speaks to them, his voice comforts them. They know they are safe because he is there.*

*When a person's heart and mind are set on Me they begin to listen for and recognize My voice.*

*Through My Son's obedience, all people have the option of allowing Me to dwell with them and in them; they can know My voice if they so desire. It takes time. The sound of My voice doesn't get louder with time, but those who choose to listen for Me become more aware of the sound of My voice. In the stillness of their hearts and minds they begin to converse with Me. I find great joy in speaking with My children.*

*In those times they mature. They learn about Me from Me. I reveal secrets to those who are willing to listen."*

My head is shaking and I am smiling as my mind wanders back over the past few weeks.

*God? Why did You start talking to me after all these years? My mind was racing and wild. I had never really changed. ...why now?*

*My Word does make it abundantly clear that if you seek Me, you will find Me, but one verse tells a secret. Isaiah 65:1. 'I revealed myself to those who did not ask for Me; I was found by those who did not seek Me'*

*In Romans I remind my people that 'I will have mercy on whom I have mercy, and I will have compassion on whom I have compassion.' It is all about My kingdom. I know the plans I have and who I will use to make sure those plans are effective. I know the hearts of all men and women. 'I reveal deep and hidden things; I know what lies in the darkness.*

# Inside My Head

*You are My child. You wanted to understand. You were not able to do so. I simply used circumstances to help you get started. You have in turn grown quickly. See, Constance, a seed needs to be put into the ground. It needs the dark, hidden places. It needs the pressure of the dirt on and around it to crack in order to begin to extend outward. It then needs water and sun to grow. Some seeds take a longer time in the darkness; some need more pressure to crack. For instance a buckeye is strong and hard, it needs to be deeper in the darkness of the cold ground; the solitude. It needs a great deal of pressure to crack. The tree it will become is tremendous. Children can play in it. It will be strong and powerful. Look at a dandelion seed. A windy day will blow the seeds far away. Laying on top of the soil and absorbing the warmth of the sun it will grow quickly.*

*Like these seeds, my children are very different and for each I know what it takes for them to grow."*

Well, I guess I needed to be in the ground for years…and a lot of pressure! Oh, my gosh, I almost gave up just before all of this started. Change has been so fast, and so powerful… I don't think I ever thought I would change. I knew something wasn't right, but I couldn't explain it. I thought I was the best I could be…

Well, honestly, I guess I knew I wasn't as good as Jade. Well, I just thought I could never be good enough. I never have been good enough at anything. Relationships are certainly not my strong point. I never kept one together. I've been so alone for so long… I just thought… I don't know… I guess I thought I couldn't keep my relationship with You either. Like You didn't really want me either. I only started the Bible study to earn points with You. I hoped You'd notice me. Maybe be happy with me. I know I don't deserve Your pleasure in me. I still don't, but I can see the changes…

*I really wanted to change, I just didn't know how. I really didn't think I could change enough to make You happy anyway, so why try.*

*Thank you, thank you, thank you for never giving up on me. Thank you for beginning to talk to me in a way that I could understand. Thank you.*

**I find delight in you, Constance, my daughter... my beloved.**

I can feel His smile; the warmth fills the space around me, like a hug. It's like Kendra's smile. I am so excited about her coming. Maybe while she's here I can learn from her; how to have God's smile.

..........

"Connie, all I could think about was how to hear God. Can you explain it now during break?" Sheila had started talking before getting next to me.

"Well, I can try. The Bible says that we are like sheep and that He is the great Shepherd and that His sheep hear His voice. God wants all of us to listen for His voice to hear Him and to know Him better. I don't know how I started hearing from Him, except that it was time."

"But, where does that leave me? Can I hear from Him? I'm just barely a Christian, I don't know much about any of this. So, how long before I can hear Him?" Sheila asks as Ron joins us with his Mountain Dew and a Diet Pepsi for me.

"Thanks," I say with more of a questioning look as I pop the top.

## Inside My Head

"Sheila, the best way to hear God's voice is in the quiet place. Oh, Connie, I'm sorry; am I butting in?" I take a drink as he continues.

"No, by all means answer away." I take another drink as he continues.

"O.K., listen, Sheila, get alone in a quiet place and then quiet your mind. The Bible says 'be still and know that I Am God.' When we want to really hear Him, we need to listen for a small still voice. It happens in our head and lines up with scripture. If it does not line up with the Bible it is not His voice. Put on some worship music if you'd like. You can even open the Bible and start reading. Sometimes we hear what He wants to say through a song or through reading His Word." Ron takes a drink and looks at me then her.

Sheila nods and thinks; her eyes close slightly and her forehead wrinkles. She'll look like me one day, aging before her very eyes. *She'll wish she didn't do that. That was a good explanation. I had no idea what I was going to say.*

Buzz, buzz, buzz

"Thanks Ron, that'll give me something to think about this afternoon. What are you doing this weekend, Connie?"

"Well, a good friend of mine is coming in from out of town for a visit. She wants to be here for week six of the study. She also has some business to discuss with Maraschino. So I will be cleaning." She nods as she starts back to work and I continue to my position on the line.

*Ron certainly understands You, God. That's cool! That's what I want in a man, someone who understands You.*

**Do you really?**

*Yes, but I want someone handsome and a bit on the wild side. Not that he needs to be a party animal, but at least fun. I don't know. Is there a man that understands You, could understand me and want me... and love me? ...and is sexy?*

"Oh, crap! Sheila my machine is down again."

"Maintenance to line 4. Maintenance to line 4." Her voice rings out across the plant. "You just wanted an excuse to see Kevin, didn't you?" Her smile is devious.

"Uh, no. Not that I would ever mind seeing him, but this one is out of my hands."

"Seeing who?" The voice from behind startled me.

*It couldn't be. Oh, please tell me he didn't hear that.*

"Kevin, it's Connie's machine again." Sheila smiled and pointed down the line at the only spot where no one was working.

*I'm going to just die now; it would be a whole lot less embarrassing.*

"What's it doing? Or should I say, not doing?" Kevin asked as we walked back down to my machine.

"I don't know. It made a loud clunk sort of sound and just stopped. All I really had time to do was turn it back on after break." I stare at the machine and bite my lip. *Maybe if I don't look at him he won't know how much I want to.*

*Oh, man, Superman is using his x-ray vision to stare into the machine. He stops for a second and just looks at the door covering the motor... he's using his psychic ability to talk to the iron monster. He notices the door is slightly ajar and reaches into his man-sized toolbox and removes the perfect tool for the job. The lock is stuck but those arms tugging at the door!!! Oh, what I wouldn't give to have them around me...*

## Inside My Head

"Here we go; a measuring stick. It had fallen in though the crack at the top. I don't even know how it got in. Did you do this just see me again?" He gives me a shy grin showing off the reason for my machine's sudden break down.

"No, here's my stick." I say holding it up like a magic wand. *Oh, if this were a magic wand, I'd wave it over him and say the perfect words to make him fall in love with me forever. 'bipity-bopity-boo say I love you.'* I wave it back and forth.

"Well, it's someone's and it will take a few more minutes to fix the damage." His green eyes put a spell on me as he watches me wave my stick back and forth.

"Trying to put a spell on me?" He asks watching my stick.

"No, oh, uhh sorry." I put it down .

*But, if I was it would be the best thing that ever happened to you. Well... to me anyway. I'd be able to have you any way, anywhere, any time. We'd both enjoy it, I can assure you.*

I continue to watch as he takes the next twenty minutes to operate on the iron machine's internal organs.

"So, Ron said you are a Christian."

"Mm hmm." *Is he really talking to me?*

"So, what church do you go to?"

"Cavalry Hill Church."

"Oh, how long have you been there?"

*No, way! He's making small talk... with me!*

"About ten years or so. My friend went there for a while then moved out of town."

"Hmm, my sister used to go there. But it was a long time ago. Maybe ten years or more, I'm not sure that you would have known her."

"Well, I didn't really know a whole lot of people then. Where does she go now? Or is she still going to church?"

"You know, I know she goes to church, but she moved out of state and I don't know. She's still a Christian though. Here you go. It's fixed and ready. Maybe we can talk sometime without having to break your machine first." He smiled.

*He's still looking at me. Does he want me to say something? He didn't ask anything did he? Maybe we can talk sometime without having to break your machine first...Oh, my gosh!*

"Yes!" I shout, and he laughs a little.

"O.K. then, maybe next Friday after work we could have dinner and some conversation?"

*Are you serious? Dinner and breakfast and everything you can think of in between.*

"O.K.?"

"Uhh, yeah sounds good." I barely get out and he turns to leave.

*I may hyperventilate. Oh, my gosh! Oh, my gosh! Oh, my gosh! Oh, my gosh!... Kevin? The all-time most perfect specimen of the male species... the most amazing looking man on the planet...Kevin! Just asked me out?!!!! Oh, my gosh! I may not be jumping on the outside... I'm not right?* I check my feet and look around and no one seems to notice that my life has just taken a turn for the greatest! Which translates into, no I am not jumping on the outside. I look down at Sheila and smile the biggest smile ever.

*How can I work? My hands are shaking. I know it's just dinner and with all I've learned lately, God, that is all I know. I want to know about his relationship with You. If he really is not all about You... ...I don't want him.*

*That's saying a lot, God. You explained lust to me and I don't want that any more. I'm trying. God, Please help me. He is gorgeous! His voice is everything that can soothe me. And those eyes, and those arms! Oh, my gosh! Help me please, God. Lust is so easy with him. I know it's wrong. This is all new to me. I've been better for the last couple of weeks, but, I'm the same me.*

**Do you really want someone who understands me.**

*I had forgotten that we were talking before he came over, I'm sorry, God. One look at that beautiful man and I forget about You. How wrong is that? I'm so stupid; and evil. I'll never change. I want You God, I really do. I want a man and sex and marriage. Marriage first, anyway... sigh I'm sorry. Do I really want You? Will I ever change?*

**I know your heart, Constance. I know you want me. Lust is wrong and taking this dinner into breakfast is wrong, but having dinner and talking is fine.**

*Thank you, God.*

Buzz, buzz, buzz

*Yay, work is done! I have the weekend to get ready for Kendra and Celeste.*

## Inside My Head

"Connie!" Sheila almost pounces me. I laugh and bite my lip.

"Yeah?"

"Uhn-uhn, what happened between you two?"

"What do you mean?" False innocence being obvious.

"No way! You are not walking out without telling me everything! That smile said something happened," she demands.

"Connie?" I turn to see him, the god of all that is gorgeous.

"Yeah?"

"I didn't get your number, so that we could discuss where you'd like to eat. Can I get that? And would you mind if I called this weekend?" He hands me his business card and a pen.

"Of course." I write fast so he can't see my hand shake.

"Thanks. I'll talk to you later then." He smiles that melt-my-heart-like-butter smile and turns back into the plant.

"Oh, my gosh, he asked you to dinner? You must be so excited! No wonder the smile was so big." Sheila dances as she talks. I only nod and close my eyes.

*The magic wand/measuring stick worked.*

**Not exactly.**

## Inside My Head

*What? God, was it You? Did You really make him ask me out?*

**I didn't make him do anything.**

*But it was You?*

**I might have had something to do with him having the courage to ask you out, yes.**

*Courage? What do You mean?*

**You'll see, soon.**

"What are you doing tonight then, Connie?" Sheila asks.

"Remember I told you my friend is coming?"

"Well, yeah, but... maybe we can work together and I can hear more. How does that sound?"

"Help clean? That is always a welcome idea."

"Cool. Let me go home and change and let the kids know where I'll be and then I'll come over. Is that cool?' She walks backward, barely missing a car.

"Sounds good, see you in a bit."

## CHAPTER TWENTY-FIVE

*Jade, Porter, the store, the bank, gas. I need bleach, cleaning stuff, and food for dinner. Kendra's going to call tonight too. Oh, my gosh! Her brother! Oh, great, what if he comes to dinner? What if he's cute? Yeah, what if I really had options? Besides, no one compares to Kevin. I can't believe he asked me out.*

*It would be fine to have Kendra's brother over. It's not even a date. He's just coming to visit his sister at my house.*

"Hi, Jade, how was your day?"

"Great! Aced the math test, got an A+ on my comp essay, and a B on the biology test. We watched movies in health and government so it was a great day. How was yours?"

"Awesome! Completely fantastic! The absolute best day I've had in ages!" I say, nearly bursting at the seams.

"Really? Wow, Mom, what happened?" She turns sideways in her seat and looks straight at me. I smile big and bite my lip while raising my shoulders to my ears. I feel like a teen again.

"Kevin asked me out to dinner next Friday." I screech with excitement.

"Kevin? He's the guy at work you really like, right?"

"Oh, yeah, Jade, he is gorgeous! He's strong and oh, my gosh! Best of all…"

"Yeah,"

"He's a Christian!"

"Wow! Mom, I'm so happy for you."

"Me too!"

"Why so happy?" Porter asks as he climbs into the back seat.

"Mom's got a boyfriend."

"Oooh! Mom, what's his name?"

"He's not my boyfriend, yet, but he did ask me out to dinner next Friday. And his name is Kevin."

"Mom and Kevin sittin' in a tree k-i-s-s-i-n-g"

"Porter, you've got to be kidding! What a baby. Six year olds say that!" Jade shakes her head.

"Whatever! Jade, I am not a baby. You're just dumb."

"Name calling? Baby."

"You're calling me a baby and say I'm calling names, but so are you. Dummy!"

"O.K., you two; enough. We're going to the store, so what sounds good for dinner?"

"Hot dogs and chips" Porter suggests.

"O.K.," says Jade, "I was going to ask if I could go over to Patty's house tonight."

"Sheila's Patty?"

"Yeah. She asked if I'd come over. I was shocked too. I haven't seen her at church the last couple of weeks and she's been stand-offish at school, but today she asked if we could talk tonight."

"O.K., what time, because Sheila's coming over to help clean in a little while. I will drop you there after the store. Porter, see if you can get a ride home from practice, and if not, just call."

# Chapter Twenty-Six

The doorbell wakes me from what was supposed to be a minute to rest my feet.

"Hey, Sheila, I was resting my feet for a minute and lost track of time."

Laughing, she wipes the hair stuck on my face. "Sleeping Beauty, I brought pizza."

"I must've sat down for longer than I had intended. What kind?" *How embarrassing. Sleeping and drooling and not cleaning, does it get worse?*

"Veggie. I think you'll like it even without the meat."

"We'll see," I jeer as she sets the box on the coffee table. "I'll get the napkins and drinks."

She follows me to the kitchen and takes the can I had already opened for her. "It looks great in here; looks like you earned your rest. Maybe I should've referred to you as Cinderella." She laughs and I yawn."

"Oh, I was upset yesterday and turned into a cleaning machine. I didn't realize it was so late." I remark after glancing at the stove. "Porter should be here any minute. Man, I slept the whole afternoon away." I shake my head in disbelief.

"Well, you are always going a mile a minute. You obviously needed it."

"Veggie pizza, huh?" I take a bite and take in a good look at the front room. *I've got so much to do.*

## Inside My Head

"What do you think?"

"I have so much to do. I'm tired and busy all the time and this place gets so messy so quick. Thanks for coming to help."

"You're welcome." She nods. "Now what do you think about the pizza?" She snickers.

"Oh, yeah, not bad. I don't know what I was expecting, but it is better than I thought."

The door slams open and Porter drags himself inside, dropping his backpack and shoulder pads just beyond the swing of the door.

"How was practice?"

"Good, the game tomorrow will be great! Are you coming? Pizza! Cool, that's better than hot dogs any day."

"Ah ah ah, hands. Wash those dirty things before grabbing food. And it's veggie pizza, Sheila brought it."

"Veggie pizza? What's on it then?" he yells over the running water.

"Veggies!" I yell back.

"Funny, Mom. What kind?"

"Onions, mushrooms, tomatoes, peppers, olives... I guess that's it." I say as I analyze the piece I am eating.

"Gross! Can I just get a hot dog then?"

"Yeah, do you have homework?"

"Math and I still gotta read more of that book."

"O.K., off the hook for tonight but after the game I'm gonna want your help cleaning."

"Cleaning what," he begins the whining and because Sheila is here I refrain from the usual yelling, whining cycle. *I have a million and one things to do and he wants to whine like that. I hate when he acts like his lazy, good for nothing father.*

"Everything! Kendra is coming and I want it spotless. It needs a good fall cleaning anyway."

He tries to get me going but I hold back. He attempts a negotiation to lessen his sentence but I don't budge. Sheila miles.

"Sounds familiar," she says softly so as to not be overheard. I shake my head. "Except I yell a lot more."

"So do I, usually."

*That was easy. Must be because she is here. I should have her over more often. The arguing gets old. I give in far too often. I've never been a great disciplinarian. Heck! I've never been a great anything.*

Sheila picks out a piece of pizza and smiles as she starts. "So... are you a kiss-on-the-first-date kinda girl or a make-'em-wait kinda girl?" She takes a bite while she waits for my answer. But I have to think so I pick a piece out.

"Hmm..." I bite so I don't have to answer yet, and she waits with a smile. "I don't know what I am anymore."

"Anymore? What does that mean?" She takes another bite. I put mine down and wipe my fingers and mouth before answering.

"Well..." *what do I say? I started young and finished young too?*

*Now's a good time to give your testimony.*

I take a deep breath, "Well, my first love was Tommy. I was 14 and we had been playing truth or dare for a long time. Each time we'd get closer to going all the way. He was a little older and so hot! It was exciting to have his attention. We had sex one afternoon. It was the first time for both of us. And I thought I was in love. We were together for a couple of years before I found out he was seeing other girls and sleeping with them too.

"After we broke up I became very popular with all the guys. Not only was I a kiss-on-the-first-date kinda girl, I was a let's go all the way yeah yeah yeah yeah yeah, let's go all the way (I sang) kinda girl." I look over to see her reaction. "Sorry, I love 80's music." I offer a shrug and slight smile to ease my tension and take another bite.

"I do too. Lotsa memories."

"Yeah, that can sometimes be a problem. Anyway, when I met Porter I was tired of going from one guy to the next. Porter was handsome and had a good job. I found out I was pregnant and took it as a sign from the gods that we were meant to be together. We got married a couple of months before Jade was born.

"A year after Porter was born he finally settled on one of the stupid young bimbos he was sleeping with and he left. He has rarely seen them. Child support is here, but it's not much and it's only here because it is automatically taken out of his paycheck."

I take a minute to eat and drink while she expresses her understanding for my disgust in Porter. She says her kid's dad was the same way, except he never bothered marrying her. I shake my head and start again.

"Well, I was completely broken, I hated him and myself. I tried three times to kill myself, but each time someone found me and saved me. Thank God, it was when the kids were young. Porter was taking them every other weekend at that time to play the 'good dad' for his bimbo, Barbie."

She chokes on her drink, trying to hold back tears. It doesn't work. "Oh, my gosh, Connie, I would've never guessed. You're so different now. How did you get past that?" She wipes tears on her hands and then her pants. So I hand her a tissue as I use one.

"Kendra was my roommate at the hospital the last time. She had a miscarriage and something went wrong and she was only there for a couple of days. We talked a lot. She told me her only reason to go on was because she knew what God said about her. That she was His treasure. His daughter. That the God of the Universe delighted in her.

"I wanted what she had. I had never gone to church. I just wanted to feel the peace and the love that she felt. So I gave my life to Christ there in the hospital. I started going to church with her and only a year later she adopted a beautiful baby girl and moved to Colorado."

"Wow! No wonder her visit means so much! She's to you what you are to me. My life saver!" I smile. *I never thought of that before. I did invite her to church. Wow, she sees me like I see Kendra? That's cool.*

"Then let's get busy and get this place ready for your savior. How about I start in here and you get going on that laundry you were telling Porter about; sounds like you have plenty." She takes charge.

"Sounds good. Thanks, sometimes I look around and it just seems overwhelming. I talk myself into postponing the start and it never gets started."

"That is my specialty." She chirps like a songbird. "I analyze the job and determine the steps to complete it as efficiently as possible." She wastes no time. Dinner is already picked up while we chat. "Where are the cleaning products?" She doesn't even look at me, just marches in to the kitchen as though she owns the place.

"Well, under the sink, and the vacuum is in the coat closet under the stairs. I will get the bleach while I am in the basement. Do you mind music while we clean?"

She begins to whistle the tune from Snow White. "No, it's preferable to my whistling, I'm sure."

"We'll do 80's stuff since we both like it." I turn on the stereo and head for the basement.

The house was spotless in no time. And as Sheila was putting on her jacket the phone rang; Patty asking for her mother. *She cleans like a cyclone! This place looks fantastic, I need her help more often.*

"Is it O.K. with you if Jade just stays the night?"

"Sure. I can come by in the morning to get her."

The two of them chat for a minute longer and Sheila leaves in her sports car. *Great car. I always wanted to drive something like that. Maybe I could get some attention then. Men could only see my head and shoulders, so maybe it would trick them into at least talking to me. Well, my van is better for us anyway.*

*Oh, my gosh, it's already 11:30, no wonder I'm so tired. I'm so glad we got so much done so quickly. Good night, God, thank You for Sheila's friendship. She really is amazing. It's so cool to have a girl-friend again. I do miss having someone to talk to.*

"Porter it's time for bed, Honey... Porter?" I open his door to find him sleeping with his ear buds in. I take them out gently waking him only momentarily and kiss his forehead good night as he turns over and goes back to sleep.

Jade and I pick up cappuccinos then instead of dropping off Porter at practice we stay to watch.

"Porter is really good." I remark as though Jade was unaware of that.

"Yeah, Mr. Johnson has been watching him closely."

"Mr. Johnson?"

"The coach at Washington."

"Yeah? A high school coach? Does that mean he could be a starter next year?"

"I think so, that's the talk around school."

"The talk around your school?" *High schoolers are talking about Porter? My Porter? After years of being teased he's being watched by the high schoolers? Wow! How did I not know that?*

"Does he know he's the talk around high school? I mean, he's never mentioned it to me."

"Well, I told him the other day that I heard some guys talking about him at school and how good he was at football."

"And what did he say?"

"He just smiled and shrugged and said yeah. He looked happy though. I'm pretty proud of my baby brother. I'm so glad you're here with us today, Mom."

"Me too, I will be here more often." *That probably seems like it's just because of what she just told me. Is that really the reason? I never wanted to watch before. Am I really that shallow? What if he never got off the bench, would I come more often then? No, I guess being honest with myself that would be a no.*

My tears well up and I shake my head in disgust and disappointment with myself. *Here's my baby playing football and I didn't even know if he was good or bad. In fact I assumed he wasn't all that great and I didn't bother to find out. I guess I felt like I would be stuck watching other guys play. I can't believe I never bothered to find out.*

*God, what is wrong with me?*

**You're self-centered.**

My tears begin to really fall and I sniff, catching Jade's attention.

"What's wrong?"

"Oh, I'm just so proud of Porter. How exciting for him." I force a smile as I take her hand for a second before drowning my sorrow in a lukewarm cappuccino. Jade smiles.

"Me too, he's so cute. And He's not acting all stuck up because of his popularity." Now I smile.

The game went by fast and Porter blocked several touchdowns. I try hugging him as he leaves the field only to

## Inside My Head

be reminded of my embarrassing presence. I glance around hoping no one caught that faux pas. Alas, a couple other players noticed and laughed. I wanted to go teach them a thing or two but, of course realized right away that it would only make things a million times worse. *Times are changing and he is nearly grown. I've missed so much because of my self-centeredness. What a fool! He can't be a "Mama's boy" anymore.*

*Anymore? When was he? Now! I am going to be here for these two now. I really am proud of both of them. They will definitely know that, starting today.*

"How about we go to the grocery store on the way home and get the stuff to make fried chicken tonight for dinner?"

"I love that deli chicken! Can I get three legs, I'm starving," Porter says.

"Yeah and I love their mashed potatoes with gravy," Jade adds.

"Well, I actually meant I would cook it all myself. And you guys can help if you want. I know it's been a long time, but I used to love to fry chicken."

"Oh… O.K. But can we get something for now? I'm **starving**." Porter adds more emphasis on the starving part this time.

"No problem, what sounds good?"

"Burgers and fries." Both agree.

Grocery store after a quick bite then home, still later than I intended. A reminder to both to clean their rooms and a short discussion about how awful that is.

"When is Kendra and Celeste coming?" Porter tries a stall tactic.

"Are, Porter. When ARE Kendra and Celeste coming? And that would be Monday evening a little before seven. That reminds me, I need to check messages; she was going to call if they are staying here for sure…"

"Connie?…" *A man? Who's that* "Well, I was hoping you were home any way, umm… if you want to call me back, uhh… yeah… OH, yeah, this is Kevin…"

*Kevin?! Kevin! I missed his call? I can't even believe he really called me. Wow! Dinner with Kevin. Does life get any better than that? Well, I could see him first thing in the morning… every morning. That would be better. Waking up with him beside me, touching me… yeah that would be the best possibility.*

"Mom, were you going to write that number down or just stand there smiling?" I turn to see both of them laughing.

"Uhh, yeah, of course, I am going to get the number and call him back." I rummage through the junk drawer to find a broken pencil, two pens that won't write, the same crayon I used last time to take a note and an envelope. I turn and push replay only to notice a woman's voice finishing a sentence.

"…all of you, Monday."

"Who was that?" I look around at the kids and they both break out into hysterical laughter.

"Wow, Mom!" Jade starts between laughs, "Kevin must be something special." My embarrassed smile tells all.

"It was Kendra," Porter adds, also shaking his head.

## Inside My Head

I go about my business pretending to ignore them, and they each go their own way. "Connie..." *that voice, so deep, suits him well. He could say anything and I would listen. I can't believe he's calling me. I've wanted that for so long, but never in a million years did I ever let myself believe it was possible. Let alone, dinner.*

*What if he wants me to go back to his place? What if he doesn't? Well, he is a Christian, so hopefully he won't make me choose, I couldn't say no.*

"Mom, you gonna call now?" Jade interrupts my thoughts.

"Oh, I didn't get the number again."

She roars with laughter and suggests that she write it down this time. "And yes Kendra will be staying here. She said her brother's house is too small."

"Oh, good! I'm so glad she and I can catch up." Jade just nods and pushes replay again.

"Connie..." I melt. "Well, I was hoping you were home, but, anyway, if you want you can call me back... Oh, yeah, this is Kevin. Uh, my number is 555-5681." I take a deep breath at the thought of having his number. "O.K., well hopefully I'll hear back from you. Thank you, bye." Jade hands me the envelope and the crayon and strongly suggests that I call before I chicken out. Her smile is teasing. As I reach for the phone it rings and we both look at each other.

*What if it's him?*

"Mom, you gonna answer it?"

"Hello?"

# Inside My Head

"Connie, hi."

"Kendra, Hi."

"I just got off the phone with my brother again and he insists that we stay there. It is small, but I feel God is doing something, so...I'm sorry and thank you for the offer. I will spend most of my time with you, but this is promising to be a very healing visit for many,"

"O.K., Kendra, I have to say that I'm disappointed, but I do understand. I'm just excited to see you anyway. Should I still pick you up at the airport or is your brother picking you up?"

"Kev said he would. Celeste and I will settle in Monday night and see you Tuesday as soon as you're off work, O.K.?"

"Of course, umm, well, I'm not sure how to ask this, but... When do you want to meet with Maraschino?"

"Well, I think it would be inappropriate just to show up Tuesday night in front of a large group of people, which is actually the other reason for my call. Would you mind calling her and setting up a meeting time and place for us? I know I'm asking a lot. I'm just assuming with this whole trip that she will want to meet with us."

"Yes, in fact I'll do that right away. Is there a preferred anything on your end?"

"No," she starts "everything is in her lap at this point. You did say that she really does love God, right?" She sounds nervous.

"Yes, very much so. She really is great. " After a brief silence I resume my thought, hoping to set her at ease,

"Kendra, I'm so honored to be your friend. You are truly the most godly woman I've ever known." I fight tears.

"Thank you, Connie. I have a long way to go, but I've been talking with Him a lot lately. He loves me and Celeste and therefore He doesn't want us to be hurt. He wants to heal us. In that same vein, He is no respecter of persons, He wants to heal Maraschino as well, and missing her daughter every day, (she sniffs) must be terrible. I'm doing this for her and Celeste; they both need the confirmation of love from each other."

"Would you like for me to call you right back with the itinerary?"

"…Yes…I'll want to plan around it I suppose…" she hesitates.

"O.K., I'll call you in a little while. I love you, Kendra."

"I love you too, goodbye."

"Goodbye." My hands are shaking as I hang up. There's that terrible feeling in the pit of my stomach. I don't know what I'm afraid of, but, I am. The church directory, "Thomas, Thomas, ahh here it is, Jay and Maraschino Thomas. 555-3192." *I can't just leave this on a message. I hope she answers. Oh, yeah, she and Fancy promised me a makeover and next Friday would be the perfect time for that, well this would be a terrible time to ask for that.*

"Hello?" Jay answers.

"Hi, Jay, is Maraschino at home?"

"Sure and this is…?"

"Oh, of course, this is Connie from church."

## Inside My Head

"Oh, hi Connie, I will get her for you."

*How do I do this? Is it rude to do this over the phone? I don't think there is a real precedence for this kind of thing. I don't really have a choice after volunteering to call Kendra...*

"Hello, Connie, how are you doing?"

"I'm good, thanks (deep breath). Maraschino, I'm not sure exactly how to do this, but, ummm, well..., umm, (deep breath)."

"Is everything O.K.?"

"Actually, yes, but I don't know... well, Maraschino, I was changed by your testimony, as you know, (deep breath, let it out slow). And since then I prayed and thought and figured something out. I went on my hunch and turns out I was right. So, ummm... I'm sorry, I don't want to be rude or whatever, I wasn't trying to be in your personal business at all. Maybe you should sit down.

"Anyway, I was in a bad place in life and my new friend at the time asked me to go to church with her. I gave my heart to God and she was my mentor. I didn't know many people at the church then. A few months later she and her husband adopted a baby. We changed churches and that is why I go to this church now, but things didn't improve and maybe six or eight months later they decided to move to Colorado. I had no idea why, but she said that it was better for everyone involved (deep breath).

"Anyway, (pause, deep breath), I think God let me put it all together last week and I called Kendra and asked if her daughter was your daughter, or if she even knew for sure."

Maraschino gasps and is bawling.

"I'm sorry if it's too much in your business. But, the reason I called you is that Kendra said yes, Celeste is your daughter."

I stop and listen as she sobs uncontrollably.

"Anyway Kendra believes it's time to let Celeste meet her birth mother… if that is O.K. with you."

"Oh, my God!" She's sobbing to the point of not being able to be understood. "I can't believe it! She wants me to meet her? Is it O.K.? Oh, my God!!!! I have prayed for this moment for years!!! Yes, yes it is definitely O.K.! It's fantastic! Oh, my God! When? I mean do you know how soon it would be possible?"

"Well, Kendra and Celeste are coming into town Monday evening and will be at Bible study Tuesday night."

"Oh, my God!! Are you serious? This week?" I can hear Jay's voice in the background.

"Is everything O.K.?"

"Oh, my God, Jay I get to meet my daughter!"

"What? What are you talking about? How?" He doesn't sound as excited, but not angry either. She runs down our conversation quickly before returning her attention to me.

"Connie?"

"Still here."

"So, when did she want to meet?" She sounds a little more pulled together.

"Well, she said she's praying and it's all in your lap. If you do want to meet with them she will be available

## Inside My Head

Tuesday any time. They won't be here until Monday evening and she would like to get to her brother's house and have dinner and stuff so it would be better Tuesday if that's O.K. And the time and place are up to you."

"This Tuesday? Three days from now? I get to meet my daughter in three days? Oh, my God! Connie! Oh, my God! How about in the morning? How long can I see her?"

"It's all up to you. You are the reason they are coming."

"Really? I could spend the whole day with her?"

"As far as I know, yes."

"O.K., where should we meet? Umm… I'm going to be a mess. In a public place would probably be best so that they feel comfortable. I don't think I could cook. Umm so… what about Bob Evans? Or maybe she won't want breakfast, or well, maybe a park. I, uhh…I don't know. What do you think?"

"Well, how about my house? It's neutral. I could put together a brunch or something. Then, if you're a mess, which I can't even imagine, it won't matter and the three of you could decide what to do from there. How's that sound?"

"Good, good, O.K., what time?"

"When will you be up and ready?" I ask putting it back into her lap.

"I don't know if I'll sleep between now and then. Anytime is fine. Not too early, they may need rest. How about 10:00? Is that too early, or too late? Does it sound like I'm putting them off?"

"No, it sounds fine. Everyone should be awake and fresh. I think it sounds fine."

"O.K., O.K., 10:00 a.m. Tuesday at your house. Incredible! Celeste, I have always loved her name. Do you know her middle name? I never knew it."

"Lynn, Celleste Lynn." She starts sobbing again.

"Lynn? Celleste Lynn? Do you know why they named her that?"

"No, I'm sorry, I don't, why?"

"Lynn is my middle name as well."

*Oh, wow, that's amazing. I was fine till now. I thought I could get away without crying, but not now.* "Maraschino, I have to call Kendra back and let her know the plans, O.K.?"

"O.K., do you think she would mind if Jay came along?"

"I'll talk to Kendra, but I don't see why it would be a problem. I will confirm everything with her and let you know if there is any problem. Bye for now, Maraschino."

"Goodbye," she sniffs back joyous tears.

Calling Kendra proved to be just as emotional. She was far from excited. What if she had made a wrong decision in haste? What if Celeste would hate the idea? What if all of them were so uncomfortable it made for a miserable trip, and cost her family a great deal of money? The very typical Kendra lost her usual laid-back perspective momentarily.

"Well, sounds nice. I guess having her husband there makes sense. I am so unsure of this whole thing. It's scary to think that I may lose something between my daughter and me through all of this. I don't know what I thought was going to happen. How hard is it going to be to go back to 'normal' after this week? God is going to have a lot to deal with for all of us, but I know He is able." She was only concerned for a moment. I knew she could handle this. If Celeste is as wonderful as her mother, and how could she not be, she will be great through it all.

# Chapter Twenty-Seven

"Kevin, I got your message and thought I would call back (sigh and swallow hard). Uhh, well O.K. I will be home the rest of the day, if you want to call me back. O.K. that's it I guess, so, maybe I will talk to you later." *What if he was screening the calls, and didn't like my phone voice or the fact that I had no idea what to say.* My head is shaking as I start toward the stairs.

"It's getting late you two, so let's get started in those bedrooms before the rest of the day gets away from us."

"But, Mom! She's not even staying here." Porter attempts to get out of the inevitable.

"Well, we've got such a good thing going, let's keep up the momentum and finish strong."

We all work with the music from K-Love blaring. We don't stop for dinner till it's all done. Then we decide not to mess up our rarely immaculately clean house, and that we deserve a nice meal so we head out. The little diner down the road is our frequent haunt and we each have our favorite picks so dinner promises to be short.

Our conversation was mostly about how much we love the diner and the food. Then Jade asked the question that set the entire evening into a new direction.

"So, Mom, why is it that you have never dated? I mean dad left years ago and he has been married for most of that time. You are beautiful, so why haven't you gone out with anyone?" *That's not exactly my favorite conversation, and definitely not with my kids, but here goes.*

"Well, most men want someone young and thin. I don't fit either of those bills. I don't have a life outside of work for the most part and don't know where I would meet men anyway." *Hope that's good enough.*

"Mom, you go to church. You could meet men at Porter's practices or games. Also, you have been quite the catch here lately, with Mark, and now Kevin from work. I just don't get why you don't make any effort to date."

"What do you mean? I am old school, the man should ask out the woman." I try to defend myself.

"Mom, you are beautiful. And me and Jade have been talking. We think you don't want to date because of us."

"That's ridiculous. First, Porter, that would be Jade and I. Second, I don't think people other than my two wonderful children think I'm beautiful. See, men think differently about women than her children do."

"That's the problem right there." Jade announces loud enough for everyone in the restaurant to hear. I look around like some kind of secret agent.

"What's the problem?" I nearly whisper in an attempt to quiet the conversation back to our table. The place is pretty full and I know I don't want everyone to know what my problem is.

"You don't see yourself as beautiful and therefore neither do others. We just studied that on Sunday. Well, they talked about it a little differently, but the same thing applies. See when Caleb and Joshua went into the Promised Land with the other guys they saw giants and they became afraid. When they returned they told all of the chosen people that their land was inhabited by giants. They said that they saw themselves as grasshoppers and so did everyone else. The giants probably didn't see them as grasshoppers. They may not have noticed them at all. Joshua and Caleb returned with giant grapes and excitement telling everyone that it was all theirs. They said all they had to do was go in and claim it. What God had promised, they could have, but the majority won. The Israelites were unable to go into the Promised Land for another forty years and... all of that generation had to die. Only their kids got to go in."

"O.K. I don't get it," I say, still looking at the other tables around us as my daughter the preacher talks away with excitement.

"We need to help you see your beauty. Let's go shopping. We can pick out a nice outfit for your date with Kevin and to see Kendra. Do you even have makeup?"

"Yeah, somewhere. I don't think Porter would enjoy a night of shopping." I try the easy escape.

"Mom, I'd do it for you; you would do anything for us. And besides, I want you to feel as beautiful as I see you." *Well that wasn't what I expected.*

"Fancy and Maraschino told me that they would do a makeover for me. I just haven't had the time to call them." I shrug.

"Cool, a real makeover! Let's call when we get home. We could go pick out an outfit now. One of these days you should think about getting a cell phone. We could've called now."

"Yeah, they are really expensive and I hear people at work complain about going over on the minutes and having a ridiculous high bill they didn't expect. It's not necessary, anyway; if people want to get ahold of me they can call our house."

"And the real thing we are discussing?"

"I guess a new outfit would be nice. Porter, are you sure you don't mind?"

"Well, I prefer a friend's house over shopping, but in this case I think you need a man's opinion." He smiles that big smile that melts my heart and I can't resist the offer.

We shop for the next couple of hours finding two new outfits that win the opinion of both of my children. One will be for Sunday and my date, according to Porter and the other for everyday and the final Bible study, according to Jade. Once home Jade took the initiative to call Fancy about the makeover. Right after work Monday, Fancy will come to the house and hopefully I will be as changed on the outside as I have become on the inside.

"Look, a message," I push the play and walk away accepting that nearly every call is for one of the kids. "I'm going upstairs to try on my clothes again."

"Hello? Connie?" That voice… "I guess I missed you again. I thought you were going to be home for the rest of the evening. Umm, well, umm O.K. uhh if you still want to talk to me I will be home." So disappointed. "I'm usually only up till 10 or so but uhh, if you are home early you can call back. Oh, yeah, this is Kevin… from work. O.K. then uhh, maybe I'll talk to you later."

"Was that it? The only message?" Porter asks without any thought of any true response.

"I guess my new outfits can wait. I don't want him to think I'm trying to avoid him." I say trying to sound passé.

"Whatever, Mom, you wouldn't miss talking to Mr. Wonderful for any reason. Don't tell him about the new outfit..." Porter pipes up before turning to go upstairs.

"Don't forget to let Duke out for a while."

He let the dog out and fed him, staying within earshot so that he would be able to listen in on my call. Jade wasn't that slick, she plopped down right beside me on the couch.

"I'm here for moral support." She snickers. I just roll my eyes and begin dialing the number I seem to have memorized. She watches in surprise and covers her mouth to laugh. "She has the number memorized already." She calls over to Porter. He laughs and shakes his head walking over to her side and plopping down to listen.

"Hello? Kevin?" *I can't believe it.*

"Connie, hello, I thought you were trying to back out nicely."

*Not a chance...*"No, I took the kids out for dinner at this diner right down the street. They are small and priced decent and we really like their food. Then we went shopping, all at the last minute. Sorry." I offered.

"Oh, no problem. Well, I wanted to check with you about a time that would be good next Friday. And find out where you would like to go."

*Does my place or my room sound better?* I smile at the thought of either and notice both the kids looking at me.

"Well, I have to make arrangements for my kids to be home from practice and school uhh, well..." Both kids look at me like I'm lying.

"O.K. Well, how many kids do you have?"

"I have two, a boy and a girl. Jade is my oldest and Porter is the youngest." I glance at them and they are cracking up. 'What?' I mouth to them; which makes them laugh all the more.

"Cool and how old are they?"

"Jade is 15 going on 30 and Porter is 13. He is playing football for the junior high team, but I was just told today the high school coaches are already looking at him."

"Awesome, I used to play football in high school. It takes a great deal of discipline."

"Umm hmm." *I wish I knew him in high school. I would have really gotten to know him. But that wouldn't have lasted long. It never did, especially with the jocks. They only wanted me for one thing and for a short time before moving on to the next challenge. I guess I wasn't* "much of a challenge."

"Hmm? What challenge?"

"What?" *I better not have just done that.*

"You said 'much of a challenge'. I must have missed the first part of that."

"Oh, I don't know. I uhh, hmm, I don't know what I was thinking. But I bet you were quite challenging as a player." *Good save.*

"I could hold my own. I was the quarterback. I had lots of challenges and saves. I still love the game. I watch it every Monday night. I have lots of favorite teams but my all-time favorite are the 'Dawgs' I can go on and on about sports, so if you are a fan that will give us something to talk about Friday."

"The only thing I ever followed in high school was boys, so I don't really know too much about sports." The kids' eyes were wide with surprise. I never talk about my past with them. I don't want them to see me that way.

"O.K., well, where would you like to eat on Friday?"

"Well, I like nearly everything, so it doesn't matter where we go, I can find something I like."

"I love steak and seafood, so how about that?"

"Sounds wonderful. Do you have any children?" I ask, not wanting to get off the phone so quickly.

"No, sadly I was never blessed with children. My wife died young and we had not yet had children. Sometimes I wish I had a son to play football with or go to the gym with. My wife was my whole life and I... I guess it took too long to get beyond her death."

*Oh, good job! Touch the sore spot. This is why dating is so hard. What do you say?*

"Well, I'm sorry. Uhh steak and seafood are fine."

"Sorry, I am past her death. The Lord was there all the time. I learned so much more about Him and about me through the years since, that I know how to move forward. I don't know what I would've done if I were not a Christian when she died. I probably would have followed. I don't mean to go on about that. It is a good memory, but I am ready to make new memories."

*What? New memories? With me? That is too good to be true. I should wake up anytime now.*

"And you called me?" I almost whisper.

"I didn't mean anything by that. Uhh... I mean that I won't be only talking about sad things or my past on our date, if you still want to go out on a date." He sounds nervous now.

"You aren't trying to back out are you? 'Cause I am looking forward to dinner." I try to make up for the touchy subject.

"No, no I guess it's been a long time since I asked anyone out and I am not very good at this dating thing. Ron told me you would probably say yes and so I thought it would be a good idea. I have seen you at work for so long but I just assumed you were married, as pretty as you are and all, but Ron said you had asked about me and then I saw you at church and thought maybe you would be willing to go out with me so I got up the courage to ask, but I don't guess I had thought about what we would talk about or have in common. But that is what dating is about, right? Finding out what you have in common... You are really a Christian, right?"

"Yes. I had wondered the same thing about you. It seems difficult to meet single Christian men. Most say one thing and live another. Ron told me you are a very godly man. I was surprised."

"Why?"

"Well," (the kids have finally lost interest and gone into their rooms) "I never thought that a Christian man would have long hair." I can't very well tell him the rest of my thoughts.

"Oh." He pauses before continuing, "Is that a problem? I'm an eighties kinda guy. I guess I loved the hair bands and the wind blowing in my hair on my motorcycle. It's easy to imagine... stuff anyway."

"No, it's not a problem at all. I too am an eighties kinda gal. Not that you're a gal but just from the eighties. I love the hair bands. The music still takes me places." *Places I shouldn't go.*

"Cool. Crystal loved my hair. Sorry. Anyway I should probably go before I mess up again. I need to get my house cleaned up. I never have time during the week. I didn't realize that getting older meant getting tired more easily."

Before I could say anything he adds, "Not that I am tired all the time. I still have plenty of energy for things I want to do. I just have company coming this week and I haven't seen her for a long time so I want to make a good impression."

I still haven't said anything. *She? A good impression? Is he dating around and I am just one of many? Of course that would make sense, kind of. I mean the dating around part, that I am one doesn't make much sense at all.*

"Well, I hope she is impressed." *I don't know what else to say. It's not like we are a thing or anything. We haven't even gone out yet and I am feeling a bit jealous. I never thought I would get to have a conversation with him and when I do he tells me he's trying to impress someone else. Oh, brother.*

"Thanks. It's my sister. We haven't seen each other in a while and I want her to see how much better I am doing since we last were together."

"Oh, O.K., well I want to go check on the kids anyway so I guess I will see you Monday."

"O.K. I will see you then. Good night."

"Good night." *I guess he is just like every other guy. I was right. I mean given the circumstances I didn't even want to*

## Inside My Head

*hear good night from him. Before now I would have given anything to hear those very words come out of his mouth. In fact I would have imagined turning off the light and having a phenomenal night with him but he just told me he wants to impress another woman, and then lied to cover that up. I knew I couldn't trust any man.*

"Well, how did it go?" Jade asked coming from out of nowhere.

"Fine. I think he is just starting to date around and I am one of I don't know how many."

"Well, after he sees you in that outfit we picked out the choice will be made for him. You're THE one I want!" Porter exclaimed as he then proceeded to sing 'You're the one that I want…' and dancing around the living room. Jade joins him and the whole scene is overwhelming. My kids are the best thing that ever happened to me.

"How 'bout you go get into that new outfit again so that you can be reminded of how fantastic you look and then maybe you will see. He couldn't possibly want anyone else." They continue singing and I laugh.

The night was much more enjoyable than it would have been a few weeks ago. My imagination can be the death of a good time or the only good time. I am so glad that I let the kids be a part of it all. And even more so, that I finally let God be a part of it all.

# Chapter Twenty-Eight

I slept well, dreaming of the best possible ways the next few days could go. I know that there is so much going on that this is the only way to do this. I would not have been able to get to sleep after last night's conversation only a few weeks ago. I realize if it were not for the conversations with God of late, I would be focused only on the date. Actually if it were not for those conversations I may not even be looking forward to a real date with the most amazingly gorgeous man on the entire planet. So much is riding on these next few days, in my life as well as my closest friends. I could not have imagined any of this as a possibility; it is so incredible how God can work things out in a matter of a few days.

Six weeks ago I was a mess. I had no real future plans and assumed nothing could or would ever change. I had no true friends and now I am overwhelmed by the beauty of so many women; not physically but more importantly their inner beauty. I am also beginning to like who I am. I have a ways to go but I am so much further ahead. The Bible study I started, so that I wouldn't look bad by saying no, is now up to sixty or seventy or something like that and will continue with the help of my new dear friends. Women I can now admire instead of hate. My mentor from years ago is coming into town to introduce her daughter to her birth mother, and introducing me to her cute little brother. And I have a real life date with Kevin! How could this get any better?

"Mom, Duke is still outside. I forgot about him last night since I was so interested in you and your dream date." Porter apologetically admits.

"Oh, my gosh, let him in and give him a really good treat. He must be so cold. Duke, my poor baby, come here. Aww, poor thing you are freezing. Here's a blanket to snuggle up in. Come up here and sit on the sick couch."

Porter went to get a treat while I tried to warm up our poor neglected dog. Jade came down the stairs and immediately began to cuddle with Duke and reprimand Porter, leading to bickering and my frustrations bursting out in a very ugly way. Everyone, including Duke, stops and stares at me.

"Look you guys, there is too much good in this world to waste another second on this petty arguing. Porter accidently forgot about Duke and no one else thought about him either, evidently, so just stop and know that his thick fur has protected him. Now let's get ready for church." The kids take off up the stairs, now arguing over dibs on the bathroom and Duke settles back into the warm blanket. I start off to the kitchen for a warm breakfast, listening to the chaos and realizing that I am thankful for the blessings I have been given in each of my children.

"Whistle while you work…" I sing followed by a beautiful rendition of the famous whistling tune. *Tommy taught me a lot of cool things and whistling was one. God, You have taught me many more very cool things in the last few weeks than I had learned my whole life. I can hardly believe the turns I have taken in my thoughts and actions since You and I began talking. Thank you.*

"Breakfast!" I call up to the kids and dig into the pancakes on my plate.

We get ready and get to church early for a change. Sheila and Joe are here with Chuck, and Patty and Joe's son, Evan. I hadn't realized he had any children.

# Inside My Head

*Those two are quickly becoming very serious. I am so happy for her. Patty looks good; I wonder if she is having morning sickness. It's sad that her boyfriend already ditched her but so typical. Lord, why do we women continually fall for that crap? What lures us into that belief that 'this one will be different'?*

Maraschino rushes up to me with tears in her eyes and hugs me without saying a word. Her hug is strong and long. Suddenly she whispers in my ear 'I love you,' and rushes back to Jay's side. I shake my head realizing the impact this will have, and I become overwhelmed with emotion. *Thank you, God.*

JoAnne hurries over and sits for just a minute so that she can let me know that she has decided to change her eating habits and wants to share that with the group as a part of the upcoming changes being made at the Bible study. She asks if we can meet later in the week to discuss her ideas and shows me her journal that will be the guide for everything she is doing. We agree on Wednesday before church and off she goes to find Jack as the music starts.

*God, wow! Wow! I can't even explain how incredible it is to be liked by others. I never thought it would be possible. I never have had girl-friends. These women truly love me and I truly love them.* I shake my head and clap to the beat of whatever song is playing, not paying any attention to the words. *You have wrecked me forever, but in a good way. I am so much happier, even when the kids were arguing this morning I was able to sing and whistle. I could get dressed without hating everything I put on. I still don't like what I look like but at the same time I don't hate me anymore. I can't thank you enough.*

"The holidays are coming up and we will all be very busy but let's not forget why we are celebrating this year. Invite friends and family to the Thanksgiving service and meal next Wednesday. We will be having a guest speaker and a special singer. It should prove to be a beautiful new tradition at our church. Also, if you know of anyone in need of help with Christmas this year please take the time to sign them up today so that we can make sure that no one goes without this year. If you would like to be a part of the seasonal blessings and sponsor a child or a family there is also a paper to sign up for that in the foyer, or simply write Christmas blessing on the tithing envelope before dropping it into the offering. Ushers," he says with a nod in each direction.

"Father, we give You thanks for those of us who have been blessed this year and are able to be a blessing. Multiply all that is given, especially this time of year, like the 5000 you fed with the five fish and two loaves of bread we can give abundantly to all those in need. I pray that each get together will bring divine appointments and see multitudes enter the Kingdom this year. Father, may your blessings fall on each one here today whether they are able or unable to give."

Music starts and Sheila leans in, "I have a sister who is out of work and she isn't sure if she will be able to buy her kids anything this year. Would I be allowed to put her name in? She doesn't go to church anywhere."

"Yes, there is a paper in the foyer for you to put her name and the kids' names and ages with ideas or needs. If she needs food we also do food baskets. Invite her for Thanksgiving dinner on Wednesday here too. It's an outreach for everyone, not just those who go here."

"O.K. I'm not sure if she'll come but I'll try; thanks."

"Today we will focus on Romans 12 verses 1 and 2. If you have your Bibles with you please turn there with me. The verses are always up on the screen as well but that lacks the same opportunity to make notes and highlight scriptures in your Bible. Today, I want to take these very familiar scriptures and read them to you from The Message version...

"'So here's what I want you to do, God helping you: Take your everyday, ordinary life—your sleeping, eating, going-to-work, and walking-around life—and place it before God as an offering. Embracing what God does for you is the best thing you can do for Him. Don't become so well-adjusted to your culture that you fit into it without even thinking. Instead, fix your attention on God. You'll be changed from the inside out. Readily recognize what He wants from you, and quickly respond to it. Unlike the culture around you, always dragging you down to its level of immaturity, God brings the best out of you, develops well-informed maturity in you.'

"I so enjoy The Message version of the Bible. It puts it right out there as plain as possible. Take everything you are, and everything you do, and lay it out before God. He wants to use it all to bring out the most effective and beautiful rendition of you.

"When we determine to adjust who we are to the world around us we lose track of the value in our uniqueness. Our world is an instant-gratification world. Romans 8:28 says in the NIV 'And we know that in all things God works for the good of those who love Him, who have been called according to His purpose.' This does not put time restraints on God and the good He wants to do in our lives. It doesn't suggest that He will immediately work it all out and there will be no struggle or trial. In fact, in John 16:33 Jesus tells us, 'I have told you these things, so that in me you may have peace. In this world you will have trouble. But take heart! I have overcome the world.' And James says in chapter 1 verses 2-4: 'Consider it all pure joy, my brothers and sisters, whenever you face trials of many kinds, because you know that the testing of your faith produces perseverance. Let perseverance finish its work so that you may be mature and complete, not lacking anything.'

"So, putting this all together we see that we will have troubles and trials which we need to count as benefits for our lives, realizing that they will all be used by God to work toward our good in His time. As we lay out ourselves on the altar of sacrifice we can trust that God will take only the bad parts and leave the good. And He will add more things into the mix that we are unable to imagine are available. See over here in Ephesians 3:20 again in the New King James version it says, 'now to Him who is able to do exceedingly abundantly above all that we ask or think, according to the power that works in us,' In the NIV it says, immeasurably more…and in The Message it says 'God can 'do anything, you know — far more than you could ever imagine or guess or request in your wildest dreams!' He does it, not by pushing us around, but by working within us, His Spirit deeply and gently within us. Glory to God in the church! Glory to God the Messiah, in Jesus! Glory down all the generations! Glory through all millennia! Oh, yes!"

The entire congregation is clapping, some are even standing.

"How exciting it is to KNOW beyond a shadow of a doubt that The God of the universe, The God who spoke into existence the entirety of the multiple universes the scientists now are saying exist, is working EVERYTHING out for your personal good!"

Again the congregation stands and applauds. It sounds like thunder as people are grasping the truth.

"So here's what I want you to do, God helping you: Take your everyday, ordinary life — your sleeping, eating, going-to-work, and walking-around life — and place it before God as an offering. Let me tell you that my life is not worth having some days. It can be difficult. My past is especially horrific; I want nothing more than to lay it down. Why God would accept it is past my comprehension.

"Embracing what God does for you is the best thing you can do for Him. At this time of year when we are looking at all the things that we are thankful for, let us not forget to give thanks to The One who takes all of our ugliness and makes it beautiful. Let us embrace all that He does for us. This brings Him pleasure. It is like one of my children, when they ask me for something special at Christmas time and I make sure it is under the tree, I wait anxiously for them to wake up and open the package. I have been known to wake them up myself because I couldn't wait any longer to see their faces as they discover that the item they wanted was wrapped up and under the tree. Their joy brings me joy. Their excitement and their appreciation makes my day complete. That's how it is with our Heavenly Father as well. When we have asked for something sometimes we get anxious and wait and wait and wait. Sometimes we almost give up on ever believing that God will give us those things we ask for. Sometimes the troubles and trials along the way deter some people and they never make it to the Christmas tree. Sometimes God has to wake us up to His generosity and His graciousness, because He can't stand to wait any longer to see the reaction. But if we don't embrace what He does, we cause Him to lose some of that joy.

"'Don't become so well-adjusted to your culture that you fit into it without even thinking. Instead, fix your attention on God. You'll be changed from the inside out. Readily recognize what He wants from you, and quickly respond to it.' Sometimes we act as though the world is where we can find our ultimate joy. We adjust our thoughts and our actions to assimilate to the world around us. We find that going to this party or that school, or joining this gym or wearing those clothes will bring us more popularity and therefore pleasure. It will fill that emptiness. But how many famous, or rich people, are found dead from overdosing? How many would tell you that the stress of having the continuous scrutiny of the entire world at their door constantly is not fulfilling? How many would say that the money is not everything they had hoped it would be? Sure, they have fancier homes or cars or nurseries for their babies, but do they have peace?

"We need to fix our attention on God and allow Him to make the changes in us. When we try to do our own fixing it doesn't always work. But 'in ALL things, God works together for our good.' He knows the entire story. He knows our end from our beginning. He longs to make the changes from the inside out. He longs to take our old stinking thinking and turn it into a glorious aroma.

"We cannot readily recognize what He wants from us if we do not spend time meditating on Him and His Word; time to just listen to hear His voice. Therefore we cannot respond. Again, if my children want pizza for dinner on Saturday and I ask them to clean their rooms in exchange for the pizza, but they never heard me over the TV, they will not have a clean room nor will they have the pizza. They will continue to stay in the filth and not indulge in the decadent flavor of their favorite meal. However, if they turn off the TV and listen for my response they will have a completely different outcome. Sure, I could clean their rooms and order pizza while they relax in front of the tube, but it would not teach them anything. I would not be much of a father if I didn't teach my children responsibility and work ethic. I want their futures to be abundant so I need to act now.

"This ties into the last of these two verses, 'unlike the culture around you, always dragging you down to its level of immaturity, God brings the best out of you, develops well-informed maturity in you.' Our spiritual maturity is what will pull us through the troubles and trials of this world and allow us to remain faithful to Him.

"His main goal and purpose is our eternity, not our right now. He let His own Son die so that our souls would never have to experience death; separation from their creator. He created us in HIS likeness and in HIS image; when we readjust our likeness to that of the world it tears holes in our souls that only He can repair. That is where the pain comes from… the emptiness.

"We just read that Jesus said that He overcame the world, and He left us peace that the world doesn't offer. And Ephesians 3 says 'God can do ANYTHING, you know — far more than you could ever imagine or guess or request in your wildest dreams! He does it not by pushing us around but by working within us, His Spirit deeply and gently within us.' When we respond to what He instructs we not only have a clean life but more than we could ever request in our wildest dreams. Let me just say that my imagination can be quite large. He doesn't force us to respond, but He gently works through us, for us, deeply and gently within us.

"Starting today, let's focus on letting God have His way. Listen for His still small voice. Be still and KNOW Him. See if things don't begin to change in your life and even in the lives of the people around you.

Let's pray, and if you would like to respond to His voice today come on down to the front, kneel at the altar presenting yourself as a living sacrifice before Him. Or if you can't get down here kneel at your seat."

Many, many people respond by going forward as he prays. I don't think I have ever seen the altar area so full. It is such a beautiful thing.

"Father, so gracious and wonderful are you. We are here before you today giving you permission to show up in our everyday lives, our ordinary mundane lives. Help us, Lord, to focus on You and what You are doing. Bless us as we stay and pray and bless us as we leave. We stand on Your word and believe that You will work all things together for our good and Your good pleasure. We love You. Amen."

The minority of the congregation leaves reverently; it's uncanny. Typically it is noisy and quick paced as dozens race off to their dinners and family, but today only half or less are slipping out without a word and finding their way toward children and cars. I don't stop to talk to anyone as Sheila and her entire family have gone forward to pray.

·········

"Jade, what was your lesson about today?" Porter begins the conversation.

"Well, we read from James and the way we should be living our lives. Brother Steve read James 1 from The Message and it took on a whole new perspective. We discussed the pressures we face at home and school and how those pressures are there to cause us to become mature spiritually and well developed. He reminded us that God is always there to help in every situation, and He loves to help. I really enjoyed the class today. I did, however, miss Patty; did she go in with you and her mom, Mom?"

"Yes, she was in there and we had such an amazing sermon about Romans 12:1 and 2 that she went down to the front to pray with her mom. I was so excited to see the reaction of the congregation today. I know God has been working wonders in my life and I could see that He was doing it all over today. How about you, Porter? What did your class talk about?"

"We talked about James, too, but it was not from The Message, it was basic, NIV. I think it was about asking for wisdom. Yeah, we talked about asking for wisdom in school and that He would give it to us and that when we ask we should not doubt that He has given it. We need to trust that He is always working in us."

"So, Mom, what was so fantastic today in the sermon?" Jade asks.

"Well, it was how the God of the Universe that created all things by simply speaking them into existence is able to do everything we could ever possibly imagine and that He wants to do things for us as long as we will listen and respond to His voice. That He is there in troubles and trials as well as the good times, causing all of it to work together for our best possible outcome and He knows the best possible outcome even though we can't begin to imagine it for ourselves. And, that when we try to become like the world we are tearing our souls causing gaping holes that cause pain. He is the only one that can repair those holes and reverse the situations causing us to change from the inside out."

"Wow, I love it!" Jade declares.

"What's for lunch?" Porter asks, taking the conversation in a whole new direction.

"I put a roast on this morning before we left and it should be done shortly after we get home. It has potatoes and carrots and I will make some green beans while you two change clothes…"

I was in mid-sentence when Porter cut me off. "What? Mom, a roast and pancakes for breakfast? Did you sleep at all last night?"

I laugh. "Yes, and got up early enough to have real food for today." I continue to laugh as Jade adds her two cents.

"That's what love does," Jade smiles at the two of us and takes back the conversation. "I am so happy for Patty. The last time I was at her house we talked for a long time and I knew she was in a better place than the first time we met. I know having a baby will be hard for her and her mom, but I think it will be a good thing." She watches out the window and we drive the rest of the way in silence.

..........

"Dinner was great if I do say so myself. I wish I could be an at-home mom."

"I don't know if I would like that," Porter comments.

"Why not," Jade starts. "With Mom at home we wouldn't have to clean anything; she would have it all done and we could have real food all the time. She could help with homework and we wouldn't have to get up so early."

"Yeah, no cleaning," Porter nods in agreement. "And she would walk Duke and clean up his poop. Yeah, Mom, you should be an at-home mom."

"Yeah, I didn't say I wanted to be your at-home slave," I add with a smile. "It's just that I could be like Beaver's mom."

"You want to be a beaver's mom? What is that supposed to mean?"

# Inside My Head

I look at Porter and realize he has no idea who Beaver is. I start to laugh a bit at my age-revealing comments and explain. "Leave It to Beaver was a show on TV in the fifties or sixties and Beaver was the younger boy in the family; I think that was a nickname. Anyway, his mom stayed home and his dad went to work and she wore a dress all the time, even when she was cleaning the house. Everything always worked out for them perfectly."

"Like a fairy tale, huh?" Jade smirks, "then I wasn't far off. Everything would be clean and beautiful, and perfect, and food would be excellent, and there would be no dog poop in the yard. I like the idea. Could we go ahead and start calling you Cinderella?"

"Whatever!" I laugh with her.

Time flies by and we enjoy the game of make believe for a while. We decide to have a family night, which we have not had in ages. The board games come out and popcorn along with hot cocoa; the entire evening is proving to be tremendous.

*God, I don't remember the last time we did this. Thank you so much for making this possible. It seems like every weekend is spent rushing through housework and preparing for the next week. I feel so prepared for this week and yet it is the biggest week in years. I don't get it, but I do appreciate the calm.*

**Constance, I have placed people in your life to help you. Ones who will love you and you can trust them. Those women you wouldn't dare let into your space are the very ones that will be there to guide you. I am working all these things for your good according to the purpose for which I have called you, because you love me.**

.........

"Wake up, you two; it's going to be a beautiful fall day. We have so many things to do today. Kendra and Celeste will be here tonight. You can have cereal for breakfast, or peanut butter toast. I let you sleep in an extra fifteen minutes so we have to hurry."

We are out the door in record time, each munching on peanut butter toast and washing it down with pop. The kids were quiet as usual on the way to Aunt Bonnie's and I am standing on the line ready for work.

I had not thought much about being home with Maraschino and Kendra tomorrow until just this minute. *I have taken so much time off lately. I have gotten bonuses for six years straight for perfect attendance and now I have been off several days in the last few weeks. But I can't let it happen without me. I will just call in sick. I can't very well let them know ahead of time in case they refuse my request. It is last minute. Oh, God see there are times when a person has to lie.*

The same old familiar tunes rolling out of the speakers, monotonous white noise. I move mechanically throughout the day. Nothing like the same old everyday nothing to bore a person to her thought world.

*"Hey girl what's going on with you lately? You look like something the cat dragged in."* Kendra always knew how to cheer me up. *I smiled a mellow dramatic smile acting as though everything should be and was just fine. I didn't know this girl very well I was barely awake after the third attempt on my own life. This time no one realized I had done it myself so I didn't have to be put on the third floor. Her moving in next door a couple of weeks earlier hadn't yet been noticed by me.*

*"No really, you can trust me."* She also knew how to read my mind. I shook my head and turned to leave the mailboxes but she wouldn't let up. "Do you need something for the babies? I could take you to the store, or heck, I might be able to buy it for

you. My husband makes decent money, we aren't rich but we are comfortable and we can't have children as you well know. I'd love to help someone with children. It was always my dream to have a little girl and dress alike, play with her hair and have tea parties. I was always the prissiest girl in school. I figured someday I'd have a daughter to teach the girlie things to, but I guess God saw it a different way."

That had my attention. "Kendra, how does this God thing work anyway?"

"Yeah, something like that. I am not the typical Christian, but I am a Jesus follower."

"What's the difference?" I figured she was trying to trick me somehow.

"Well, the typical Christian religion gives a bunch of rules to live by, and leaves out the best part of why anyone would want to follow Jesus." I looked quizzically at her eyes to see if she was just leading me on but didn't detect any sign of jest. "I have a personal relationship with Jesus. He hand-picked me to be His bride. I trust my whole being to Him. I talk with Him daily and meditate on His Word. I used to say I went to church, but found it was so dull I dreaded the time I spent there. I said I was a Christian, but had never had a change of heart. It's kind of like being a car and having a junk body but a 4 speed in the floor ready to travel 0-60 in 30 seconds flat. I lived like a junk car because that is how I saw myself until I truly got to know Jesus. Now I can go 0-60 in 30, and since realizing that I have had such a dramatic change that my outside has begun to match my inside. Sorry, it's the only way I could think to describe it." She must've noticed my scowl. I wasn't angry or anything just trying hard to figure out what in the world she meant by all of that.

"Anyway, you being in here and sick and all and a single mom, I don't know I just thought maybe you could use some help."

## Inside My Head

*"How did you know I'm a single mom?"*

*She laughs and replies "I moved in next door two weeks ago. I thought it was amazing how God worked things out that we could be in the same hospital room. I guess you just didn't recognize me. You have been pretty out of it since you got in here."*

*I listened more to her faith story. I asked God to change me and give me a reason to live. She invited me to church and I saw no reason not to go. I only went a few times before quitting. I thought of every excuse under the sun.*

*"Kendra, how are you?" I asked at the grocery store one Saturday morning. She admitted that she barely recognized me. "I am very well, thank you. The question is how are you?" I was grateful that she didn't bring up the obvious lack of self-care on my part. I had been drinking myself deeper and deeper into that pit for several months. I could barely recall my last relaxing bath or even whether or not I still had a razor at home. My hair had been pulled into a ponytail every day so that I wouldn't have to find a brush. But she acted as though I looked the same as ever and that she was really concerned about me as a long-time friend.*

*"I have been going through a lot. I guess you saw the break up and the police at our house a few months ago. He finally left with the latest bimbo. I don't know if I'm coming or going lately. I get the kids up and to school and then I don't know what to do." To my great dismay I began to cry, right there in the store. I had never thought that kind of thing would ever happen to me; I felt unloved and unlovable. I knew of no other person that had noticed, or even pretended to be concerned. I guess it wasn't fair since I didn't have any girl-friends and burned every bridge with guy-friends when I got pregnant.*

*"Sweetheart, come home with me. Let me hear it all. Get it out, that helps start the healing process." We left together and had tea at her house while I told her everything. She was right about that being the beginning of my healing. Her friendship proved to*

*be exactly what I needed. She invited me back to her church and this time I kept going. I gave my heart to Jesus for real this time, soon after our first 'tea party'; not at church but at her round dining room table over a hot cup of chamomile tea and homemade sugar cookies.*

*I love her so much, God, thank you for her friendship. Thank you for putting her into my life. I would have died had it not been for her. My kids would have been raised by their cruel and insensitive father. God, she showed you to me at that table. She didn't judge me, or preach at me, she just listened. She invited me back day after day and listened. I enjoyed those cookies, and the tea. I am so excited about her coming. Please, Lord, for her sake let this go well.*

**No worries, my dear, I love her more than you do. I have this under control. I shared this with you so that you could set it all up for me. Thank you for being a willing vessel.**

*I never understood that saying, God.*

**I am like a master potter, and you are the most wonderful clay. I mold and shape you into exactly the perfect size and shape of vessel I desire. Then I use you in this world to take my living water to others. Some people don't allow me to use them and therefore they are like empty vessels sitting on shelves. They may look beautiful, but they are of no use to anyone. Some vessels have allowed themselves to be used by the enemy or by other people, they have cracks and chips and breaks, they are no longer able to hold that fresh life-giving water. Instead they leak out all over everyone around them. Or they are filled with hard heavy burdens in order to feel full. Either way they are not satisfied because they are not being used for their ultimate purpose. I know that purpose and can restore them, if only they will allow it. You, my precious, were a very broken vessel, and it has taken a little while to repair the damage**

*done by others and yourself. You are becoming more beautiful every day.*

Wow, God, thank You. Thank You for using me, and for making me, and for fixing me. Thank You for being there when I was not thinking about you or even wanting to do so. I was such a mess, why me?

**My Word makes it very clear. Deuteronomy 7:9 says 'Know therefore that the Lord your God is God: He is the faithful God, keeping His covenant of love to a thousand generations of those who love Him and keep His commandments.' My dear child, your great-great-great grandmother was a favored child of mine. She spent hours in my presence. She called out to me regarding her family forward ten generations. She knew what it meant to go through hard times. She was a slave. She had been sold to a terrible man and his hateful wife as a housemaid. Her owners beat and raped her many times before selling her to a traveling team of thieves. They had fallen on hard times, as my punishment for abusing my child and they refused to repent. She was pregnant when sold to the cruel team of bandits and they wanted nothing to do with her once her pregnancy could no longer be hidden. They dropped her off in a small town several miles from here and a kind family took her in. She was nursed back to health and offered her services to them as a way of repayment for their kindness.**

O.K., God, I know you are in the middle of this story, but I am white and I have never heard anything about having a black heritage. I am not sure this is my story.

**Of course you aren't, but I am acutely aware of everyone ever born and everyone who should have been. I know their family history from the beginning. I have no time restrictions, so to me it was like yesterday. She was named Constance as well. She was in constant**

communication with me. She asked me to save her family from the same fate she had been subjected to.

*Her new family only allowed her to be one of them, not as a slave, but as a daughter. She was a mere 14 when she had your great-great grandfather. He was a strong, godly man born into a freedom that the enemy tried to take from him. He was, however, light skinned and living in a free part of the country. He married a mixed young woman and their children were even fairer skinned. Your great grandmother was the fairest of them all.*

Was her name Snow White? I giggle at the silliness and at the fact that I can joke around with God. It's as though He giggled back.

*No, it's not a fairy tale that I am telling you, it is your story. She was named Shekinah to represent my glory on the earth. Her beauty was fantastic to me. The men of earth noticed her as well. She chased after the attention they offered. She was given twelve children and held her heart from me until her later years.*

I'm sorry Your glory was wasted on her.

*My glory is never wasted. Her twelve children represent the twelve tribes of Israel. Your grandfather, who died before you were born, was a farmer. He tended the ground and prayed fervently everyday as he worked to take care of his family and others in need. His wife was a faithful woman who raised your father to be a well-loved young man.*

*Your mother led him astray and to cover up her sins she lied to you about him abusing her. He called out to me on his bed at night asking me to be merciful to him and to his children and grandchildren. He begged me for forgiveness and asked me to bring him home realizing his weakness. I did so for his sake. Now, there is you. I have been there always; I moved Kendra next door, put her in your hospital room and brought you to the place of calling out to me. I am faithful and patient. I care about the eternal repercussions of individual lives rather than the temporal moment. I know what it will take for those I have called and I work all things to that end. You were chosen as a precious gem to be placed into the perfect setting of space and time to represent my glory in the most incredible way. I have had my eye on you for eons. Jade will bring my glory back to the masses and Porter will be a quiet replication of my Son, doing all that I ask, seeing miracles, signs and wanders.*

My eyes fill with tears and I am overwhelmed by such humility. *I don't deserve any of this favor for me or my children. I have been so judgmental, not at all portraying my God in a positive manner until recently.* Incredible joy overtakes me as I make my way home. This has been a day without interaction other than that of me and my heavenly Father. He must have put a bubble around me. I never have a day like today.

I try to share my experience with the kids but miss some key points I am sure. I can hardly believe the history I have and plan to confirm it all online to be sure I am not making up such tremendous greatness. Both kids are excited to help with the task.

Pizza for dinner allows for easy cleanup and time to rest before going to the airport. Computer exploration begins, and with the names and times He gave me, we are able to confirm quite a bit before leaving the house. Excitement and a new comprehension of God's eternal favor is mind boggling. I could never have imagined the alignment from my past to God's divine purpose for me and my children. The prophetic words about Jade and Porter are staggering. I can hardly stay seated as we head west to the airport. The long ride and wait there are filled with anticipation which is met satisfactorily upon the sight and embrace of my dearest friend.

The kids chat most of the way home and I try to recall all of the conversation with God from earlier today. "It was so extensive, Kendra, I could hardly take it all in. His words were kind and gentle as He described my family even those who didn't follow after Him. Shekinah, what a beautiful name! And she didn't follow Him. I don't get it."

"I can't say that I do either. But, if I have a girl then I would like to carry on that glorious name and train her up to represent Him in such a way as to delight Him." I stay still for a moment as I soak in what she just said.

"Was that your way of telling me you are going to adopt another child?"

"Not exactly, it was my way of telling you that I am pregnant." She looks over at me to catch any reaction. I am numbed at the thought.

"I thought you couldn't have children. I was just remembering today the first time we met and you were telling me about the sadness of not being able to have any yourself. Did I remember that all wrong?"

She smiles tenderly, lightly giggling as she begins, "No, you remember perfectly, I'm sure. I was at a church service a few months ago and was praying for a woman to have a child safely since she had been diagnosed with cancer while only four months into her pregnancy. That night I went home and the Lord gave me a dream. In it He showed me a picture of me very pregnant. I assumed it was a spiritual dream and brought it up at our ladies group to see if anyone else could tell me what they felt that it could have meant. An older saint came to me afterward and told me that God had given her a word for me during her personal prayer time a few days earlier and she had waited till that meeting to tell me. She was afraid that she was wrong and that it would hurt me to hear such a word if she had missed the mark, but this dream was her confirmation. She told me that God told her that I would have a child of my own because of my faithfulness and my willingness to accept anything He had planned for me. I found out three weeks later that I was indeed pregnant."

I screech with excitement, this is too much to imagine. God is giving Kendra a baby of her own! "Oh, my gosh, Kendra! You held back telling me, why?"

"I hadn't heard anything from you in many months and wasn't sure that you were concerned with my goings on anymore. I was so glad to hear your voice, but when you told me your news I decided since I would be here I would tell you in person. I am due by Christmas." She is glowing with such pure radiance it lights up the darkness.

"A Christmas baby! That is tremendous! I am so excited! Oh, Kendra, I couldn't be more excited if it were me having the baby." You don't look very big for having a baby in a few weeks."

"Well, the baby and I are doing very well. I had to check with the doctor before coming and she said it was fine. I have only gained twelve pounds so far and am still able to do everything I was doing before."

"Boy or girl, do you know?"

"No; we have chosen to be surprised."

"Oh yeah, you did say 'if you have a girl' earlier. Oh, my gosh, Kendra, I am so excited! God is doing some amazing things."

## Inside My Head

"He most certainly is. My brother lives only a few miles from here. I can hardly wait for you to meet him. What if you two hit it off and you become my real sister?"

I take a deep breath and begin telling her all about Kevin at work and how long I have wanted to go out with him. I leave out all the parts that no one else should ever hear about, and conclude with the date coming up. "I don't know if now is the best time to meet someone else as a potential boyfriend, but I would definitely love to be your sister."

"It's O.K., God's perfect will for you is all I want." We conclude as we pull into the driveway of a cottage-style home. Its simplicity is perfection, reminding me of every fairy tale happily-ever-after ending.

The doors of my van all open and Kendra and Celeste slowly saunter toward the door. Suddenly it opens and a man runs out and picks Kendra up swinging her around. They laugh as I bring the baggage toward them planning to gracefully invite him to dinner tomorrow evening with all of us hoping that he refuses, so as to not have an awkward conversation with a strange man.

"You have put on a bit of baby weight, Kenny, I am so excited for you." He touches her tummy looking at her closely in the dim light of the porch.

*That voice...*

I look up into the eyes of the most incredible man I have ever seen in my life.

"Connie?" He says with great surprise.

"Kevin?" I say with even greater surprise. *My Kevin is Kendra's brother?!!! Oh, my gosh! How is this possible?*

## Inside My Head

"Uhh, yes," I stammer. "This is Kevin from work. The one I told you about." Kendra begins laughing hysterically. She wobbles, nearly falling off the corner of one of the perfectly placed stepping stones near the exquisitely hewn stones making up the porch. Kevin catches her as he looks at me.

"You were talking about me?" He smiles shyly.

"Well," Kendra begins, "she was letting me down easy about meeting my baby brother since she had finally been asked out by the man of her dreams." She laughs some more, he stares at me in disbelief and I want to crawl under the nearest stone to escape.

"I have to get the kids home. I guess I will see you two tomorrow." I say nodding toward Kendra and Celeste. "And Kevin, you are welcome to come for an early dinner tomorrow right after work, if you'd like."

"That I would, thank you, and thank you for picking up my sister at the airport. I really do appreciate it."

"No problem, good night." I wave at everyone and turn to go to the van.

*God, that was totally unexpected. Wow! You knew that all along.*

God must be smiling, with the sound of His voice comes that familiar lilt. *Oh, I could hardly wait for you to get there. This has been in the making for many of your years. I was just waiting for you to catch up. He is perfect for you. Sleep well tonight, my princess.*

I can hardly believe all that has taken place in such a short time. All the years of begging God to do something and He was already doing it. He knew all along that I was going to end up with Kevin and yet He made me wait. But

## Inside My Head

oh, he is so worth the wait.

# Chapter Twenty-nine

I called into work at 4:00 a.m. letting them know that I had been up all night throwing up. I am so sorry but I will not make it in today affording all of us extra sleep. Both kids look forward to meeting Kevin at dinner. We leave for school following an expected attempt at bargaining for the day off. I explain the importance of solitude for the parties involved and remind them that they will have only a three day week anyway. They understand, but continued to plead to the very last second.

"God, you are unfathomable. I cannot comprehend your greatness, and your overwhelming love for us. That You would put into place the pieces of the puzzle and I would not even realize that You were involved completely blows me away. You don't just align the stars and the moon, You align my life; You find pleasure in Your people. That You relentlessly pursue us is incomprehensible, especially when we are unfaithful to You. I didn't even know that You cared at all until a few short years ago, and then I didn't get it. It didn't click until a few short weeks ago. God you are so patient. Your pleasure is my delight. Thank You for Your pleasure, Your constant supervision of my life. You are more than I have the understanding to speak. I am speechless."

I sit in silence the rest of the way home, as I absorb the sunlight, feeling closer to Him in this moment than ever before.

Thanks to Sheila, the house was already prepared. I simply need to pick up some fruit and muffins. I made coffee and poured orange juice into a pitcher. It has been years since I have entertained so again I complain to myself about the mismatched flatware and cups. Duke was put outside and music is on in the background so that the atmosphere is never awkwardly silent. I ate a small plate and now wait anxiously.

"It's not even my life that is about to change forever and I am so nervous." I pace as I wait.

Maraschino is the first to arrive. Jay is not with her. We chat nonchalantly and I offer the continental breakfast. She declines stating that she cannot eat if she is nervous. I can't fathom not eating the entire house when I am nervous, so I eat another muffin. She looks incredible and checks her face for red eyes, and her hair for smoothness several times before the arrival of Kendra and Celeste. Kendra had borrowed Kevin's car, a cute little Sebring Touring with a convertible top. She begins the meeting with a very stable hello.

I expected some stammering from all parties involved, but the first thing suggested by Maraschino was to open in prayer. This was welcomed by Kendra.

She breathed deeply, in through the nose out through the mouth, classic sign of calming nerves. "Daddy, we are here for the most important meeting of my life. I am so grateful for this time together with Kendra and Celeste. I ask that Holy Spirit be present causing peace and grace to abound. Thank You for keeping Celeste in Your sight and holding her close to Your heart forever. I love You." She waited quietly in case anyone else wanted to add anything.

"God, thank you for using me to intercede on the behalf of these amazing sisters of mine. Bless this meeting today and give wisdom to each person here as to how to proceed from this meeting." I pause in case Kendra wants to add.

## Inside My Head

"Thank you, Jesus for letting me meet my birth mom and thank you for an amazing mother." Celeste spoke with strength beyond our expectation.

Kendra sobbed quietly and didn't speak so Maraschino said amen. Everyone stood for a second holding hands, as time stood deathly still. Celeste was the first to speak.

"What should I call you?" She asked Maraschino.

"Maraschino is fine." She replies, wiping tear-filled eyes.

"O.K, my mom told me all about this day. I am thankful that you wanted to meet me. I want you to know that my mom and dad love God first and then love me. I have had a good life. I have my own room and I don't always get everything I want, but I don't actually need anything. I just want to set your mind at ease."

Silence permeates every inch of space in the house; even with soft music the silence is deafening. Tears cover each face. No one knew what to expect and still do not know what to do. I offer breakfast and take another scoop of fruit salad. Celeste politely takes a muffin but the other two simply shake their heads.

Maraschino looks at Kendra and begins "Kendra, this is truly the most amazing gift anyone could do for another person. I don't take this lightly. Thank you for this." She turns to Celeste and continues in her soft, tear-filled voice, "Celeste, I have thought about you often. I celebrate your birthday every year. I have set aside birthday cards with notes to give to you." She turns and removes a large plastic bag filled with cards from her purse and offers them to Celeste. Celeste smiles at the package and takes it gently from her shaking hand.

"I'm sorry that I missed the opportunity to be there when you were scared or sick or sad. I'm sorry about not being there for you while you went to school on the first day, or brought home those precious crafts for parents and learned to write your name, which I love by the way," she turned to Kendra and smiled. "I realize the tea parties and playing house days are over, I wish I could have played peek-a-boo, and chase, and taught you how to ride a bike, but I want you to know that I prayed for you so many times. I was unable to pray for the first few years because my relationship with God was not there. I also brought a gift, I don't think this buys your love, but it is all I could think to do to let you know about your bloodline, in case it is ever needed." Her bag was like a magician's hat; she pulled out a large book and opened it like it was a priceless treasure as she scooted closer to Celeste to show her the pictures and notes accumulated over decades. "My mother kept up on all the family history and everything going on. She said it was like our family Bible, like in Matthew how there was the genealogy of Jesus." She smiled as she went page by page pointing out antique prints, Polaroid shots, handmade notes about family members, letters sent from grandparents and aunts and cousins dating back to the mid 1800's. From there it was more of a he-said she-said kind of notation naming couples and babies and deaths. This was obviously a family treasure. The first entry was from a young girl questioning 'where did I come from?' and continuing to answer her own question with a family tree/journal. I would love to have the opportunity to study every note and card and entry.

"It's been in my family for all these years, passed on to the oldest daughter or to a son if a daughter was not available. We can trace back to the original persons that came to the U.S. in 1645. I know that the software exists to continue backward and find out even more if someday you are interested in doing so. I want you to have this and continue the tradition if you don't mind. It is a big responsibility but after hearing you this morning, I know you're up to the task. Pass it down to your daughter someday, letting her know her heritage."

Kendra is looking at the book with surprise, I can't read the face. That's unusual for me; I'm usually good at that.

*Is she good or is she hating that. It is a constant reminder that Celeste is someone else's child. That her heritage is different and lets her know Celeste will not carry on her bloodline. Her grandkids will technically not even be her grandkids. That does have to be disheartening.*

Suddenly her face lights up. "Hey, that's a picture of my Aunt Betty!" She exclaims pointing at a Polaroid from the 70's. Sure enough, the woman's name is Betty and she lived in Houston Texas in 1978. She had long brown hair and a small build, but was taller than the other girls in the picture. I assumed it was a growth spurt she had gone through before her friends or siblings.

Maraschino leaned in and remarked that she was also her aunt. They began to look at each other in disbelief. "Your Aunt Betty? Who's your dad?"

"My dad is Bill. Betty was the youngest of the eight children and my dad was the oldest. I always loved when we visited her. She was my favorite because she was close to my age. We had so much fun together. I haven't seen her in years but we continued to write for years until one day she never returned a letter. I supposed she grew out of being a pen pal to her niece. Who is she to you?"

Maraschino begins to cry. "She was my mother." Her sobs are louder than her voice. With that Kendra begins to cry. Celeste and I take more food as the reality hits that these two really are related and that Celeste will continue the blood line of her grandmother. The thought finally takes hold in my mind and I can no longer hold back the tears.

*They are cousins and didn't know it? How is that possible? They went to the same church for a while when Maraschino was a kid and still no one knew? How strange is that? What about the letters? How did she not know about her aunt's move? Strange, God, Oh, my gosh! I can't wrap my head around how You wove this blanket into existence. The years and precision...*

"When did she stop writing you?"

"Well, let me think... I remember this picture being taken in '78 I was in town with my parents for Grammy's birthday. She was about my age so we played and had a great time. This picture is one of several taken with the brand new Polaroid Grammy got for her birthday. It was so much fun to take a picture and see it develop in your hand we went through probably three packs of film." She shakes her head and snickers, "Aunt Betty was a star in the making. She sang songs and danced and we laughed till early morning hours and got up to start all over the next day. I think it was the funnest week of my life." She sits for a moment introspectively.

"Anyway, we promised to write and to someday get together but Grammy died the following year. We were unable to attend the funeral as a family so only my father took the trip back to Texas. I sent along some letters and gifts for Aunt Betty and she returned the favor. We had been so close for that year. After her mother died she seemed distant, I mean we still wrote back and forth but the letters were further and further apart. I heard scuttlebutt about depression and then a marriage but she didn't keep up with the family. They were against her marriage to..." She pauses realizing she was talking to her daughter and not wanting to hurt feelings she contemplates her next words.

"I'm sorry." She looks at Maraschino, "It was all just rumor. I didn't know what to believe. She married young and I heard she went back to church and that she had a daughter, but she stopped writing before she got married. I heard they had moved to the Midwest but I didn't know where. We lost track. I have continued to pray for her all these years. I didn't even know she had died. Her family was unable to contact her because of her husband." Again she looked apologetically toward Maraschino who was lamenting as she heard stories she never knew about her mother as a young girl.

"I didn't get to know my mother very well. I lived with her but my father was controlling and secretly abusing me for years. He told me she knew and I didn't trust her. She went to church and that would be the worst times for me. She came back happy and I cried myself to sleep. She didn't know until it was too late. That sent her back into a depression that she never recovered from. She prayed continually for death until God took her home. I became very angry with God for a long time. I blamed Him for my abuse, and my mother's eventual death. I felt so alone. Not one family member showed up for the funeral. I thought I was alone in the world." The sobbing became uncontrollable and Kendra leaned in to comfort her.

Celeste doesn't fully understand. She is barely ten and this is not what she expected. She leans in to join the hugs and they wrap their arms around each other; a true family hug. I go to the kitchen to give them privacy.

*God, I can't believe this. How far-fetched is this? I don't see how any of this could happen. How intricate the workings of this family have become, or should I say, have been. It is amazing to me that these women are long-lost cousins. It's something you'd see in a movie.*

## Inside My Head

Again I feel His smile. *Constance, as you are aware, I am a God of consistency. I love to watch the plan unfold. It is a joy to watch how everything works together for the good of those who love Me and whom I have called for a purpose. I never took my eyes off of the 'sparrow', Betty, nor did I remove them from her family. Her granddaughter bears the name Celeste Lynn, meaning Heavenly Hope, she was born for such a time as this, as was Hadassah.*

Hadassah? Who is Hadassah?

*Most people knew her as Esther, the queen of Persia. She also brought hope to a dying nation. Celeste is part of a bigger plan, so she needs to understand My intricacies and ability to be precise in My workings. Her life is being woven into the masterpiece of the end times. My Son will return soon and this meeting is necessary for many. These three have been aligned from the beginning of time to do my will. And you have been purposed to pull it all together.*

What? I don't get it. I didn't even know You hardly at all until recently. I lived a boring life according to a bunch of rules that I resented. I was wicked, condemning, judgmental and let's not forget, lustful. How was I part of the plan? I feel like I just stumbled onto something and it panned out.

*It was truly all planned, ALL planned. Nothing catches me by surprise, Constance. Wickedness is rampant and others need to know they are not trapped by it. They are not left out there to fend for themselves. I see every one of my children and know their deepest thoughts, and desires. I have a plan; I don't sit and wait for it to be figured out. Would you have figured this out?*

Not a chance.

*Your ways are not my ways and your thoughts are not my thoughts; they are far too lofty for you to comprehend. I Am a Big God, and no one can understand Me fully. But today is a start to a better understanding of how much I Am a part of everything. I will NEVER leave any one of you totally alone, even though at times it feels like I do. I will NEVER turn my face from any of you, even though you don't see Me. I Am the essence of love, and grace abounds with Me.*

*Tell the ladies tonight at the Bible study that My Son will return soon. The time has come to rise up in their faith and know that I Am is in the earth. I Am taking care of them and their situations, but I do so with the thoughts of eternity in mind, not just the here and now. It is not for them to be able to fully understand. Tell them the theme verses this week are Proverbs 3:5-6. And don't forget to read 1 Corinthians 13.*

*I will. What do they say?*

…silence

*I will look them up in a bit, God. Thank you. Actually I will look them up now; maybe they mean something for this situation as well.*

I take my Bible off the coffee table and open it to a familiar set of verses. "Hey, you guys, I was just talking to God. He gave me these verses and a huge message. Do you mind if I read them aloud?" They all shake their heads no and I begin. "Proverbs 3:5-6 Trust in the Lord with all your heart and lean not on your own understanding: in all your ways acknowledge Him and He will make your paths straight."

Smiles and nods from each person. I proceed to explain as best as I can recall the words He told me about Celeste and all four of us. And tell them that tonight at the Bible study I have a message for everyone. I am so excited to tell people about this.

We talk for hours and decide that we could work together at making food for the kids and I suddenly remember that Kevin is coming over for dinner.

"Kendra, I can't believe he's your brother, all these years I have had my eye on him and had no idea. You never talk too much about him. Is there something I should know? Is he a trustworthy guy or are there some hidden secrets I should be concerned about?"

She laughs, "He is great. I didn't have much of a relationship with him after I moved. We had been so close and our sudden decision to move threw him off guard. He was disheartened at being here without anyone. I reminded him that he was married and that he no longer needed me. But I was his best friend. His wife was amazing! She loved him and she loved God. She carried him through the times of loneliness. They tried for a couple of years to have children before she found out that she had cancer. He then found meaning in every second. He tended to her like a priceless treasure. His love deepened as they got closer to the end. He lashed out at God and me when she died. He wouldn't respond to letters or phone calls. He had married later than I did and she was his everything. Then she was gone. We couldn't understand why. He continued to work and go to church. But outside of that he hid himself away. It took about a year before he slowly came around to accepting calls.

"He continued to lash out at my concern. He accused me of preaching at him; he will still quite angry with God. I feared for his salvation. A few months ago I heard God tell me that he was placing a new love in his path and that he would be fine. That God had everything under control and He gave me several verses that helped to comfort me. Proverbs 3:5-6 were two of them. He also reminded me of Jesus' words in Matthew 10:29-31 about the sparrow selling for less than a penny and He still sees when even one falls to the ground, and that we are worth more than several sparrows. He even knows the number of hairs on our heads. I gave these verses to Kev in a letter and he wrote back a thank you note in a nice card letting me know that God had given him the same verses. He still sounded off somehow, but last night we sat up and talked for several hours just like old times. He told me that he has drawn far closer to God in the last year than he knew was possible and that he has a new lease on life. He thanked me for all the prayers and letters and let me know that not one went without giving him comfort.

"All the times I had thought he was cold was because he had been working overtime and becoming very tired. He also had done some remodeling. He felt as though it would need to be ready for a family. He is not sure if it will be his family or if he will be moving but he has done a fantastic job."

Dinner was coming along stupendously so I dipped out to get the kids.

"Hey, Jade, how was school?"

Same ol' same ol'." She announced "And how was the reunion?" She asked with far more interest.

"It is going very well."

"Is? Is it still going on?"

"Yes. Everyone is at the house cooking dinner. We will eat early enough to get ready for the Bible study and I am expecting you and Patty tonight still, right?"

"Yeah, I talked to her today and she said she is looking forward to it. God is sure working in her life. What is for dinner and who all will be there?"

## Inside My Head

She really just wants to know about Kevin. I don't want to look too feverish about the whole idea of having dinner with the man of my dreams.

"Well, Maraschino, Kendra, Celeste, Me and you and Porter, and uhh, I guess Kevin is going to come too. But dinner will have to be somewhat quick so that we can get to church early for the study, God has given me a specific word for everyone tonight." I barely crack a smile in hopes to seem very blasé about everything. Inside I want to get up and dance and sing with pure ecstasy.

"Mom, I don't know what to ask first... What are you going to wear? How will you do your hair? Aren't you excited about Kevin or are you nervous? And...a word from God? What about? I mean you never say you have a word from God. I am so excited."

Porter gets into the back seat and injects a "What for?"

"Kevin will be at dinner tonight and Mom is hearing words from God for other people. It all seems so surreal."

"Surreal? What does that actually mean? Or do you even know? I think you just like to make yourself sound more intelligent so you use big words."

"It means kind of like a dream, stupid. I am intelligent and obviously you are not."

"O.K. you two, stop now. This will be a very important meal for many reasons. You two will not act up or out tonight. Jade, you know much better than to call your brother stupid. He is not stupid and he does not need you saying such cruel things."

"I know, Mom, I just hate that because I love to read and have a much higher level of vocabulary than he does, he feels like he can criticize me. I haven't done anything wrong just because I choose to pursue intelligence and he does not."

"Like I said, it is over now." The van is quiet for the remainder of the ride.

*I know this is not our date, but I really wish I could have had a little better notice about dinner with him. I wanted to look my best when I saw him outside of work and here I saw him last night and I will see him again in a little while. The very least I could do is wear something nice. Ew! Maybe the new Bible study everyday outfit, I almost forgot about that shopping trip.* Nodding I silently agree with myself and determine to change immediately.

"I'm going up to change for dinner, well, and Bible study, anyways I will be right back down." I call down as I ascend the stairwell.

Finishing the last touches to my hair I hear the doorbell. I breathe in through the nose and out through the mouth. *He's here.* One last look in the mirror and off I go. He catches sight of me as I walk down the stairs and I see a smile. *Did he really just smile at me?* I look to see if someone is behind me and conclude that it must be him.

"Hello," I can barely get out clearly. Everyone else just looks at the two of us and hide their laughs. I simply smile and fake serenity. "Were you able to finish dinner while I was out?" Jade may bust a gut. I look to see Porter and he is no better. I scowl at them both and ignore their laughter.

"Kendra and I finished up and the three kids set the table and got ice and drinks ready. We were simply waiting on you."

# Inside My Head

My eyes close. *Did I really take that long? How embarrassing. Do I look like I took forever? Well I hope I at least look like I took enough time. I seriously didn't want to let him know I was upstairs preparing for his arrival.*

She must have seen my expression and giggled and revised her previous statement. "I was joking, we just finished."

"I love homemade food. I don't cook all that well and this is such a treat, thank you for inviting me," Kevin said just before taking another bite. He has a plate full and eats slow and steadily.

I expected him to eat a lot, but I thought he would scarf it down quickly. I wonder if he does everything slow and steady. O.K., that needs to stop now. Jesus, help me to take every thought captive.

"You all did a wonderful job. Man, I love Italian food. This lasagna is great."

"Yeah, thanks." Both Kendra and Maraschino reply with snickers.

"Frozen is always our favorite." Celeste commented, giving away the secret. We all laugh.

Dinner chat turned its focus to tonight and the last Proverbs 31 study.

"Well, I feel like God wants to take this into a totally different direction tonight. I want to take the time to allow the women to respond to what God told me this afternoon. I also plan to give a glimpse of the future of the study."

"What is it that God told you?" Kevin asks.

## Inside My Head

"Well, He told me basically that He is sending His Son back very soon and it is time to rise up in their faith and KNOW that He is here. He made it very clear that He is in control of everything and that nothing takes Him by surprise. He is actually the one aligning people and events in order to have His purposes fulfilled." Everyone stares me.

"Way cool," Porter finally says.

"Yeah," Kevin agrees and everyone nods. "So what is Porter doing while you're all gone?" Kevin asks as he takes another bite.

"Well," I look at Porter, "do you have homework?"

"Nope," he says as he shovels more into his mouth.

"Would it be O.K. if he comes over to my house and we play some video games?" I obviously look concerned because he continues. "I don't play those hunt and kill games, but I do have a WII and we can do some bowling or something," he turns to look at Porter's response, "if you want to."

I also look at his response and the smile my direction says it all. "O.K."

Dinner cleanup is a breeze with everyone's help. We all shuffle out and decide Kendra and Celeste will ride in my van and meet Maraschino there.

The van is filled with singing old and new songs as well as promises to keep in touch from Jade and Celeste. Kendra smiles and stays in deep thought. We arrive as Chris goes to open the door. There are ladies already waiting to get in. Some brought sandwiches or salads and finish them up inside. I overhear a group talking about this being the highlight of the week and others concerned about how it will continue from here.

## Inside My Head

I get the front ready for me to present what I have been mulling over in my thoughts since God spoke to me this afternoon. *God, I want to get it all right. I don't want to say something that was not what you said. I don't remember it word for word and I'm afraid I will not do it all justice. Holy Spirit, bring it all back to my remembrance, please. Speak through me as I reveal to these ladies God's heart for them.*

The sanctuary begins to fill up and Pastor John and Trula arrive. *I had no idea they would be here. I wonder why he came. Oh, here they come.* I look down to check my clothes and wipe my hands on my pant legs before shaking hands.

"Connie, I am thrilled to be able to come tonight. I know it is only for ladies, but I felt like God told me it would be good to be here tonight. It looks like you draw more followers than the service on Sunday mornings." He laughs and shakes my hand as he nods in the direction of the pews. I look out at the biggest crowd so far. I can hardly believe my eyes. "There must be about 75 or 80 at least and they are all early! I must have your secret," he jeers.

I smile and shake my head, "I don't know." I reply honestly. "I haven't done as much study as testimonies from each other. I believe God is calling us to share what He has done so that we can gain strength to believe that He will continue to do stuff."

*Oh yeah, that sounded profound. He will do stuff... duh! Yep God, that is proof enough that it is all You and none me.*

"You are so right," Trula adds. "He has been telling us the same thing. We need to share the testimonies of what He has done recently to build up our faith. You are hearing straight from the throne."

*Wow, that's cool. I mean I know that I have been hearing You lately, but it is nice to have that confirmation.* "Thank you, I have seen my life changed by those testimonies and I believe others are seeing it too. I want it to continue so that women all over can, not only share their testimonies here, but be encouraged to share their own and others everywhere they go."

"I am proud to say that you are my sheep." He smiles and takes a seat in the back to watch and listen without disturbing the study.

"It is time to start the final Proverbs 31 Bible study." I begin and ladies all over rush back to their seats. "Tonight is extraordinary because we have planned to study, of course, the end of the chapter; however, I am simply going to read from verse 10 and then tell you all what God has laid on my heart to tell you. Let's open in prayer.

"God, you are great beyond our understanding and able to accomplish more than we could ever imagine possible. I am so thankful that You used me in this place at this time. Thank You that You have never stopped moving in the Earth. We are so humbled by Your choosing us to be a part of the chosen ones that will fulfill the end-times prophecies. Bless each of us here tonight and impart new understanding of Your promises to us, amen.

"The wife of noble character: 'A wife of noble character who can find? She is worth far more than rubies. Her husband has full confidence in her and lacks nothing of value. She brings him good, not harm, all the days of her life.'

"This was so important to so many of the women in the beginning weeks of the study. We realized that we are of great value to the marriage. We, acting in God's direction are able to cause our husbands to have peace and faith in all that we do. That we are responsible from the very first of our lives to begin to lift up the man God has for us in prayer and do him good even before we meet him.

"'She selects wool and flax and works with eager hands. She is like the merchant ships, bringing her food from afar. She gets up while it is still night; she provides food for her family and portions for her female servants.'

"This is a reminder that this woman made money saved money and did so with an excitement. Her husband was a leader in the community and she respected him.

"'She considers a field and buys it; out of her earnings she plants a vineyard. She sets about her work vigorously; her arms are strong for her tasks. She sees that her trading is profitable, and her lamp does not go out at night.'

"She is wise and full of understanding for the market. Today that could translate into having enough understanding of the stock market and the retail market that she can provide what is best for sale. Buy low and sell high. She is not lazy and she does things with strength.

'In her hand she holds a distaff and grasps the spindle with her fingers. She opens her arms to the poor and extends her hands to the needy. When it snows, she has no fear for her household; for all of them are clothed in scarlet. She makes bed coverings for her bed; she is clothed in fine linen and purple.'

"She makes high quality clothing; today we would be purchasing our clothing at a top of the line store or designer. She doesn't have to worry about the bills or the weather she is well prepared and has prepared her household. She is kind and generous.

"'Her husband is respected at the city gate, where he takes his seat among the elders of the land. She makes linen garments and sells them, and supplies the merchant ships with sashes. She is clothed with strength and dignity; she can laugh at the days to come. She speaks with wisdom, and faithful instruction is on her tongue. She watches over the affairs of her household and does not eat the bread of idleness.'

"She and her husband have become respected members of society. She is well known for her work and her honesty. Merchants of the day would not take the wares of just anybody, only those they trusted. If they took it once and came back with bad reports they would no longer carry their items because they could not make money from them. She was an entrepreneur.

"'Her children rise and call her blessed; her husband also, and he praises her: "Many women do noble things, but you surpass them all." Charm is deceptive, and beauty is fleeting; but a woman who fears the Lord is to be praised. Honor her for all that her hands have done, and let her works bring her praise at the city gate.'

"We found in the beginning that this was an accumulative of many women. One woman, no matter how awesome she is, could probably not accomplish all of this. It was to say that any of these things could be the amazing woman of the king's dreams. She could and would do all that she was able in whichever area she was talented. For instance, JoAnne will be continuing as a leader of this study, and will present many types of things we as women can do to make and save money. She will be able to teach us how to put together a workable budget and she will teach us how to cook from scratch so that we can become stronger and healthier.

## Inside My Head

"Fancy will also lead some of the studies, teaching us how to decorate the home and how to do so with that budget in mind. We don't want to work hard for the money (I sing) and then just watch it fly out the window just to have a beautiful home. We want our husbands and children to love bringing people home, but we don't want our husbands to wish h never gave us access to the money. We need to do him good and not evil all the days of our lives.

"We will also have cleaning techniques from another woman and beauty tips from another. We want to be the essence of the Proverbs 31 wife and learn how to respect someone, not just be emotionally invested in that moment. It needs to last so that we can share with the rest of the world that loving God helps us to love ourselves and our husbands. We need to stand up and say enough is enough! I am no longer conforming to the world's picture of what I should be. I want to be transformed by the renewing of my mind. And we need to know the author of the book so that He can personally teach you how to be the wife to that husband." Everyone is clapping and shouting and many women are standing.

"I want to tell you something that God told me today. I may not get it word for word but I have asked God to remind me so that it will be what He wanted you all to hear. He said to the women tonight, I want you to tell them that I am sending my Son back soon. It is time to rise up in your faith and know that I Am is in the earth. I Am taking care of them and their situations, but I do so with the thoughts of eternity in mind, not just the here and now. It is not for them to be able to fully understand. Tell them the theme verses this week are Proverbs 3:5-6.

"And He said, 'It was truly all planned, ALL planned.' Nothing catches Him by surprise. 'Wickedness is rampant and others need to know they are not trapped by it.

They are not left out there to fend for themselves. I see every one of my children and know their deepest thoughts, and desires. I have a plan; I don't sit and wait for it to be figured out.'

"'Your ways are not my ways and your thoughts are not my thoughts, they are far too lofty for you to comprehend. I Am a Big God, and no one can understand Me fully. But today is a start to a better understanding of how much I Am a part of everything. I will NEVER leave any one of you totally alone, even though at times it feels like I do. I will NEVER turn my face from any of you, even though you don't see Me. I Am the essence of love, and grace abounds with Me.'

"Tonight I was going to allow one last testimony. I decided to let it be His testimony. He wants to teach you all that He works ALL THINGS out for the good of those who love Him and those He has called. It is all according to His purpose. We each have a role to play in the end times. We need to stand up and take our positions.

"We need to stop leaning on how we understand things to be and fully trust in Him and His ability to work EVERYTHING out, even when we cannot see how it would be possible. He has intricately woven the blanket of our lives. Be still before HIM and know that HE is GOD! He does have a plan for each of us. It is to be with Him for eternity. He loves each of us in ways that we don't recognize."

I look out and ask if I can share what happened today. Both Kendra and Maraschino agree with nods. Jade takes Celeste to the bathroom so she is out of hearing distance. (I had set that up with her earlier while getting ready.)

"Years ago, God saw me in my self-centered, dying mess and moved a woman next door to minister to me and to love me into His Kingdom. She invited me to church, and just loved on me. I stepped back out of fear and she let me do what I needed to do. Eventually, I came to Him." I pointed up, making the point clear.

"She was unable to have children and decided to adopt a baby that had been birthed out of horrific circumstances and then for the sake of the baby, moved hundreds of miles away.

"About three weeks ago, Maraschino gave her life changing testimony. She told of how her father had forced himself on her many times as a young girl and from there she became very well known around school as the easy one. One night after a traumatic time of gang rape by some boys from school she went home to her father who also raped her. It was devastating and she became very ill.

"To make matters worse, in a few short weeks she was found to be pregnant and had to reveal the secret horrors to doctors and her mother. She was only fourteen. Her father was found to be the father of the baby. The downward spiral was excruciating for her and her mother. The baby was given up for adoption and her mother finally died as a result of the overwhelming depression and guilt." Sobs can be heard all over the room.

"As I prayed, I felt that God revealed to me that Kendra had adopted Maraschino's baby. I called and asked for confirmation and was correct. Today Maraschino was reunited with her little girl. A child she had not seen in many years. Years of regret and pain were washed away in an instant as the three of them sat in my living room talking and laughing.

"Then the story got even better. I could never have imagined this. A picture Maraschino brought to give to her daughter was recognized by Kendra, as her aunt. She recalled her love for her favorite aunt; one that had been about her age and had once been her pen pal. Maraschino broke; Kendra's Aunt Betty was Maraschino's mother." Sobbing is more overwhelming than before; tears of sadness and joy blending.

"God asked me if I could have put all of those things and people and places together. I obviously said no. I couldn't have figured that out in a million years. He said His eye is on each of His children and nothing gets past Him. Nothing catches Him off guard. He has lined it all up from generations past.

"I say all of that to say this. Be still and KNOW, KNOW, KNOW, beyond a shadow of a doubt that God is real. AND that HE is the great I AM.

"Before closing I want to read one more set of verses that God asked me to read to you. You have probably heard of 1 Corinthians 13, but let's read it with a twist. We all know the verse, God is love so here we go…verse 4: 'God is patient, God is kind. He does not envy, He does not boast, He is not proud. He does not dishonor others, He is not self-seeking, He is not easily angered, He keeps no record of wrongs. God does not delight in evil but rejoices with the truth. He always protects, always trusts, always hopes always perseveres. God NEVER fails…'

"I will close this night with prayer and I ask that if any of you that want to know Him more, pray. Talk to Him as though you were talking to your best friend. Do it tonight. He has EVERYTHING lined up; you just need to step out in faith.

"God, You have given us this day, this time and we were born for just this time. It is hard and yet exciting to know that the prophecies of thousands of years ago are coming to pass right now and that we will see Your Son coming in the clouds. Jesus, we are your bride and we say to You, come quickly. We ask that you use us in whatever ways you so choose. Holy Spirit, thank you for your full-time presence. You are always here and You intercede on our behalf before the throne day and night. You cry out for us and with us to the Father; reminding Him of His calling for us and reminding us of His call and purpose for us. Help us to learn to be still and hear the small still voice. God, give us exponential growth in our faith as we heard tonight how You think of everything, and work it all for our good. Give us wisdom in all that we do so that we may truly become the Proverbs 31 wife to You and to our earthly husbands. We love You."

Women are making their way toward the front.

"Ladies, if you are here tonight and you do not know God in a real sense, as The I Am, I Am the husband, the father, the friend, the provider, the protector, the encourager, the one who loves unconditionally and forever without end, the creator of all things, The One and Only Living God; you can talk to Him at your seat, up front, or even in Your bedroom tonight. It says in 1John 1:9, 'If we confess our sins, He is faithful and just and will forgive us our sins and purify us from all unrighteousness.'

"Proverbs 28:13 reminds us that whoever conceals their sins does not prosper, but the one who confesses and renounces them finds mercy. I know this for sure because for years I hid all the anger, judgment, bitterness, self-hate, depression, fear, and lust and once I began to confess those sins change was evident. God's mercy and grace became a real part of who I am, and that began only a few weeks ago.

# Inside My Head

I had believed for years that God is real, I had come to church and lived by the rules yet I still lived according to a lie. I didn't understand that change was possible so I lived according to what I could do on my own. God began to show me that change is not only possible it is inevitable when I allow Him to work.

"Anyone who wants to know what change is like needs only to begin to talk to Him. If you are here tonight then there must be a level of belief. God sent His only Son to live and die and be raised again taking all the sins of everyone who had or ever will live; and every disease known and not known. He now is sitting at the right hand of His Father, the place of strength and honor, where He intercedes for each of us day and night. He loves each of us enough to die for us. There are no magic words, it is simply you reaching out and talking to Him and then listening to hear Him. It is a relationship not just a matter of living according to your understanding of a series of rules.

# EPILOGUE

Kendra and Celleste are home now with Shekinah, (which after researching they found is the majestic presence or manifestation of God, a pure light). They are in constant communication with Maraschino and Jay, who is now accepting Celeste and is growing closer to Maraschino through the whole matter. He has joined a men's group which directly came from the Proverbs 31 study having to do with being the right husband, Biblically speaking.

Kevin and Constance are dating. Both Jade and Porter have welcomed his presence as a part of their daily lives. Kevin is practicing football with Porter and they are reviewing high school teams to improve his plays as he looks forward to starting on a high school team.

Sheila and Joe are enjoying being grandparents to Patty's son, Kabod (a Greek word meaning glory of God). Patty is finishing high school online so that she can be at home with her son. He has been a large part of the healing in their lives. Chuck is going to Seminary and looking forward to traveling as a missionary or evangelist, he has yet to decide.

JoAnne gave her husband an ultimatum and began an entire new journey in life and is making that journal style story available soon. She began to teach at the New Life study (renamed after the final verses of Proverbs 31 were done).

Pastor John and Trula are enjoying a brand new marriage, like a full-time honeymoon. And the church is growing with leaps and bounds. Small groups are being implemented to accommodate the growth.

## Inside My Head

GOD is moving all over the world, and His Son, Jesus will be back very soon.

www.ingramcontent.com/pod-product-compliance
Lightning Source LLC
Chambersburg PA
CBHW071645160426
43195CB00012B/1363